Philip Freneau

The Gale Library of Lives and Letters
American Writers Series

Philip Freneau

The Poet of the Revolution

A History of His Life and Times

By
Mary S. Austin

Edited by Helen Kearny Vreeland
Great-granddaughter of the Poet

Descriptas servare vices, operumque colores
Cur ego, si nequeo ignoroque, poeta salutor
HORACE.

New York
A. Wessels Company
MDCCCCI.

REPUBLISHED BY GALE RESEARCH COMPANY, BOOK TOWER, DETROIT, 1968

Library of Congress Card Catalog Number: 67–23885

DEDICATED

TO THE

SONS AND DAUGHTERS

OF THE

AMERICAN REVOLUTION

Author's Preface

THERE is nothing new in this book, kind reader, for, if Solomon proved to his satisfaction that there is "nothing new under the sun," presumptuous indeed would it be in me to think to have succeeded in that wherein the wisest of men has failed.

M. Bautain, in his admirable treatise,[1] speaks of two methods of conceiving a subject: the one direct by means of illumination, the other indirect and within the reach of ordinary minds. He says it is difficult to be original upon subjects already treated of; but a second sort of originality consists in giving forth ideas that have become incorporated in one's own, and have been quickened with the life of one's own mind, which is called "taking possession in the finder's name."

This latter process, he continues, consists in acting as does the bee, which extracts from the flowers the aromatic and oleaginous particles, that serve to form the honey and the wax. "Be it well observed," he says, "that the bee first nourishes itself with these substances by the process of absorption and assimilation."

Therefore, kind reader, if in perusing this imperfect work you should find that which is familiar to you, remember it is not solely with the intention of giving

[1] Bautain on "Extempore Speaking."

you the new that it is written. "*Non nova, sed nove*," says Vincent of Lerins — not new, but in a new form. I claim no originality in the treatment of my subject; my efforts have been directed rather to presenting in the best light the character and times of the subject of our biography, than to the endeavor to appear original. When this end could be the better attained by making use of the words of others, I have done so; as most of the information they have received has emanated from the same sources as my own; namely, the relatives of the subject of this work, and likewise of the author.

An author[1] has deplored the fact that there are hundreds of names of men who have rendered the most important services to their country, that have been suffered to sink to the grave "unwept, unhonored, and unsung," and in a great measure it has been this thought that has prompted me to do what lies in my power to keep alive the memory of one who, born almost a century and a half ago, had an influence in the colonies during their struggle for independence that is said to have been very great.

I speak of Philip Morin Freneau, the "Poet of the Revolution."

Although in Freneau's case we may not hold as strictly true the words of the author above quoted, inasmuch as from time to time able and interesting articles upon his life and writings have appeared, still from paucity of data these have been fragmentary and somewhat erroneous, owing in part to the disastrous fire

[1] Thomas.

that consumed Mont Pleasant, the poet's homestead, in which were consumed, along with much of his unpublished poetry, many valuable letters and manuscripts that would have given abundant matter for a most interesting work.

Since undertaking the task of giving to the public the Life of Freneau, some unexpected data in the form of notebooks and marginal notes have thrown light upon some hitherto unaccounted-for years in the poet's life, and have served to link together the portions already given to the public, as well as to correct many misstatements.

Appreciating the fact that the life of a man is in reality a history of the times in which he has lived, and that the value of history depends as much on its veracity as upon the matter, I have endeavored to gain an accurate insight into the times, as well as the life of the man. I am enabled, consequently, to say that what I have stated as facts are in accordance with history, whereas such things as have not been proved are given as probabilities.

As one can judge of the works of a person being great or small only by comparing them with those of others, as well as by their effect upon posterity, I leave all judgment to my readers, contented with merely supplying the facts.

As no less than fifteen authors, possibly more, have written upon this subject, most of them being authors of repute, I have drawn entirely upon them for the matter contained in the chapter devoted to Freneau's poetry and prose compositions, bestowing all eulogy in their words, as praise comes not well from interested parties, and criticism is not pleasant to one to whom the object is endeared by association with loved ones. With Mr. Julian Verplanck, his friend and reviewer, one would rather —

> "With full applause in honour to his age,
> Dismiss the veteran poet from the stage;
> Crown his last exit with distinguished praise,
> And kindly hide his baldness with the bays."

Table of Contents

List of Illustrations

PHILIP FRENEAU

The Poet of the Revolution

Chapter First

IN relation to the revocation of the Edict of Nantes, much has been written by authors holding very different sentiments.

With some, we should deem the Huguenots an inoffensive and deeply wronged people, persecuted solely on account of their religious convictions; according to others, we should look upon Louis Quatorze as a forbearing monarch, — one who, being in imminent danger of having his kingdom wrested from him and its religion subverted, was compelled to act upon the defensive.

Some represent the Huguenots as bearing injuries inflicted upon them with fortitude, and suffering persecutions even to martyrdom for their religion; others depict the king as pursuing his rigorous course through the purest of motives, and to such an extent only as to repress the continual revolts of his rebellious subjects; they would cause us to hear him say to his intendants, "Je vous recommande surtout de menager avec douceur les esprits de ceux de la dite religion;" and to listen to his censure of one governor for pursuing a different course; and to learn of the recall of another for the same offence.

In the year of our Lord 1685, that which saw the Edict of Nantes revoked, France was divided into two parties; the dominant one being that of the Crown, headed by Louis Quatorze, — a prince as scrupulous and inflexible in matters regarding the faith he professed as he was unscrupulous and lax in the morals he practised. Intolerant of any opinion not his own, he condemned freedom of conscience in his subjects as tantamount to rebellion against his kingly authority. In religion, as in other matters, he would be absolute.

The minor party, that of the Huguenots, or Calvinists, still retained the characteristics sternly impressed upon it by its founder; which caused its adherents to live a life as totally at variance with that of their countrymen as was their belief. The severe and inflexible decrees of Almighty God, and the impotence of man's will in influencing his own destiny, being the basis of the Huguenot's creed, it produced in him a rigid severity of morals which, repressing all the natural instincts and emotions, caused a corresponding austerity of manner in his private life; while his natural independence of character, joined to the conviction of the hopelessness of his cause, gave him an air of defiance in his public demeanor and intercourse with the outer world. The former party, powerful and all-important, were as arrogant as such characteristics usually cause their possessors to become; while the other, no longer of political importance and consequently possessed of no influence at court, bowed to the inevitable, and, although subdued, were not conquered.

Cardinal de Richelieu, upon his elevation to the prime ministry, set himself to the accomplishment of three things; and having already effected two of them, namely, the humiliation of Austria and the extinction of feudalism, turned his attention to the one that lay nearest home, — the subjugation and conversion of the Huguenots.

Their subjugation he had effected in the year 1628 by the siege and possession of La Rochelle, which had been followed by the reduction of Montauban, the last stronghold of the Huguenots in France.

The terms of capitulation at La Rochelle had been

liberal in the extreme, far more so than the besieged had dared to hope;[1] and since the treaty signed at Alais in 1629 difference in religion had never prevented the cardinal from rendering the conquered all sorts of good offices, nor had it caused him to make any distinction between Frenchmen in the fulfilment of the duties of his office.[2] Notwithstanding the late revolt of the Rochellese, he had continued to protect the religious as well as the civil rights guaranteed to them by Henri Quatre in 1598, in what is known as the "Edict of Nantes."

But in regard to their conversion, even the sagacious Richelieu was mistaken, perhaps for the first time in his political career. The peaceful submission of the Huguenots was only the result of necessity. Their ambitious hopes crushed, their numbers depleted by the many wars they had undertaken, as well as the abandonment of their cause by the greater number of their nobility, had combined to oblige them to relinquish all hopes for the future, and set themselves to the work of repairing the sad effects of the last war; consequently those districts of France inhabited by them soon began to present their former appearance of fertility and thriftiness.

Excluded from higher pursuits, those of the Huguenots whose means permitted them to do so, lived in retirement; devoting themselves to the management of their estates, or else engaging in commerce, which they soon controlled to a considerable extent. Others turned their energies toward the development of the different manufactures in which, by their close application and enterprise, they soon excelled to such a degree as to cause some of its branches to become almost a monopoly with them.

With returning prosperity and a steady increase of population, the Huguenots began to raise their heads

[1] Ozaneau. [2] Richelieu's own testimony.

again; and, as their religious as well as civil rights were secured to them, their academies soon became national synods; and they have been charged with infractions of several of the articles of the Edict.

Deprived, by death, of the counsels of the sagacious Richelieu and the prudent Mazarin, and likewise of the politic advice of the displaced Colbert, Louis, encouraged by the fanatical, war-loving Louvois, determined upon taking more effective measures to hasten the conversion of the Huguenots which he was so desirous of bringing about.

By degrees many of the privileges guaranteed to them were curtailed; and they, fearing lest in time they might see the Edict rendered null, began to hold their assemblies as in days gone by; and, as in those times, force was now likewise used to prevent them, sometimes indeed to such a degree as to cause bloodshed. Symptoms of insurrection in the southern and western portions of France caused Louis to realize that the spirit of Calvin yet lived; and that the Huguenots were still a political body which might give cause for alarm. "It is necessary to recognize this fact," says Poole, "in order to render the attitude of Louis towards them intelligible. This has been denied persistently by them and their descendants, and its assertion is stigmatized as an attempt to vindicate conduct which, judged by its results, is in a supreme degree indefensible. But the truth is that, from this point of view of the national disaster, the recall of the Edict, setting the whole world in an attitude hostile to Louis, stands at so indefinite a height among the follies of statesmen that no exaggeration of fact can aggravate it; for this very reason we should grasp at anything which, while it cannot palliate it, may serve to explain its stupendous mistake."

At the king's council held October 2, 1685, the Act of Revocation was passed by a unanimous vote, and Louis signed the declaration to be sent to the different intendants of the provinces, to be read by them in public.

In concert with his minister, Louvois, he now set about the prosecution of the work with all the vigor of which he was capable. The dragonade was established, and cruelty succeeded cruelty. Threats, imprisonment, and death followed each other, the latter by single murders and public massacres, until it seemed that the heresy would be extinguished in blood.

The only alternative for the proud-spirited Huguenots was to abjure their faith or suffer the penalty. Escape was prohibited under pain of the galleys if they were caught in the act. Many of the Huguenots that lived in the shadow of the court abjured their religion; others, along with gentlemen living in the provinces, men of commerce and manufacturers, determined to leave their native land, however hazardous the attempt might be.

The depopulation of his kingdom had no part in the king's intention; therefore he ordered the ports to be closed and the frontiers to be closely guarded, thinking thus to prevent the threatened exodus; but determined men are not easily thwarted in their designs, and many ways were devised to elude the vigilance of the officials.

In many cases gold proved the "open sesame" of closed ports and guarded frontiers; disguises also and second-hand passports served to pass many across the boundaries, and frequently bales of merchandise came to life when safely stowed away in the holds of friendly ships.

As the Protestant countries offered hospitality to the refugees, some sought homes in Holland and others in Switzerland. They were obliged to make their way thither during the darkness of the night, concealing themselves by day, and crossing the frontiers by the least frequented roads. Many found means of crossing to England, notwithstanding the precautions taken to prevent them from doing so.

Certainly, the migration of such numbers of industrious people could not but make itself felt throughout the kingdom, and it did paralyze commerce and manufactures to a great extent. It being impossible to ascertain the exact number of refugees, each historian seems to have set down figures according to his own conjecture; consequently the numbers are in some cases undoubtedly exaggerated. Hume has estimated the exodus to have cost France half a million of her subjects, and many have accepted his statement. Larrey, Jurieu, and Benoit give as a total two hundred thousand, Basnage, one hundred and fifty thousand, Caveirac fifty-five thousand, and others seventy, and sixty thousand. The Duke of Burgundy, of whose opportunity of ascertaining the nearest approach to the correct figures and of whose sincerity in stating them an historian has assured us,[1] asserts their number not to have exceeded sixty-eight thousand.

There can be no doubt that the loss of even the least of these numbers of subjects did affect the material prosperity of France; and this fact was most probably the cause of the unwillingness of Louis to have the Huguenots leave his kingdom. And here likewise historians differ. Some assert that their migration was the ruin of the country, while, on the contrary, others say that the disadvantage to France has been greatly overstated. Tessereau, the king's intendant, says: "Although the refugees from La Rochelle were from amongst the principal inhabitants, both in regard of substance and reputation, the generality of the emigrants were those who either had little

[1] Fredet.

or nothing, or were compelled to leave what they had behind them." Certainly the majority were obliged to receive assistance from the countries in which they sought refuge, instead of enriching them as some would believe.

They did take with them, however, a vast amount of energy, industry, and a knowledge of manufacture, along with the germs of the principles of the democratic government they afterwards helped to establish in the new world, and a corresponding love for freedom, and hatred of monarchial forms of government, and all that savored of royalty.

With their loss agriculture declined, and likewise the culture of the vine; consequently the domestic supply and the foreign trade in wines were cut off. Imports failed, as the links of commerce were sundered; weaving also suffered greatly. Yet, notwithstanding all this, some writers have declared that, instead of being a misfortune to France, the king received congratulations because this emigration freed his kingdom from rebellious subjects whose loss would soon be made good.

The greatest misfortune would seem to lie in the fact of a mother country so treating her children as to oblige them to seek a home on foreign shores, even were the reproach of one of the exiles to his fellow refugees merited, — of having caused these extreme measures by their own conduct; to which he added a second, saying that the laws of most of the Protestant countries against Catholics were more severe than those of Catholic princes against Protestants.[1]

Those of the refugees that reached Switzerland immediately became incorporated into its civil as well as religious life, while those that succeeded in reaching Holland joined the Walloons, and some of them eventually reached the shores of the new world in

[1] Avis aux Refugiés, Baylé.

Dutch ships. Others again that sought permanent homes or a temporary asylum upon the English coast found in some localities French Protestant churches with the surplus of a fund, raised some years previously, and which was now devoted either to their maintenance or to defray their expenses to some of the British colonies in the new world.

Those of the exiles that settled in England adopted the established religion, alleging, as a reason for so doing, that the kindness received from the country as well as the church made such a step a duty for them; but others, so long as they were not obliged to renounce it, clung to the form of religion in use in their native land. Those that intended to make their future home in the colonies adopted, for the time being, the form of the established church.

During their sojourn in England, the wealthier and more intelligent of the refugees had the opportunity of gaining information regarding the different British colonies, and had leisure to mature plans for their future. Many of them had relatives or acquaintances in the new world, and, after some correspondence with them, their future course was decided.

Such of the refugees as had foreseen their flight, had left their property in the care of friends, who afterwards contrived to transmit at least a portion of it to the owners. To such, although saddened by reverses and separation from friends and country, the future did not present such a dreary aspect as it did to those who had only their passage money, or not even that. The latter were obliged to trust their future in the hands of some captain willing to convey them to the sometimes very distant port to which the vessel was bound.

None of the French vessels being of sufficient size to cross the Atlantic, the poor Huguenots were usually landed upon some European coast, were they fortunate enough to reach it alive; for the voyage was full of danger, and the captains often unskilful. Many of the exiles found homes in the bosom of the deep.

The American colonies were desirous of receiving the refugees. Massachusetts and South Carolina had agents in England to make proposals to them. William Penn would fain have their assistance in the forming of his new colony, and Virginia offered them land at trifling cost and even as a gift, provided they would settle upon it.

Many of the refugees took out papers of naturalization before they left England. Others, loath to cut the slender tie that united them to their native land, deferred the act until they should reach the precise locality in which they should decide to settle.

When Charles II. first invited the Huguenots to England, he led them to believe that by one general act, they all would receive the benefits of naturalization; but this idea was not realized. For a long time they were allowed to obtain under the royal seal a grant by which they might secure to themselves and families all the rights, immunities, and privileges enjoyed by free-born citizens; the only obligation being that of actual residence in England or within its dominions: but several exactions were made; among which was a certificate proving that they had received communion, and another promising they would take the oath of allegiance and supremacy within a year.

In 1671 Virginia passed an act giving to all aliens, that desired to become citizens the liberties, privileges and immunities of those born within the British dominions upon their presenting a petition to the Assembly, and taking the usual oath of supremacy and allegiance. New York passed a similar act in 1686, and South Carolina did the same in 1691.

Escape from their country was not, however, the sole solicitude of the exiles. By it one step might be accomplished, but other steps were yet to be taken before their lives could assume a peaceful tenor. First was the passage across the great ocean that lay between them and the new world in which they hoped to plant their "vine and fig tree;" after which some time must elapse before they could hope to eat their fruits and rest beneath their shade.

The passage of the Atlantic was fraught with many dangers. No two vessels ever pursued the same course, as Maury had not yet planned his wind and water-current charts. Chronometers and quadrants were unknown to navigation, the compass being the captain's sole assistant. Sometimes, indeed, the ship would be found many degrees out of its intended course, and again approaching to the very coast it had lately quitted. Steam not having been impressed into the service, the small and inferior vessels were the sport of every wind and wave. One moment raised on a mighty billow, the next would find them engulfed in its depths, to be tossed upwards just as the passengers thought to find a watery grave.

Pirates infested the waters; consequently, however distant, every sail caused a tremor of anxiety to captain, passengers, and crew. Every vessel was obliged to carry guns and ammunition, which occupied the room needed for provisions for such a lengthy voyage, and sometimes they were reduced almost to starvation. Frequently deaths ensued from lack of food as well as from want of medical attendance and the simplest of remedies.

"Land ho!" was a joyful cry; but often it was only the beginning of new dangers, as no pilots were found awaiting them, and no friendly lighthouse warned them of dangerous rocks; and in case of shipwreck no saving life-boats manned by willing hands and fearless hearts were there to save them. What wonder if many of the poor exiles required no earthly home.

Provided the landing was successful, who shall describe the homesickness of those who had left the most luxurious of all the modern countries, with the refinement of its society and the comforts of the family hearthstone, with its well-known faces and familiar language, to meet the inconveniencies and privations of a new land, with its strange tongue and unfamiliar countenances?

But brighter days were in store for these poor wanderers. To whatever part of the new world they came they brought their industry and enterprise, and probably no other class of emigrants contributed more, in proportion to their number, toward the prosperity of the country of their adoption than they. In whatever station of life they belonged they were remarkable for their kindliness and courtesy, as likewise for the refinement, and even elegance of their manners, as well as their mental calibre.

Of the seven presidents of the Continental Congress, three were of Huguenot parentage: Henry Laurens, John Jay, and Elias Boudinot. In New York city and in its vicinity the names of the French refugees are amongst the most prominent ones.

Chapter Second

"NEW YORK is settled upon the west end of the island having that small arm of the sea which divides it from Long Island on the south side of it, which runs away eastward to New England, and is navigable though dangerous. For about ten miles from New York is a place called Hel Gat which being a narrow passage, there runneth a violent stream both upon ebb and flood, and in the middle lieth some Islands of rocks, which the current sets so violently upon that it threatens present shipwreck; and upon the flood is a large whirlpool which continually sends forth a hideous roaring, enough to affright any stranger from passing any further, and to wait for some charm to conduct him through; yet to those that are well acquainted little or no danger, yet a place of great defence against any enemy coming in that way, which a small fortification would absolutely prevent and necessitate them to come in at the west end of Long Island by Sandy Hook, where Nutten Island doth force them within command of the Fort at New York, which is one of the best Pieces of Defense in the north parts of America.

"New York is built most of brick and stone and covered with red and black tile, and the land being high, it gives at a distance a pleasing aspect to the spectators. The bay upon the south side which joins to the sea, it is so fortified with bars of sands and shoals, that it is a sufficient defense against any enemy. Upon the south side of Long Island in the winter lie stores of Whales and Crampusses, which the inhabitants begin with small boats to make a trade, catching to their no small benefit. Also innumerable multitude of seals which make an excellent oil. They lie all the winter upon some broken marshes and beaches or bars of sand before mentioned, and might be easily got were there some skilful men would undertake it. Hudson River runneth by New York northward into the Country towards the head of which is seated New Albany (a place of great trade with the Indians) betwixt which and New York being above one hundred miles is as good corn land as the world affords."

Such was one of the first published accounts of the colony of New York, written much in the style of Mandeville, and it is probably as accurate a description of Manhattan Island and environs as may be found.

The "hideous roaring" of Hell Gate has moderated its tone; the seals that once basked upon the marshes of southern Long Island have taken themselves to more congenial shores: and the whales and grampuses that frolicked in its waters probably continue their sports in quieter places. The bar, once such an obstacle to navigation, is there no longer; it has subsided into the harbor bottom or else continues its "moanings" in some other locality, allowing vessels of the largest size to approach the city except at the lowest tide: this has proved of great benefit to the young colony.

As a violent storm makes itself known by ripples breaking upon far distant shores, so the great disturbance in France occasioned by the revocation of the "Edict of Nantes" caused itself to be felt even in the insignificant little colony of New York; the majority of whose inhabitants had scarcely recovered from the shock occasioned by the fact of being handed over, like so much merchandise, into the hands of another sovereign.

During the years 1685–6 a continuous tide of immigration poured into this obscure colony. Every vessel arriving in its port brought some of the refugees; which fact caused a considerable amount of puffing in the long pipes of the Dutch inhabitants, and of increased loquacity amongst the English portion of the colony.

Not indeed that these good people were unwilling to extend the hospitality of the new world to their unfortunate fellow-creatures, there being quite a sufficiency of room for all; but even the best-tempered people are apt to be discomposed at innovations in time-honored customs, and certainly many would be necessitated by the admission of so great a number of persons of a different nationality.

Indeed they had already commenced. The first and most important of which was a change in the established postal system.

Although more than a decade of years had passed since the government of the colony as well as its name had been changed, its members still retained the characteristic trait of its former proprietors,—evidenced in a degree of phlegmatic temperament rarely met with outside of those in whose veins flow the blood of the settlers from Holland, or perhaps in others who, from constant and intimate association with them, had contracted the same peculiarity.

The New Yorkers were certainly a slow people. The "hideous roaring" of Hell Gate on the one side of them and the harbor bar on the other, may account for foreign commerce and domestic trade having passed to other ports, thereby increasing the importance of the sister colonies of Philadelphia and Boston: nevertheless its best friends could call it nothing else but slow.

In the year 1686 the discontinuance of their postal system called the "Coffee House Delivery," considered sufficiently good for the past onc hundred years, was the immediate cause of the present disturbance of the even tenor of community life.

One should have lived in the days of coffee houses to fully understand the inconvenience of this innovation.

During the early days of the Dutch settlement, the population of Nieu Amsterdam being small and communication with the mother country limited, there had been but little epistolary correspondence, and that little mostly confined to merchants respecting their cargoes.

It was the custom in those days to hoist the flag of the "Privileged West India Company" upon the flagstaff in the old fort, whenever a vessel appeared in sight; and its orange and blue decoration was the signal for a general turnout of the masculine portion of the community to watch and speculate upon the approach of the ship.

Upon its arrival, this correspondence was immediately consigned to its respective owners. Those who expected any news of either personal or general nature received it by hand in the former case, and in the latter contingency by word of mouth. If, perchance, there should be an unclaimed missive it was left in the care of some responsible person until an owner was found to claim it.

In time, however, the captains of the vessels, finding sufficient to occupy them besides answering questions and delivering letters, placed the latter, upon landing, in the most popular resort in those days, which was the coffee house. From there they were quickly claimed, read, and discussed over cups of fragrant coffee. The finding of owners for unclaimed missives was greatly facilitated by the custom of fastening them upon a board hung in some conspicuous part of the public room. The endeavor to decipher the almost illegible, and in some cases all but undecipherable, superscriptions helped to pass an idle moment away and also give basis for speculation.

This custom had been continued even after the

English had possession of the settlement, as in the coffee house met all the great and learned men of the place, as well as the wits and visiting celebrities; and great was the flow of wit and reason over the favorite beverage, as they discussed the news that was interchanged and circulated to an extent that would cast into the shade the far-famed locutionary powers of the fairer portion of the community — but of course men will never admit this.

In the year of '86 all this was changed, for an official order had been issued that all letters coming by ships should in future be sent direct to the Custom House; consequently the "Coffee House Delivery" became a thing of the past.

American spirit, however, was not to be thus easily conquered; for when later on the British government started a post office, continental post was likewise started, and patronized to such an extent that the governmental one had very little to do.

Although letters were no longer distributed there, the coffee houses still held their own in the public affection as places of general resort; holding amongst our ancestors the place the club houses of the nineteenth century do to their descendants. There, matters of great importance as well as matters of no importance at all were discussed, from wars and rumors of wars abroad to a runaway horse at home. Every ship arrival supplied a stock of news to be exchanged or retailed in greater or lesser quantities as suited the will of the giver and the moderate or immoderate desires of the recipient.

When the subject of taxation without representation was discussed, and, later on, that of an independent government mooted, the meetings, formerly of a social nature, assumed a seriousness befitting the matters discussed, and sittings were long and frequent. It was in the coffee house known as "The City Arms," which faced Bowling Green that opposition to the Stamp Act was first started. This old building stood until a comparatively late date, when it was taken down to make way for modern improvements. It was built partly of brick, the sides and rear being of wood, and was surrounded by a garden in which musical entertainments were given. Tradition says that Benedict Arnold lodged in this house after his treason.

During British occupation, the coffee houses merely existed. Fraunce's held its own, however, although it was more of a hotel than coffee house proper. This old building is still standing at the corner of Broad and Pearl streets, and has been enlarged, it being at that time only three stories in height; it is of brick and was built in the early part of the eighteenth century by Mr. S. Delancey, who resided in it. It is still quite firm and may be identified by the green marble slab set in the corner, stating that within its walls Washington delivered his parting address to the army. After that event it declined in importance.

After the War of the Revolution, nationality seemed forgotten, and the descendants of the English, Dutch, and French met in a loving brotherhood born of their late common grievances; and they chose for their place of mutual resort the "Merchants' Coffee House," which stood at the corner of Wall and Water streets. It is described as a three-story building, a store occupying the lower part. On the second floor was the "Long Room" in which public meetings were held. Here statesmen and politicians, merchants and literary men, discussed the affairs of the nation over their cups of coffee or tea.

Amongst its frequenters might be seen the majestic figure of Washington and the angular one of Thomas Jefferson, his political opponent, the brilliant Alexander Hamilton and the intriguing Aaron Burr, Ben Franklin, who never contradicted any one, and Gouverneur Morris, who found fault with every one except General Washington, the refined Chancellor Livingston and that rock of sense, John Jay, George Clinton, the anti-Federal governor, and John Adams with royalistic tendencies, John Morin Scott, the versatile lawyer, and William Bradford, the first public printer of New York, Hugh Gaine , the champion of the free press, and his insatiable satirist, Philip Freneau; these, and many others perhaps as well known, found ample subject for present discussion and future conjecture. Here Washington was received upon his arrival in the city for the inaugural ceremonies. The Chamber of Commerce held here its first meetings, and the insurance business was started within its walls, as was also the first bank of New York. The compilation of a city directory, "the size of a Westminster Catechism," was herein essayed, and the "Loyal Sons of St. Andrew" and the "Grand Lodge of Free Masons," as well as many other associations, held their meetings inside its doors; but with the removal of the national government to Philadelphia its sun sank to rise no more.

The year 1686 was a marked one in the little colony. The mother country had seemed to awaken to the fact that its infant, and future prodigy, was still acting under the seal of Holland; and forthwith a larger and more elaborate one was granted it. The same year Governor-General Dongan, who had accorded a kind reception to the Huguenots since 1683, deemed it necessary to extend the city limits to meet the requirements of the increased population; he therefore ordered a survey of the northern boundary of the settlement, and a removal of its walls to a more remote locality.

Hitherto the line of the present Wall Street had been defined by a palisaded work erected as a means of defence against the Indians; it extended the entire width of the island from the shipyard of Rip Van Dam, now comprised in Trinity churchyard, but at that time the western limit of the island, to "Bucther's Pen," adjoining the river on the eastern limit. At the head of Broadway was a large gate, which was closed every evening by the city watch; and nearer the river on the eastern side was another, called the "Water Gate," through which ran the road to the ferry to Breucklin, now Pearl Street. Beyond this gate stood the ferry-house, by the door of which hung a tin horn; any one desiring to cross, by winding the horn, would summon a boatman to conduct him to the opposite shore, for the moderate sum of one-half cent.

In many places the works had fallen down; which rendered the duty of closing the gates at night quite a nominal one; except that the fact of doing so gave the inhabitants a certain sense of security; which was a great thing in itself. The guns too had disappeared, and the ditches and trenches were in a ruinous condition.

By the governor's orders, the palisade was removed to the present line of Chamber Street, running from the river bank on the west side to the old Ferry house on the east side, now Catherine Street; at every short distance a block-house was placed. The line of the old palisade was laid out into a street, which took its name from the wall that had once occupied its place. The streets, that same year, were paved, and they were also lighted by means of lanterns suspended from every seventh house; and a watch patrolled them all the night, who sang out the hours as they passed.

The city limits were at that time more circumscribed than at the present; Greenwich Street then formed the western boundary, and Pearl Street the eastern one. All ground beyond these streets has been made by filling in.

Recently, in excavating in the lower part of Front Street, the ribs of a vessel were unearthed; they were thought by some to have been those of the "Morning Star," a powder ship blown up in the harbor August 7, 1778. This fact goes to prove the encroachment of the city upon the water limits.

The French refugees were relegated to the eastern side of Broadway below Wall Street, and in the vicinity of the "Bucther's Pen," this being an unfavored part of the city, where the laboring portion of the community dwelt, and there were many unused lots.

The frequent Indian incursions had caused the settlers to centre around the fort to such an extent as to endanger its safety; so much so that certain officials complained to the home government that it might be easily scaled by placing ordinary-sized ladders upon the surrounding houses.

This old fort deserves a word for itself, it being the first and oldest structure of the settlement; and, according to the author already quoted, "one of the best Pieces of Defence in the north parts of America." I am inclined, however, to the opinion that Mr. Lamothé would have said of it the same as he said of an old fort on the Jersey side of the river, "It is no great things."

This venerable piece of Dutch antiquity, that was destined never to hand down its name to our republican times, — indeed, to bear none for any great length of time, — was erected in the year 1614 by the Nieu Amsterdamers as a defence from the attacks of the Indians. It is described as a mere palisaded work, but its form and dimensions have not been stated; it went by the name of Fort Manhattan until 1626, when its increase in extent, and number of inhabitants, caused a more substantial work to be constructed, which upon completion was called Fort Amsterdam. It is most probable that the plan of De

Razieres was not carried out to the full extent of his designs, as we find Governor Stuyvesant alleging, as an excuse for ceding it so easily to the English, that it was an untenable place, and not fit to bear an assault from European firearms. The walls, furthermore, on its northern and northeastern part, although much higher than those of its other sides, were, nevertheless, lower than the ground beyond. So much higher was the latter, he added, that people sitting on it could see the very soles of the shoes of those who might be standing on the esplanade, or bastions of the fort. Indeed, its walls for some eight or ten years were merely ramparts of earth, from eight to ten feet high. The buildings within it, occupied by the officers of the garrison, were composed of planks, or bark only, with roofs of reeds.

In 1633 Governor Van Twiller came to Nieu Amsterdam invested with full power to better this state of things. Under his administration a guard-house and barracks were constructed, and a wind-mill erected for grinding the grain for the garrison. A substantial brick house took the place of the former governmental building, which lasted during the successive administrations of the Dutch dynasty.

The condition of the walls of the fort, however, does not seem to have been improved, as we find the governor in his Council of 1647 deliberating as to the advisability of having them repaired. This was to be accomplished by means of "stones laid in mortar to make of it a lasting work;" and for this purpose it was suggested that every male inhabitant between the ages of sixteen and sixty should devote twelve days of labor in the year; or give instead, the sum of eighty cents per day.

Within the fort and adjoining the gubernatorial mansion there stood a stone church of peculiar structure, consisting of two peaked roofs with a steeple between them. Beyond this edifice stood the prison, and further on the guard-house, barracks, etc. These buildings occupied the eastern side of the fort; on the western side was the gate, defended by four small brass cannon.

On the southwest bastion of the fort, at the junction of the present State and Stone streets, stood the windmill and also a large flagstaff, upon which floated the colors of the "Privileged West India Company" whenever a vessel might appear in sight. By the river outside the fort stood the gallows and whipping-post.

The governors varied in their way of living as well as in their manner of entertaining,—these being influenced to a great extent by their former social position in the mother country. As each incumbent furnished the gubernatorial mansion himself, it varied considerably in appearance under each administration. At times the state carriage with gay livery would drive in and around the fort, and the evenings were enlivened by music from the band, and other entertainments.

The fashionable part of the community resided along the lower part of Broadway facing Bowling Green, or on the environs of the fort.

In 1664 the fort passed into the hands of the English, and was called by them Fort James, in honor of the Duke of York, and a battery was added by the river. The interior was likewise greatly improved, and the mansion rebuilt.

In 1673 the Dutch regained possession of it, and its name was changed to that of William Henrick, which name it bore for an entire year. Under Governor Andros the name was changed again to Fort James. This governor erected an armory between the mansion and church; also a stockade around the exterior to protect it from wild animals.

In 1683 Thomas Dongan, an Irish Catholic, formerly Lieutenant Governor of Tangiers, and afterwards

Earl of Limerick, was appointed governor of the colony. Dongan was a highly accomplished gentleman, upright in all his dealings, and firm and judicious in his policy. His strict integrity won the affection of the people, and caused him to be one of the most popular of all the royal governors.

Governor Dongan's first act upon entering his administration was to summon the freeholders to the fort to elect representatives to meet him in council, which resulted in giving to the colony its first Legislative Assembly. This Assembly was to consist of the governor, ten councillors, and seventeen representatives chosen by the people, and its first act was to give to the province its first Charter of Liberties. By this charter it was decreed that the supreme legislative power should be permanently vested in the General Council and people, met in general assembly. Second: that each freeholder and freeman might vote for representatives without any restriction being laid upon his vote. Third: that no freeman should be punished save by the judgment of his peers, and that all trials should be held by jury. Fourth: that no tax should be imposed, under any pretence whatever, without the consent of the Assembly. Fifth: that no martial law should exist. And sixth: that no person professing belief in Jesus Christ should, at any time or in any way, be made to suffer on account of difference of opinion in matters of religion.

This charter still forms the basis of the municipal rights and privileges of New York.

These liberal measures caused great rejoicings, the more so because of the great unhappiness accruing from the tyranny of the late Governor Andros.

In 1689, James II. having been dethroned, the fort was seized by the train-bands or militiamen; and one of their captains was appointed to hold it until the will of the Crown should be known.

Leisler having been the one selected, he took possession not alone of the fort, but of all the prerogatives of the administration. He changed the name of the fort to that of William, which it retained for the period of two years. During his administration, a half-moon fortification was made on the west side of the fort; upon which seven guns were placed to defend the landings of both rivers.

Leisler, having had a taste of power, desired to retain it, and refused to surrender possession of the fort when required to do so. He was in consequence immured in the very prison he once commanded, and was finally executed as a rebel.

The fort now had the name Henry added to it. The old Dutch church was demolished and an English one was erected on its site.

In 1702 the name was again changed to that of Anne, which it bore until the Georges ascended the throne. It never had another.

In 1741 the mansion was burned down and the fire was attributed to the slave population, the famous "Negro Plot" having originated in this year. The mansion was rebuilt and an additional battery added to the fort; but in 1773, while Governor Tryon was the incumbent, the building again took fire and was entirely consumed in two hours' time.

At the close of the Revolutionary War, the entire fortification was removed, to make room for the presidential mansion, which was planned to face Bowling Green. At that time the exterior appearance of the fort was that of a green sloping bank, about fourteen feet high; and above it arose the walls to an additional height of twenty feet. A portion of the materials was used in building the mansion.

In the early days of the colony the houses were mostly built of bricks brought from Holland. These were of different colors and set in patterns and glazed, the prevailing colors being red and black. The ends of the houses always faced the streets; the gables, rising by successive steps to a point, were always surmounted by a weathercock. Under the projecting eaves was a "stoep," on either side of which were seats adapted to social intercourse. The lower windows of the houses were made quite small, as a precaution against the incursions of the Indians.

The interiors of the houses were kept scrupulously clean; the planed floors were well scrubbed and sanded, and traced with delicate designs; the oaken rafters were polished and carved in devices and mottoes; and the doors were perforated with bull's-eyes and well scrubbed with sand.

Furniture, in those days, was more for use than comfort or ornament. Chairs were high-backed and rush-bottomed, and made of red walnut or mahogany. Tables were round, and turned by means of a pivot to a fan shape and were usually placed against the wall when not in use. Couches were covered with worsted damask, and clocks extended from floor to ceiling. In the corner of the best room there usually stood a buffet with glass doors, containing, as well as displaying, the family plate and china; conspicuous amongst which was a huge punch-bowl, also tiny cups and saucers, and tea and coffee pots with silver handles and spouts. Sideboards were not introduced until after the Revolution, and were very small.

Stoves were unknown; but open fireplaces, with shining fire-dogs, gave a cheerful appearance to the rooms. Small bits of carpet, usually imported by the family, were sparingly laid in the "best room." Coaches were rare, there being for some time only four or five in the entire settlement.

As time wore on and means of communication with Europe became less difficult, the wealthier settlers were enabled to import their furniture; and carpets began to make their appearance in most of the better class of dwellings, which soon began to assume a degree of luxury hitherto unknown.

A certain John Miller, chaplain to the fort, seems to have kept the statistics of the colony. He computed the number of families in New York, in the year 1692, to have been three thousand. Of these, one half, he says, were Dutch and rich, but sparing; the other half was composed of English and French, of whom the former outranked the latter in numbers, and were neither rich nor economical, and the last mentioned were poor and necessarily penurious.[1]

This worthy dominie depicts things from a rather dismal standpoint. He calls the inhabitants an ungodly people, who have no care for heavenly things; but instead turn everything to drink or money to buy it with. "Even the crops," he says, "are usually such as will yield some kind of liquor, cider, perry, etc."

A more cheerful writer of the gentler sex, on a visit from Boston, describes the same city as "a delightful place; where the inhabitants are courteous and hospitable; where families interchange invitations to dinners and suppers, at which times the tables are crowded with provisions; where the families mostly dine at one o'clock, and never later than two in the day; and games of cards engross the post-prandial hours of the more leisurely part of the community."

There were no theatres, to be sure, as in Boston; but concerts were given by amateurs, and there were assemblies for dancing which met in a large hall, the entrance being by subscription. As unanimous consent from all the members was necessary to secure a membership, the affair was very select. At these assemblies the stately minuet and sprightly cotillion were

[1] The West India Company incorporated Nieu Amsterdam as a city in 1653, and modelled its government after that of Amsterdam.

the order of the evening, the latter dance having been introduced by the French.

Marriages and funerals were public; but notes of invitation to them were issued. The funerals were followed by long processions on foot, as no public conveyances were used prior to the year 1789, and very few families owned a "leathern conveniency" as Robert Murray styled his carriage.

Without a doubt the French refugees bore a prominent part in the great change in the colony, and they undoubtedly infused new life into its veins.

As we have said, the Dutch were a slow people. They were noted for the slowness, perseverance, and the plodding tenor of their lives; they had got into a groove and they steadily persevered in it. Their social life had always been simple, domestic, and unostentatious.

The English were formal, and held strict ideas of caste, which consisted of a lower, middle, and upper class; the barriers separating each were impregnable and insurmountable. Some of the wealthier Dutch families held aloof from strangers, and formed a distinct class by themselves; but the majority met the British officers and attachés at public entertainments; and after a time adopted their idea of caste.

The Huguenots were naturally romantic, vivacious, and chivalric; and, freed somewhat from the overshadowing vigilance of their founder's spirit, and having no party feeling like the others, they formed, as it were, a bond of union between them.

The original settlers, finding no reason for alarm at the inroad upon their hospitality, and shaken out of the narrow groove in which the course of their existence had formerly run, could not but acknowledge the beneficial effect of the leaven from France. Immediately upon their arrival, the Huguenots had commenced to ply their industries, and very soon that portion of the city which, through force of circumstances, they had been compelled to accept — the vicinity of Bucther's Pen, it having, in all probability, moved away with the city's limits — gave evidence of their thrift and consequent prosperity.

Moreover, the first destitute refugees had been followed in course of time by others; who had been more fortunate in bringing with them some of their patrimony. Nearly every ship of those that arrived once a month from England brought over families of wealthy, and even noble ancestry.

The refugees of the better class had mostly engaged in mercantile or commercial pursuits. They had erected comfortable and even handsome dwellings, and the elegance and refinement of their private life caused the aristocracy amongst the Dutch and English to welcome them to their entertainments, and to take pleasure in being entertained by them.

The style of architecture likewise had greatly improved. Pearl Street, at that time the first one west of Broadway, and which between State and Whitehall streets was extremely narrow, contained some handsome dwellings.

At Coenties Slip stood the municipal buildings, up to the time of their removal to Wall Street, in the early part of the eighteenth century. There, also, stood a celebrated inn for the reception of visitors to the city, this spot having been chosen on account of the exceeding beauty of its prospect, and its aristocratic surroundings.

At the slip, Pearl Street curved to the north, widening considerably at Hanover Square; it also changed its name at different stages in its course, assuming first that of Dock Street, then Hanover Square, Queen and finally Magazine Street.

On this street the gable ends ceased to face the street, and "stoeps" and benches yielded to roof balconies, which formed pleasant and more retired localities for rest, recreation, or sociability. From these elevated pleasure gardens might be seen the beautiful shores of Nutten[1] and Nassau Islands,[2] with Staten Island and the highlands of the North, or Hudson, River forming a background.

Here one might enjoy at evening the fresh ocean breezes wafted over the lovely bay, and from the Sound through South River;[3] and the gentle lapping of the water in Countess' Slip[4] made itself heard in the quietness of the night.

In course of time Bowling Green and Lower Broadway, which had been par excellence the aristocratic part of the city, gave precedence to their rival Pearl Street, just above Hanover Square.

This square was then the fashionable shopping locality; and there might be seen old Dutch and high English dames, mingling with the fair daughters of sunny France, to admire the fashions from over the sea — six months old or more.

Dress at this period was greatly attended to by both sexes, — the ladies attiring themselves quite elegantly, and the young men appearing Beau Brummels of a Sunday, with coats of every color and indeed of several colors combined. The skirts of the coats were frequently lined with silk and satin of delicate hues, and the collars were of velvet or silk, of quite different colors from the garment. Sometimes, indeed, instead of collars the coats were finished off with several small capes. It is probable the young men were as frequently met in Hanover Square as were their lady friends, mothers, sisters, and loves — on business matters of course, for men are never frivolous.

In 1754 Mr. Walton,[5] who had accumulated a for-

[1] Governor's Island. [2] Long Island.
[3] East River now. [4] Coenties Slip.
[5] Mr. Walton married a daughter of Mr. Delancey.

tune in foreign trade, built, in Pearl Street, a house of such elegance as to compete with the Kenedy mansion, No. 1 Broadway. Its fame, we are told, reaching the mother country, was the innocent cause of preventing any scruples from arising in the maternal breast, in regard to the taxation of her infant colonies; for, she argued, if provincial children can build for themselves such elegant mansions, they may well afford to pour some of their surplus gold into the maternal coffers.

This house was built of yellow Holland brick; and its spacious gardens bordered on South River. In this residence, in after years, Antien Genet wedded the daughter of Governor Clinton. Later on, in No. 119 of this street, General Moreau[1] lived when an exile in this country; and his family remained in it while he fought for the Allied Army. After his death his widow resigned it into the hands of the executors, and there was a sale of his beautiful furniture and curios. A friend[2] of the writer's has still in her possession the elegant crystal chandelier that hung in the drawing-room of his house.

The wealthy merchant Jumel, who loaned of his fortune so largely to France in her need, also resided in this street.

Although the lower portion of Manhattan Island was composed of sandy soil, it nevertheless bore a good supply of elm, maple, and sycamore trees, as also Normandy poplars, that stood like grim sentinels along the streets.

[1] There is an amusing anecdote related of General Moreau while in this country. He was invited to a concert, during which a piece was sung, the refrain being "to-morrow, to-morrow." The general, understanding English but imperfectly, supposed the song was composed in his honor and the refrain to be the repetition of his name; he consequently thought it obligatory to acknowledge the mark of respect. The audience were consequently astonished by seeing him rise and bow most respectfully on all sides as often as the refrain was repeated. Many of them did not know the illustrious man by sight.

[2] Mrs. Julius G. Caryl.

In 1732 walks were laid out in Bowling Green, and bordered with shade trees; it then took the place of a modern park. Shortly after, however, fashion changed its location to Pearl street, and thus began its march up town which it continues to the present time.

Chapter Third

ALTHOUGH a French congregation had been established in the early days of the colony, it had ceased to exist before the year 1678; or that in which the Rev. Peter Daillé, the first minister of whom we have any record, began to hold French services. It is not probable that the first congregation had any distinct edifice, as Mr. Daillé was obliged to make use of the old church in the fort; he holding his services between those of the Dutch in the forenoon, and the English in the afternoon.

In the year 1687 the Rev. Pierre Peiret arrived amongst a band of refugees, with the intention of ministering to their spiritual interests. As their number was constantly increasing, it was deemed fitting, and even necessary that they should have a church for themselves. Mr. Peiret consequently proceeded to erect a small building on Marketfield Street. It was a very humble beginning, certainly, as its entire length was only forty-eight feet nine inches, by a front width of twenty-seven feet seven inches. A passage taken off from the width rendered the greater part of the building only twenty-five feet wide.

Upon Leisler's usurpation of the administration, the Huguenots divided into two parties; one of these being headed by Mr. Peiret, the other by Mr. Daillé. The former party opposed Leisler's administration; but the latter favored it to such a degree as to endanger his adherents in their efforts to have him released from prison, and saved from death by execution. Party feeling ran so high that the French congregation never again became thoroughly united.

After Leisler's death, Mr. Daillé removed to Boston; and it is probable that his representation of the state of affairs in the New York congregation helped in a great measure to cause the misunderstanding between Mr. Gabriel Bernon and the French congregation in that city.

The colony by this time, counted some two hundred families; and, although all of them had not located in New York city, sufficient had done so to cause the population to be about one-fourth French.

Before Governor Dongan's withdrawal from the administration, the refugees had petitioned him for the right of free trade in the colonies; and he, having forwarded the petition to the king, had received a favorable answer.

In 1689 the administration had devolved upon Richard Coole, Earl Bellemont; who, upon assuming control of the colony, sided with the Leislerites or people's party; thus rendering himself very unpopular with Mr. Peiret and the majority of the French congregation. This unpopularity was increased by the belief that he had misrepresented some matters, thereby injuring their interests with the Board of Trade. So bitter was their feeling, that he found it necessary to take some means of conciliating them, to regain their support; which he recognized as very necessary for the success of his administration, the French having become important factors in the colony, by the rapid increase of their numbers.

Being on intimate terms of friendship with Gabriel Bernon, the founder of the Huguenot colony in New Oxford, Massachusetts, Bellemont thought to gain the support of Mr. Peiret's party through his influence. Inviting him, therefore, to New York for the ostensible purpose of consulting with him about matters relating to the Crown, he laid before Bernon the opposition he experienced from the French congregation; causing it to appear like rebellion against the king.

Misled by his representations, and acting in good faith, Bernon endeavored to become a mediator between the two parties; and for this purpose met Mr. Peiret and the principal members of the disaffected congregation. Expressing his deep regret for the feeling existing between the several nationalities and the administration, he urged the French congregation to cultivate a more kindly feeling.

To his exhortations they replied that they would prefer to go to Mississippi than to live under Bellemont's authority. Bernon, now fully convinced of their disaffection, returned to Boston chagrined at his want of success in his pacific endeavors. Before leaving New York, however, he essayed one more attempt to remedy matters. Penning a letter full of regret at their conduct and expressive of his hopes for their amendment, he left it with his host to be given to Mr. Peiret after his own departure.

The minister, as well as the congregation, conscious that they had given no just cause for offence in the beginning, and that the fault lay rather on the part of the governor, waited upon the latter in a body, and, laying before him the subject of their grievance, protested their innocence.

Bellemont, like a shrewd politician, recognizing his mistaken way of gaining his end, strove to pacify them. Disowning his share in the transaction, he left Bernon to bear the brunt of their displeasure as having misinterpreted the sentiments of the governor towards them.

But notwithstanding his fair face in the matter, Bellemont was greatly displeased with the Huguenots; and he took the petty way of revenging himself by suppressing the annual stipend granted by the government for the support of the minister.

The bitterness between all parties only terminated at the death of Bellemont in 1701.

Gabriel Bernon's letter to the Consistory of the French Church in New York, 1699.

NEW YORK 25^{m} Mars, 1699.

Messieurs, Premier, partir, de cette Ville, Je me trouve obligé comme etant tous fréres Refugiez, de vous dire, qve Monseigneur Le comte de Bellemont ma fait venir ici pour discouvrir, avec son Excellence, de certaines, affaires qui Regarde le service du Roy. Apres qvoy son Excellence moi aussy entretenu de la bonne volonté qvel a pour vous; qvel voit avec douleur L'animosité contré les Englais les francais et hollandois. Que son Excellence se fait du plaisir de Ramenir avec clemence ceux qvi s'eloigne du D'voir, D'eu a sa majesté et a L'etat, &c. Que son Excellence na favorisé aucun parti: qvel n'a d'acception qve pour Les bons sujets du Roy Guilleaume puis qve son Excellence na pour But Principal qve le plus service de Dieu la gloire du Roy, et la prosperité des Peuples; son Excellence nous exhorte comme de bons sujets de nous aymer afin qu'etant unis D'amitié nous soyons fidelle a son Majesté pour leqvel nous D'vons prier Dieu de benir ses entreprises et Luy donner une vie Longve et heureuse. Amen.

Pour moi J'ai comme vous pour La Religion, A Bandonné Les Biens et notre patrie, ainsy qve plusieurs de nos freres Refugiez en divers endroits du monde, nous D'vons, chaq'un de nous, nous soumettre sous Le govvernement ou nous Rencontrons. C'est pour nous un grand Bonheur et un grand honneur de nous povvoir dire et Reclamer bons sujets de notre sovveirain le Roy Guillaume, qve puis qve Dieu nous Commande de nous assujettir au puissance Royale, qu'on ne peut avoir trop de veneration pour un sy grand, sy bon et sy l'Lustre prince, n'y trop de Respect pour ses govverneurs qvi nous Le Represente: On peut qvelqve Lois Bien avec Respect se familliariser avec Les puissance; mais; on ne peut Jamais sans Crime, Pasquinir ou felonir L'Autorité Royale ceux qvi agissent par felonie et Pasqvinerie qve Les Loys d'Engleterre Condamne, meprise L'Etat &c. (*sic*). J'ay vue avec Douleur qvelqu'un s'eloigner du D'voir qve nous D'vons a son Excellence Monsigneur Le Comte de Bellemont.

Ne croyez pas qve je sois assey temeraire pour meriger en Senseur, ny pour vous Rien Prescrire. Mais J'ai Creu en frere pouvoir vous dire mon veritable sentiments cette Diversité de goust, s'accorder; vaus etes pour Mischipipi? Je suis pour Road 'Island. Je vous offre mes services La et par tout ailleurs. Je feray tousjours gloire de vous assurer, Qve Je suis avec Respect,

Messieurs,

Votre tres humble et tres obeissant serviteur
et frere Refugié,

GABRIEL BERNON.

Messieurs D'L' Eglise francoise,
de la novelle York.[1]

Answer of the Consistory of the French Church in New York to Gabriel Bernon, 1699.

YORK, Le 22e May, 1699.

Monsieur, Vre Létre qve vous avez ecrite a Mr Jamain nous oblige a rompre Le silence sur un sujet qve nous avions résolu de laisser dans l'oublir c'est une mechanté Libelle qve Mr. Gabriel Bernon (*sic*) laissa icy en partant entre les mains de son hote, avec ordre de la rendre aprés son départ a messrs de l'Eglise françoise da ce lieu, nous le regardames comme la production d'un esprit malade et privé de jugemt plustot digne de pitié qve d'indignation et nous creumes qu'au lieu de le relévér il valoit mieux l'ensevelir sous le voile de Charité, mais comme il a lui meme publié sa honte en distribuant des Copies de cet ecrit nous avons lieu de croire qu'il avait eté pousse a le faire par un autre motif qve celui de l'indiscretion qvi lui est si naturelle et qve nous povvons prendre l'accusation qu'il fait contre nous comme une calomnie dont il a voulu salir ce troupeau de refugiez vous trouvéréz dont bon s'il vous plait qve nous dision qvelqve chose pour (*sic*) notre Justification et qve nous vous addression ces Lignes tant pour vous affermir dans le sentiment qve vous temoignez avoir de son procedé, qve pour détromper ceux qvi en ont en de mauvaise impressions contre nous, vous priant de les faire voir a messrs du consistoire de votre Eglise et a tous ceux qui peuvent etre prévenus.

[1] The Huguenots in France and America, vol. ii., p. 118.

Cette homme suppose comme vous avez veu dans la Copie de la lettre qu'il vous a remise qve nous sommes ennemis du Roy tratres au Gouvernement et violateurs du Respect qvi est deu a Monseig^{r}. Le Comte de Bellemont et il nous fait espérer de trovver l'impunité de nos Crimes dans la Clémence de ce seigneur pourveu qve nous rentrions dans notre dévoir, et il nous a fait entendre qve n'ayant rien peu gagner sur nous par ces Exhortations de ces Crimes odieux dont le moindre merité sans doute un chatiment sévére il a été obligé de laissér cétte Lettre pour tenter d'obtenir par son écrit ce qu'il navait peu obtenir par ces paroles et qve ce qu'il a fait a cet égard il la fait par ordre de Monseigneur le Govverneur.

Mais premierement il est faux qve le Govverneur lui aye Jamais donné aucun ordre sur cela et nous le soutenons hardiment parceqvenous etans presentez déux fois a son Excellence en corps de Consistoire accompagnéy de qvelque chefs de famille pour nous élancir la dessus elle a eu la bonté de nous déclarer qvelle n'avait point aux parler de cela et qve si elle eut connu qvel' qu'un coupable de ces crimes elle l'avait poursuivre selon la rigeur de Lois sans imputer au corps le crime des particuliers, qve les expressions de cette letre etaient horrible et qve Mr Bernon avait mal fait de rendre sa Letre publiqve il ne sçaurait dont des avouer qve nous ne soyons en droit de la revetir du titre de menteur et qve sa hardiesse a mentir ne soit d'autant plus impudente, qu'il commet l'honneur d'une personne pour laqvelle il nous accuse de manqver de respect, cependant c'est par le profond respect qve nous avons pour Monseigneur Le Comte de Bellemont qve nous n'avons point voulu entreprendre de nous justifie par cette ecrit qu'apres en avoir obtenu la permission de son Excellence.

Il est encore faux qu'il ait tenu a aucune de nous pendant le séjour qu'il a fait ici, des discours; nous ne disons pas semblables a ceux de sa létre, mais approchans en aucune maniére s'il nous eut veu veritablement engagez dans les Crimes dont il nous accuse ou qve l'imbécilité de son esprit eut pris des phantomes pour des réalitez, il devait nous reprocher nos rebélions et nous répresenter nos devoirs entant de rencontres ou nous avons ou avec lui des conversations longues et familieres et dégagé de toute craintre: au contraire ayant été soubçonné d'avoir rapporté a my Lord qu'un de nos françois avait tenu des discours trop libre touchant le Gouvernement il entreprit de se justifier; et n'oublia rien pour eloigner tout le soupçon. N'était ce pas la le Lieu de s'ovvrir et de nous dire ce qu'il a ecrit cependant il na la point fait ni rien d'approchant, mais voulant pourtant nous charger et nous rendre odieux en nous imputant des Crimes dont il a bien veu qve nous n'etions pas coupable, puis qu'il na osé nous les reproacher par les voye naturelles, il a laissé cette libélle difamatoire entre les mains de son hoté avec un Ordre premier de ne point nous la rendre qu'apres son depart semblables a ces láches assassins qve se cachent afin d'oter la vie a ceux qu'ils n'aiment point le voila dont deux foix a menteur sur un méme sujet, pour le fond de son accusation il ni eut Jamais rien de plus contraire a la verité, il n'est pas nécéssaire qu'il nous passer des Leçons pour nous remontrer l'obligation ou nous sommes d'honorer le Roy Guilluame nous le scauons et nous serions les gens du mondes les plus ingrat et les plus uniqve si nous manqvions en ce devoir car nous recoinnaissons qve nous sommes redevable a cette incomparable Prince de tout le repos dont nous jouissons et qve Dieu la fait naitre pour la Conservation de son Eglise et pour la Consolation de tant de pavvres qui ont echapé au persecuteurs de france mais on de doit pas craindre qve nous Tombions dans cette ingratitude nous serions bien plus capable de faire notre idole de ce grand et glorieux monarque qve d'oblier la veneration la fidelité et l'obbeisance qve nous La devons.

Il n'est pas non plus necessaire qu'il nous avertisse qve nous devons respecter ses Gouverneurs, nous le scauons et nous le practiquons comment pourrons nous ne pas avoir du respect pour des personnes qui representé dans Leur Govern[t].—Le Roy Guillaume qui est l'object de tout ce qve nous pouvons concevoir d'estime, d'amour, et de veneration dans l'ordres des affaires humaines, nous respectons Monseig[r]. Le Comte de Bellemont et nous honnorons sa personne et son charactere et nous receverons toujours ses ordres avec soumission. Pour le Gouvernment nous nous y sommes toujours soumis avec plaisir tout parceque la proffession du Christianisme nous y oblige qve parceqve le Comparant au Gouveren[t] de france sous laqvel nous avons gemi si longtemps, nous le trouvons extremement doux et humain et proportioné au droits de la nature nous protestons qve nous serons toujours prest a la deffendre de tout notre pouvoir contre tous ceux qvi entreprendront de le troubler ce sont la nos veritable sentiments opposez comme vous le voyez au accusations de M^{r}.. Bernon et nous ne doutons pas qve tout ce qu'il y a d'honnété Gens ne fut disposez a nous rendre ce temoinage s'il etait necessaire comme il nous fut rendu il ny a qve peu de Jours par le procureur du Roy qvi recconut devant monseig^{r}.. le Govvern^{r}.. lors que nous pleignisme a son Excéllence des accusations de M^{r}.. Bernon qve nous nous étions toujours montrez fort affectionéz au Gouvernment et qve le Roy n'avait pas de meilleurs sugets qve nous en Effet si il en avait quelqun parmi nous qui parut animé des pensées qve cette homme nous impute nous le retrencherions de notre Corps comme un monstre indigne de notre Société nous vous prions Monsr.. de les faire connaistre a tous ceux a qvi les discours de M^{r}.. Bernon peuvent avoir donné des préventions contre nous, c'est la toute la vengeance qve nous voulons prendre de lui encore qu'il nous soit fort dur de nous voir accusez par un homme qvi porte avec nous le titre d'Exilé pour la religion et qvi veut icy nous faire de feintes protestations d'amitie nous lui pardonnons de bon cœur lui soubsistant une Conduite droité a l'avenir et un judgement plus solide et a vous la Benediction de Dieu &c

(sic)

Monsieur Votre &c

PEIRET *Ministre*
JEAN BARBARIE
ELIE BOUDINOT
PAUL DROILET
GABRIEL LE BOYTEULX

The family of Bernon,[1] or, de Bernon, as it was known in France, was originally from Burgundy, and is one of the most ancient families of the kingdom. It claims its descent from the younger branch of the Counts of Burgundy, several of whose princes have borne the name from the year 895. Its

[1] As Bernon was a connection of Freneau's family, we give a short sketch of his life and labors for his countrymen in America.

arms [1] from the fourteenth century were borne by the Counts of Maçon.

That branch of the family of which Gabriel Bernon, the refugee, was a descendant, has or had, in its possession all the documents necessary to prove its identity from the time of Raoul de Bernon. This house is allied to some of the most illustrious families of France. It has rendered distinguished services to its country, and has numbered amongst its members superior officers of great merit in the army, as well as in the navy. Several of its names are found in the "Livre d'Or de la Noblesse" as belonging to the Order of Saint Louis.

The name of de Bernon is found amongst those of the families that were represented in the Crusades in the year 1191. In the sixteenth century it is seen contributing towards the ransom of the sons of François 1st, who were held as hostages by Spain after the battle of Pavia. It also sent money by the hands of Duplessis-Mornay to Henri Quatre, to assist him in his efforts to obtain the throne.

Besides the claims to nobility entailed by their Burgundian ancestors, the Bernons of La Rochelle possess still another claim to distinction, several of the mayors of that city having been furnished by them. To have held the office of mayor of that city, according to the customs of the time, conferred rank, not alone to the person who had held the office, but to his heirs forever.

Raoul de Bernon, who served with distinction in the wars of his time, married Charlotte de Talmont and their son, Nicolas, was mayor of La Rochelle in the year 1357. His son held the same office in 1398. Jean Thomas, son of the latter, founded the two

[1] Azur à un chevron d'argent surmonté d'un croissant de même, accompagné en chef de deux étoiles d'or et en point d'un ours passant demême.

gentilhommières or manors of Bernonière and Bernonville, the former deriving its name from a small château near Pouzauges in Poitou, now the department of Vendée, and the latter, from a château on the Isle de Ré. Jean Thomas had a son named André, who had two sons: Pierre, sieur de la Bernonière et l'Isleau, and Jean.

Jean's son André married Catherine du Bouché in 1545, and their son Léonard married Françoise Carré, 1578, and had two sons: Jean, sieur de Bernonville, and André. The latter married Jeanne Lescour, and, after her death, Marie Papin in 1605; their two sons were Léonard, sieur de Bernonville, and André, the latter being the father of Gabriel the refugee.

The branch of the family to which André belonged was distinguished as de Bernonville, and was amongst the first in La Rochelle to embrace Calvinism. The other branch, de la Bernonière de l'Isleau, also adopted the same belief.[1]

André, Gabriel's father, was one of ten children, five of whom were sons, the remaining five daughters. André was a prosperous banker, and ancien of the Huguenot Church. He did not long survive its destruction and the dispersion of his brethren, but died soon after the Act of the Revocation of the Edict of Nantes was passed, and was buried by night in his own gardens at Périgny.

Samuel and Jean de Bernon, André's second and third sons, became zealous converts to the Catholic faith. Some of the letters written by the former to Gabriel, in reply to his severe reproaches, are still extant; they prove the sincerity of his convictions, and give the reasons for his conversion. As sieur de Salines he lived in luxury in Poitou. Jean, sieur

[1] Bernon famille habitant la Rochelle après avoir embrassé l'hérésie de Calvinisme n'a Jamais voulu se faire réhabiliter; elle a toujours été riche et considérée.—FILLEAU.

de Luneau, resided before and after his conversion in San Just. Ester escaped to England, and Jeanne married Jean Allaire, brother to Alexandre Allaire, the refugee, and one of the founders of New Rochelle, Westchester County, in the State of New York. Another sister married a Mr. Du Pont of La Rochelle, and her son Jacque, along with Jeanne's son, Louis Allaire, accompanied their uncle Gabriel Bernon to America. André and Benjamin Faneuil, connections of the de Bernons, accompanied this party in their flight.

Gabriel was forty-one years of age at the time of the revocation of the Edict, and was one of the leading merchants of La Rochelle. He married Ester Le Roy, the daughter of a landed proprietor whose residence faced the royal palace. He was an inflexible Huguenot and had materially assisted the refugees who had settled in Quebec. Gabriel attempted to settle in Quebec, but on account of his religious convictions was obliged to leave Canada. Upon his return to France he was arrested and thrown into the prison of la Lanterne, from which, after an imprisonment of several months' duration, he was released through the influence of his Catholic brothers, Samuel and Jean.

After his release, Gabriel disposed of his remaining property, but he received only about one-tenth part of its value. He managed to escape with this into Holland, where his wife was to meet him; but she was arrested in her attempt, and was only set at liberty upon feigning conversion. She speedily joined her husband, however, and they sailed to England, landing in London, where they were met by their relatives Louis Allaire, Jacque Du Pont, and the two Faneuils.

Bernon, with the intention of settling in America, had sent several sums of money to his agent in that country, who purchased a tract of land of twenty-five hundred acres not very far from Boston; and later on he sailed for his new home with his wife and relatives, along with forty other refugees whose expenses he paid to his colony.

Arriving in Boston, he was put in possession of his grant by the custom of investiture of twig and turf, by Chief Justice Dudley. Bernon and his nephews remained in Boston, leaving his agent to act for him in the colony called New Oxford; in which houses, and a fort and church were soon built.

The community all together amounted to about eighty persons; amongst whom was the family of Lydia Sigourney's husband. To all appearance there was every sign of success and an increase of the infant colony, as other refugees frequently joined it.

During King Philip's war, the Nipmucks ravaged the surrounding country, and the Oxford colonists became greatly alarmed. Bernon's agent, foreseeing danger, disposed of all the stock and furniture Bernon had provided, and made off with the proceeds to unknown parts. A visit from the Indians, attended by the usual massacre, caused the colonists to take refuge in the fort, which they soon after abandoned to return to Boston. The minister also went off, carrying with him the books provided for the use of the colony, and all papers of importance.

All that remains to mark the spot of the once prosperous settlement is a huge cross bearing the following inscription: —

IN MEMORY OF
THE
HUGUENOTS
EXILES FOR THEIR FAITH
WHO MADE THE FIRST SETTLEMENT
OF
OXFORD
1680

WE LIVE NOT FOR OURSELVES ONLY
BUT FOR POSTERITY.

"I might have remained in France and kept my property, my quality, and my titles if I had been willing to submit to slavery," wrote, in his old age, Gabriel Bernon the refugee.[1]

The family of Allaire, to which Louis belonged, was another ancient family of France; and one long identified with the Huguenot cause in La Rochelle. This family was represented in their congregation, at the time of the revocation, by several prominent members, viz., Antoine, sieur du Bugnon, Jean, the royal secretary, and Henri, Councillor and Lieutenant General in Admiralty, who were brothers.

Belonging to a younger branch of this family was Pierre, whose son Alexandre Allaire came to America by way of St. Christopher in the year 1686. He finally came to New Rochelle, of which settlement he was one of the most prominent members. Pierre's grandson, and Alexandre's nephew, Louis, as we have already stated, came to Boston with his uncle, Gabriel Bernon, and his other relatives, Jacque Du Pont and the Faneuils. Louis remained some time in Boston carrying on business between that city and southern parts under the name of Louis Allaire & Co. He afterwards removed to New York City where he died of a lingering illness.

André Faneuil located in Boston, of which city he became a prominent member. His descendant Peter Faneuil was the founder of the building bearing his name, and given by him to the city for a town hall and market. In this building, located on Merchants Row and Faneuil Hall Square, were held all the town-meetings during the dark days preceding the Revolution which inspired and kept alive the spirit of liberty. Benjamin settled in New York City, from which place he exported goods to London.

[1] Huguenots in America, Baird.

In 1707 the mate of a sloop that had been captured by a French privateer while on its way to England, set the report afloat that the French inhabitants of New York were plotting for the capture of that city by the French; and that Captain Benjamin Faneuil bore a prominent part in the matter. Also that they were in correspondence with the French government to that effect.

The Huguenots, upon hearing the slander, addressed a petition to His Excellency Lord Cornbury, requesting that the mate, Morris Newinhuysen, as well as any other person implicated in the slander, might be examined; and if it was found that any one had given just foundation for the report, he should be punished and the innocent freed from suspicion.

The petition was headed:—

A Full & Just Discovery of the weak &
slender foundation of a most Pernicious
Slander
Raised against the
French Protestant Refugees
Inhabiting the Province of New York generally but more
particularly affecting
Capt. Benjamin Faneuil
person of considerable note amongst them

The captain of the vessel, John Van Brugh, testified that the mate had told him that a boatswain found some letters on board of the sloop which were addressed to France under cover to persons in England. That the contents of the letters were to the effect that the French would find the condition of things in New York in great disorder if they chose to avail themselves of it. That upon questioning the said mate as to his knowledge of the writers of said letters, he said there were no names signed but that the handwriting in one letter resembled that of Captain Benjamin

Faneuil. The mate being sworn, made in effect the same statement. Whereupon the governor issued the following proclamation: —

At a council held at Fort Anne in New York
the 4th *day of March* 1707–8.

Present His Excellency Edward Viscount Cornbury

Rip Van Dam Thomas Wenham	Esqrs.	John Barberie Adolph Phillipse	Esqrs.

His Excellency and council having considered the Depositions of Maurice Newenhuysen and John Van Brugh concerning a Letter writ from hence to France, and taken in the sloop Constant Abigal, giving some account (as is said) of the condition of this place, do declare unanimously, That they do not think that there is any ground to suspect Capt. Faneuil of holding correspondence with France nor to prosecute him here on the aforesaid Depositions

By Order of His Excellency in Council

Geo. Clarke.

Another petition was laid before the governor, requesting that his secretary should provide the Huguenot congregation with a copy of the "minits and Entries" relative to the search and inquiry, along with the opinion of the governor and his council, and also a license for the printer to imprint the same; that their reputation might thereby be vindicated, which was granted.

The signers of the two petitions were Stephen D'Lancey, Elias Nezereau, Abraham Jouneau, Thomas Bayeux, Elias Neau, Paul Droilet, Auguste Jay, Jean Cayale, Benjamin Faneuil, David Cromelin, Jean Auboyneau, Francis Vincent, and Alexandre Allaire.[1]

Although many other names of the refugees are of sufficient interest to insert here, we have only selected from them such names as belonged to relatives of the family of Freneau.

[1] Doc. Hist. N. Y., vol. iii.

The Huguenots, having sold their diminutive church in the year 1703, were authorized by an Act of the Legislature to purchase a building lot, and the site selected was that on the northeast corner of King[1] and Nassau streets. In the following year they erected a stone edifice with a tower in the rear. Sir Henry Asshurst presented a bell to be hung in it.[2] Over the portal of the church was a tablet bearing the inscription: "l'Eglise du St. Esprit Gall: Prot: Reform: fundat 1704: Peritus Reparat 1741."

This old church, for the first hundred years of its existence, was the place of worship for the Huguenot families of New York and environs. Those who had settled in New Rochelle also worshipped in it, although this act of piety obliged them to leave their homes before light, in order to reach it before services commenced.

Tradition points to an old building one and a half stories high, which stands near the Kingsbridge about a mile to the northward of Crosskeys tavern, or the place where it once stood, which bore for its sign a blue bell, from which it took its name. This it declares was the veritable place of rest where these men, of sterner stuff than now, were wont to halt over night on their weekly journeys from New Rochelle to New York for the sabbath services.

In the year 1724 some defection on the part of the minister gave great displeasure to the consistory and a part of the congregation, who consequently gave him his dismissal. He and the remaining portion of the congregation resisted; and the matter was laid before the governor, who decided in favor of the minister, and he was retained. This proved to be very prejudicial to the interests of the church, as most of the congregation left it for either the established

[1] Pine St.
[2] This old bell is now in New Rochelle.

church or that of the Dutch. It was consequently neglected and became sadly in need of repair.

In 1812, Bishop Hobart, of Trinity Church, offered to have the Huguenot church thoroughly repaired and set upon a firm footing, if the minister and congregation would enter the Episcopal communion and use its liturgy. The parties agreed to this proposal and the edifice was repaired, and a fair congregation seated.

The old church was totally destroyed in the great fire of 1776, but had been rebuilt. It has since, changing its liturgy, removed to West Twenty-second Street, New York City.

Chapter Fourth

ALMOST two centuries have rolled on their course since André Freneau, the founder of the family in America bade farewell to the quaint old city of La Rochelle in France to face the shores which were thenceforward to be his home.

The pitiless hands of time and fire have obliterated nearly every trace of his existence. The family records, along with much that was valuable in the way of letters and manuscripts, perished in the flames that consumed the family residence of Philip Freneau at Mount Pleasant (now Freneau) in Monmouth County, New Jersey, in the year 1818.

One old relic, piously rescued from the relentless flames, remains, and mutely seems to say, "I alone have escaped to tell you." This heirloom in the form of a Bible, published in Geneva in the year 1587, has been in the Freneau family, perhaps before, but certainly ever since the year 1590. The first record on its time-worn pages tells us that it was in that year it began its journey from father to son, as was the custom in the Huguenot families in France.

It alone remains to tell us of the hands it has passed through, until the present time, when, for want of male heirs, it has come into the possession of a great-granddaughter of Philip Freneau, the Poet of the Revolution.

Its record runneth thus :—

Ce livre fut donné par Philip P. Fresneau à son unique fils Jacque. Janvier 3^{d} 1590.

De Jacque Fresneau à son second fils Jacque Fresneau Janvier 1eme 1605.

De Jacque Fresneau à son second fils Thomas Fresneau Janvier 1re 1630.

De Thomas Fresneau à son frère Jean. Janvier 1653

De Jean Fresneau à son fils André Fresneau mon second Janvier 1re 1680

De And. Fresneau à son second fils André Fresneau Jan. 1re 1702

De André Fresneau à son second fils Pierre Fresneau Jan. 1re 1725

De Pierre Fresneau à son première fils Philip Fresneau Jan. 2d 1752 (O S)

Philip Morin Freneau reçoit ce livre de son père Pierre Freneau.

Philip Morin Freneau departed this life Dec. 18th 1830. aged 80 yrs. 11 mo. & 13 days.

It is a remarkable coincidence that its first and last possessors of the name of Freneau should have borne the name of Philip, and that of its nine owners they should be the only ones that bore that Christian name.

This Bible, being a Protestant version, was expatriated along with its owners.

The family of de Fresneau belonged to La Rochelle, once famous in the history of the Huguenots — now so changed in their regard. This name, we are told, was of some note amongst the Rochellais, but how it happened that its members escaped the fate of so many of their compatriots, we are not told; the flames have guarded their secrets well.

That the family residence of André the refugee was named "Mont Plaisant" is the only fact of transatlantic days that has been transmitted to his descendants.

It must have been a dreary place, that La Rochelle, and like a city of the dead to those remaining there like the grapes left from the vintage! How all things around them must perforce have brought up sad memories of those who had once lived and loved amongst them, but were now wanderers on the face of the earth.

There was la Lanterne,[1] in which Gabriel Bernon and so many others had been imprisoned; and not far from it stood the former dwelling of Pierre Jay. The residence of Ester Le Roy still faced the king's palace, but the voice of Ester was no longer heard within its walls. Of the Bernons, one alone was left in the old mansion, so veiled in mystery, and in which the remaining Huguenots met for their secret services. The dwellings of the Allaires and Du Ponts, even if not entirely without occupants, yet lacked some of the former members of their families, who were now numbered amongst the aliens of the land of their birth.

There were yet to be seen the old Scriptural inscriptions, or verses from Marot, over the small, plain doorways that gave to the street, but opened inwardly into residences in which evidences of wealth, refinement, and elegance met the eye.

The narrow, crooked streets, where formerly the tokens of recognition were so frequently interchanged, were peopled with strange faces. No wonder, then, that hearts should sicken and desires awaken to leave these sadly suggestive spots,—and that André Freneau should bid good-bye to his native land.

We may imagine the sentiments he experienced as the sombre towers of la Lanterne and Saint Nicolas faded from his view, and the receding shores of the isles of Ré and Oleron told him that he was henceforth a stranger to the land of his fathers.

We would infer from his age at the date of his death that at the time of the revocation of the Edict of Nantes, in 1685, he was but ten years of age, and from the fact of the ancient Bible having been presented to him in the year 1702 it would seem like a parting gift from his father.

[1] La Lanterne was built for a lighthouse, but was used as a prison during the persecution of the Huguenots.

It is most probable that he first went to England, and from there directed his course to the port of Boston, but we do not hear of him in the new world until the year 1705.

In this year rumors of copper being discovered in the township of Suffolk, Connecticut, caused the proprietors in that locality to appoint a commission to institute a search, which proved successful. The news travelled to Boston and caused some capitalists there to interest themselves in excavating.

The land had been the hunting ground of Indians, and being unclaimed property the proprietors of the town of Simsbury assumed its control, and leased the ground to some private individuals as well as companies. André Freneau proceeded thither and, leasing a mine, began to excavate.

According to the laws regulating the colony, smelting of ore was prohibited; therefore, loading a vessel, Freneau shipped it to London. The ship was captured by a French cruiser, and his enterprise resulted in total loss. So great were the disadvantages attending mining at that time, it is not surprising that Freneau, in the year 1707, relinquishing all hopes of realizing any profit from his enterprise, left the mining district and turned his thoughts to the city of New York, where Benjamin Faneuil had already commenced commercial business.[1] It is not certain whether Louis Allaire preceded or followed him to that city.

Upon arriving in New York André engaged in the shipping business, and also acted in the interests of the "Royal West India Company of France," in which he was associated with Etienne Delancey, Auguste Jay, Benjamin Faneuil, René Het, and others.

[1] This mine was afterwards converted into a prison called Newgate, and was the first state prison in Connecticut. The excavations served for the safe keeping of the convicts. The prison was afterwards removed to Wethersfield, and the mine is now used as a show place. It retains the name of Copper Hill.

On the seventeenth of June in the year 1710, André married Marie, the eldest daughter of Pierre Morin, or Morine, whose name appears as the head of a family in the records of the Church of St. Esprit. He was the maternal grandfather of John Morin Scott, the prominent Whig lawyer, of whom we will speak hereafter.

After his marriage, André and his young wife, who had just entered her seventeenth year, resided on lower Broadway facing Bowling Green, which was at that time the aristocratic part of the city, and it is said he entertained in considerable style. His name appears in the records of the French Church as the head of a family, and an ancien of the church.

It had always been the custom in the temple, or principal religious edifice, of the Huguenots, for the anciens, or elders, to have, along with the consistoire, prominent seats reserved for them during the services. In the mother country, the consistory was composed only of the pastors of the churches in a certain district, and one ancien chosen from each congregation, to represent it in the assembly. As such members were charged with the oversight of the flock and its temporalities, as well as their spiritual interests, the office was one of considerable responsibility, as well as honor. In New York, there being but one congregation, the elders formed the consistory. They were elected every three years.

In the year 1713, a robbery having been committed in Trinity Church, of which the Rev. Mr. Vesey was rector, the minister and consistory of the Church of St. Esprit, fearing a like sacrilege, presented a petition to the governor that the perpetrators should be apprehended and brought to justice.

The petition being of no great length, and its quaintness amusing, we will insert it. We have failed to find any method amongst the colonial writers generally, whether English, French, or Dutch, for the use of capitals, consequently we are almost led to think that such letters were thrown promiscuously amongst the type, finding, wherever they chanced to lodge, "a local habitation and a name." However, as we never remember to have found them in the middle of a word, there may have been some rule to govern such a contingency.

It would not be surprising if this promiscuous and generous use of big letters first caused Lindley, the son of Robert Murray, proprietor of the "leathern conveniency" of colonial days, to project his grammar.

Address of the Minister and Elders of the French Church in New York.

TO THE HONN^BLE^ HER MAJESTIES COUNCELL FOR THE PROVINCE OF NEW YORK.

Wee the Ministers & Elders of the Reformed Protestant french Church within the city of new york cannot sufficiently express our abhorrance of that Wicked, and Sacrileges Fact, committed the Night Between Tuesday and wednesday Last, by some Impious Persons in Trinity Church within this Citty: Being a structure built and dedicated to the service of God, the discovery and Punishment of wich hainous crime, wee estime ourselves, so deeply concerned in, to the end it may deterr others from attempting the Like on that, our, or any other Building sett apart for divine worshipp within this citty; That wee humbly take Leave to offer to your honnours, That iff his Excellency, or your honn^ble^ board, shall think fitt to Issue a proclamation with a Reward to the Person that shall make a discovery of the said wicked offense; we shall Cheerfully contribute the sume of tenn Pound towards an Incouragement for the Person that shall make such a discovery, and in duty bound wee shall pray, &c.

LEWIS ROU.\. *Minister of the French Church in N.^o^ York*
JOHN BARBARIE *Elder*
LOUIS CARRÉ *ancien*
JEAN LAPORT *ancien*
ANDRÉ FRESNEAU *ancien*

New York 16th
February $17\frac{13}{14}$

The date of André's marriage is not recorded in the register of the French church, which is explained by the fact of the frequent interruptions in its services. Marriages and baptisms were frequently performed for the Huguenots in Trinity or in the Dutch church. André's marriage does appear in the register of the Dutch church, but the baptisms of all his children are registered in the French church, and in the following order: —

Baptême. Auiourdhui dimanche 29e de Juillet 1711 mons^{r} Louis Rou notre pasteur a Baptisé André Fresneau né le 24e de ce mois à 3 heures du matin fils de André Fresneau et de Marie Morin presenté au St Baptême aprest la priere du soir par la Sr Morin et Judith Jamain Parein et mareinne.

L. Rou *Pasteur*

And^{É} Fresneau
Pierre Morin
Judith Jamain

Baptême. Aiourdhuy dimanche 8e fevrier 17$\frac{12}{13}$ aprest la priere du soir monsieur Louis Rou a Baptisé Marie Fresneau née le 4^{m} de ce mois fille d'André Fresneau et de Marie sa femme presentée au St Baptême par le dit André Fresneau et Marie Morin Parein et marienne.

L. Rou *min.*

And^{É} Fresneau
Marie Morin

Baptesme. A la nouvelle york de 9me d'octobre 1715 auiourdhuy dimanche aprest la priere du soir mons^{r} Louis Rou a Baptisé Marguerite Fresneau née de 8e de ce mois fille de André Fresneau et de Marie son Epouse presenté au St Baptême par Alexandre Allaire et Marguerite Morin parain et mareine.

L. Rou *ministre*

And^{É} Fresneau
Alexander Allaire
Marguerite Morin

Baptême Le samedy 11me Janvier 171$\frac{7}{8}$ avant mydy Est né Pierre Fresneau fils d'André Fresneau et de Marie Morin baptisé par Mons. Louis Rou en sa maison la dimanche 19ᵉ du même mois presenté au Sᵗ Baptême par Monsʳ René Het et Mad. Ester Charron Parain et maraine.

L. Rou *Pasteur* — André Fresneau, René Het, Ester Charron

Baptême. A la nouvelle york ce 11ᵐᵉ de Mars 171$\frac{8}{9}$ Auiordhui mercredy aprest la priere du matin Mons. Louis Rou a Baptisé Thomas Louis Fresneau né le 5ᵐᵉ de ce mois fils de Monsʳ André et Marie Fresneau presenté au Sᵗ Baptême par Monsʳ Thomas Bayeux et Madˡᵉ Ester Morin Parrain et marraine.

L. Rou *ministre* — André Fresneau, Thomas Bayeux, Ester Morin

Baptême, a la Nouvelle york ce 24ᵉ de Juillet 1720 Auiourdhuy dimanche aprest l'action du soir Monsʳ Moulinars a Baptisé François Fresneau né le 2ᵈ de ce mois fils de monsieur André Fresneau et de Marie son Epouse presenté au Sᵗ Baptême par monsieur Louis Allaire et Madᵉ Judy Morin parain et marrainne.

J. J. Moulinars *Pasteur* — André Fresneau, Louis Allaire, Judith Morin

We find the name of André Fresneau mentioned in the Journal of John Fontaine, a kinsman of the celebrated Commodore Maury. As this Journal depicts the condition of New York City, as well as its society, at the time of Mr. Fresneau's residence there, we will copy that particular portion of it. A few words as to its author may not be out of place as an introduction.

The family of John Fontaine, or de La Fontaine, were Huguenot refugees who left their native land at the time of the revocation of the Edict of Nantes, taking up their residence in England. At the age of seventeen, and in the year 1710, John de La Fontaine received the appointment of ensign in Lord Shaw's

CHURCH DU ST. ESPRIT
Rear View, 1776

regiment of infantry. After serving three years in the British army, he retired from the service and in the following year emigrated to America, settling in the State of Virginia.

In 1716 Fontaine visited New York in company with Mr. Michael Kearney, a member of the family of Kearneys of New Jersey, combining business purposes with those of pleasure, as he was desirous of seeing something of the country of his adoption.

The Journal commences with his departure from the English coast, but we give only that portion which relates to the family whose history we are giving.

October 22d, 1716. In the sloop at anchor under Sandy Hook. The weather was so foggy all day that we could not see the shore, nor landmarks, so we could not hoist our anchor, for this is a very dangerous bay to come up without one has fair weather to see the landmarks. There are several banks and shoals of sand which are very dangerous. There is a great deal of water fowl of all sorts on these shoals.

24th. Calm weather, but such a fog that we could not see half a mile. We had a mind to go ashore, but the master and sailors were afraid that they could not find the sloop again with the boat, so we consented to remain on board. The fog is occasioned by the burning the woods, for at this season the inhabitants set the woods on fire, and the Indians also about this time of the year go a fire hunting.

25th. Still at anchor, weather very foggy, so that the master will not venture up with his sloop. About twelve it cleared so that we could see the land, and we got out the boat, and the men landed us in Staten Island. We were obliged to walk about four miles, not being able to hire any horses. This island is mostly highland and rocky, and that part of the land which is good is mixed with small stones. There are some good improvements here; the inhabitants are mostly Dutch ; the houses are all built with stone and lime; there are some hedges as in England. The chief increase is wheat and cattle. They breed large horses here. About five of the clock we came to the ferry between Long Island and Staten Island, which is about one mile broad. The main body of New York River runs between these islands. We crossed the ferry and came upon Long Island to a small sort of village, where, it being late, we put up at the house of a Dutchman, one Harris Hendrick. We were well lodged and had a good supper.

26th. About eight of the clock in the morning, we hired two horses to go to New York. It is about eight miles from this ferry by land, but not near so much by water. Long Island is generally very plain ground, bears extraordinary good grass, and is an excellent place for cattle. It produceth wheat and all English grain in abundance. The chief part of the inhabitants are Dutch, but there are some few French. Amongst them are several good improvements, and many fine villages; the woods are mostly destroyed. Besides the plentiful produce of the Island, there is every advantage for fishing and fowling that can be wished. About seven o'clock we came to a fine village[1] opposite New York, and we crossed the ferry. The river is about a quarter of a mile over, and runs very rapidly; there are good, convenient landings on both sides. As soon as we landed we went and agreed for our lodgings with a Dutch woman named Schuyler, and then I went to see Mr. André Fresneau at his house, and he received me very well.

27th. About nine I breakfasted at the Coffee House, and at eleven I waited upon Governor Hunter, who received me very kindly and invited me to dine with him. After dinner I walked with him about the

[1] Brooklyn.

fort, wherein he lives. It is a small square situated upon a height above the town, and commanding it. The one side of it fronts the harbor, and hath a small curtain and two bastions; the land side hath but two half bastions to it, so that it is a square composed of two whole and two half bastions. There is a ravelin toward the land that lies on one side of the gate. It is but a weak place, and badly contrived. There is a regiment here, and the Governor always hath a guard, and this is all the duty they have, which is very little. From the Governor I went to see the Mayor of the town, one Dr. Johnson, and was kindly received by him; thence to Col. Delarty's.

28th. About eight of the clock in the morning Mr. Kearny and I hired horses and went about seven miles out of town to see one Colonel Morriss,[1] who lives in the country, and is Judge or Chief Justice of this province, — a very sensible and good man. We were received well by him and remained with him all night; and we saw a great many fine improvements that he had made, and he showed us several rare collections of his own making. He lives upon the river that comes down to New York.

29th. We were invited to dine with Mr. Hamilton and Mr. Lane. After dinner I visited Mr. Fresneau and had a great deal of discourse with him about the trade of Virginia. From thence I walked round the town. There are three churches, the English, the French, and the Dutch Church; there is also a place for the Assembly to sit, which is not very fine, and where they judge all matters. The town is compact,

[1] Judge Lewis Morris, son of Richard Morris, a former captain in the Parliamentary army, who settled in Westchester County, where his son Lewis was born and resided in later life. In 1715 Lewis received a commission as Chief Justice for the Province of New York, which position he held until displaced for political causes by Governor Cosby. In the exciting public affairs of the period, Judge Morris was the leading man in the liberal party. He was subsequently Governor of New Jersey.

the houses for the most part built after the Dutch manner, with the gable ends towards the street; the streets are of good breadth. The town is built close upon the river, and there is a fine quay that reigns all round the town, built with stone and piles of wood outside. There are small docks for cleaning and building small ships. At high water the vessels come up to the quay to lade and unlade. In winter the river is frozen, sometimes all over, and abundance of ice comes down, that it often cuts the cables of ships, but it cannot hurt those near the quay. The town is built on ground that gradually rises from the water, so it is amphitheatre like. The French have all the privileges that can be, and are the most in number here; they are of the Council and of the Parliament, and are in all other employments. The chief produce of this province is beef, flour, pork, butter, and cheese, which they send to the West Indies, and sometimes to Lisbon. They drive a great trade with the northern Indians for skins and furs. There is plenty of all sorts of fish, oysters, and water-fowl. The climate is very cold in winter, a great deal of snow and frost for four months, and very hot in the latter part of the summer.

31st. At ten went to the Coffee house and walked upon the Exchange, which hath pillars of wood all round, which support the roof and leave it open on all sides. I dined with Mr. André Fresneau and remained with him till four of the clock, and at six to the French Club, where they treated me.

4th Nov. 1716. At ten I went to Mr. Fresneau, and with him to church. I returned to his house and dined with him, and at half an hour after two we went to church again. The church is very large and beautiful, and within it there was a very great congregation.

5th. At ten in the morning I carried Mr. Fresneau a memorandum of the prices of goods.

6th. Visited Mr. Fresneau. The Postmaster General, Mr. Hamilton, invited me to dinner.

7th. At ten waited on Governor Hunter and drank tea with him. At four I went to the coffee house, where I met with Mr. Fresneau and at six we went to the French Club.

14th. At six we arrived at Philadelphia, a town which is situated upon rising ground on Delaware River. The inhabitants are mostly Quakers. I visited Mr. Samuel Perez and gave him Mr. Fresneau's letter, etc.

19th. At eight of the clock set out from Mr. Patterson's, which is about sixty miles from Philadelphia, and at twelve arrived at the Court House of the county of Kent, where we baited our horses. About three Mr. Kearny and I went to his brother's house in the neighborhood, where we put up and remained all night.

20th. It being rainy we remained where we were, and had good entertainment. This gentleman, Mr. Kearny hath a plantation and an extraordinary good tannery.

It is not certain in what year the Freneau family left the French congregation. The last of their baptisms was registered in its records in the year 1720; consequently it was not before that date. There is no record of Mrs. Freneau's death, which occurred in the year 1721; but this is not a conclusive proof that they severed their connection with it before that date, as, in looking over the register, we find only one interment recorded during the entire forty years of Mr. Rou's pastorate, except the burials of his own five children; these are most carefully noted.

André's death occurred in the year 1725. As he was buried in the family vault of Trinity churchyard, it is probable that he joined that congregation during his lifetime. It is not improbable that the difficulty between the minister and congregation in the year 1724 was the cause of his leaving the communion of the French Church, and joining that of Trinity, as many prominent families joined the congregations of the other churches at that time.

It would seem that "Aunt Allaire" took charge of the orphaned family, as the eldest child, André, was only thirteen years of age at the death of his father, and the youngest, François, only five. It also appears that she remained ever after with them, keeping house first for André, who never married, and after his death living in Mount Pleasant, New Jersey, in the home of his brother Pierre.

Upon reaching man's estate André carried on the Bordeaux and Madeira trade. The only record we have of him is that of being witness to the marriage of his cousin, Marie Allaire, which took place in the house of her parents in the year 1754. Although this marriage occurred in the year mentioned, it was not registered in the records of the church of Saint Esprit until the year 1761. If we mistake not, only one marriage was registered during Mr. Rou's long pastorate.

Mariage. En vertu d'une Licence de Mr. James de Lancey Lieutenant Gouvernour dans la province de la nouvelle york et terres qui en dependant datée le 6me Septembre 1754 et le 28me année du Regne de notre legitime souverain george 2d. Roy de la grande Britagne etc. Jay Beni ches made. Alaire, le 8me de Septembre 1754 le mariage de Louis Pavez officier dans la Compagnie de fort George de cette ville et Marie Allaire les temoins etaient Marguerite Allaire mere de l'Epousée, Jean Morin Scott, et André Freno ses cousins germains et demoiselle Marie Morin grandmere de l'epousée ce que je declare et enregistre pour servir come de Besoin sera a la Nouvelle York ce 7me Juillet 1761.

Jean Carle *Pasteur.*

A small pencil sketch, with the words, "Andrew Fresneau's House 1756. Cor. Pearl and Wall streets," which goes to prove that he lived there in that year, and a statement that he died in the same locality, are all the data we possess in regard to his later life. The house seems to have been a large and handsome one for that time, but when the family removed there from the vicinity of Bowling Green is not known; most probably it was when the tide of fashion began its northward march. Time has obliterated the date of his death from the vault in which he was most probably buried.

The fate of André's two sisters is very remarkable. Marie, the eldest, was two years older than Marguerite; and between the dates of their deaths, which we find in an old note-book, there was an interval of precisely two years; consequently both died at the same age, that of twenty-two years, and of the same disease, that of the heart. One died in October of the year 1736, the other in the same month of 1738.

A note adds that they were both beautiful; and that each died shortly before the time appointed for her marriage; the one, with a son of her father's business associate, Etienne Delancey; the other, to a member of the Desbrosses family.

Pierre Freneau married Agnes Watson in the year 1748. All that we know of this lady's early life is that she was twenty years of age at the time of her marriage, and that she was related to John Fanning Watson, the antiquary.

Thomas Louis died at the early age of three months, and François married Helen Provost, a relative of the Right Reverend Samuel Provost. Some writers have said the lady was his daughter, but this is not very probable, as François was many years older than Bishop Provost. She may have been his sister or aunt.

François had no children.

In Bishop Provost was united French and Dutch ancestry. His father was of Huguenot descent and his mother was Eve, daughter of Herman Bleecker. He was one of the first seven graduates of King's, now Columbia, College, New York City. His class was that of 1758. It is said that, although he was the youngest of all the graduates of that year, he carried off the honors. He afterwards entered Cambridge College, England, having for private tutor John Jebb, a scholar of great attainments, and one in favor of civil, as well as religious liberty. Provost was ordained in King's College, Whitehall; and, after his ordination, married the daughter of Thomas Bousfield, a wealthy Irish banker.[1]

Mr. Provost was appointed assistant minister in Trinity Church, but resigned in the year 1774 on account of his political sentiments. He was proposed as a delegate to the Provincial Congress, but declined it, as also the offer of chaplaincy to the Convention of 1777, which met to consider the great Constitution.

After the evacuation of the city by the British, in 1784, he was unanimously elected rector of Trinity Church, and was one of the Board of Regents of the University. He was appointed chaplain to the Continental Congress in 1785. He received the title of D.D. from the Pennsylvania University in 1786, and in the following year went to England for his consecration, which took place in Lambeth Palace.

In 1789 he was chaplain to the United States Senate and officiated in the services held in St. Paul's Church, New York, at the inauguration of Washington as first President of the United States. He was also one of the trustees of Columbia College. He

[1] Mr. Bousfield's son Benjamin was a member of the Irish Parliament, and wrote an able reply to Edmund Burke's celebrated work on the French Revolution.

died of apoplexy in the year 1815, and was buried in Trinity churchyard. As a scholar, Bishop Provost was versed in Greek, Hebrew, Latin, and German, and conversed fluently in French and Italian. It has been said that he translated Tasso into the vernacular. His sermons were full of character and force; he is said to have had no peer among American contemporaries. He was so indifferent to literary reputation that he never permitted his sermons to be printed.

In his funeral eulogy it was said of him that what he undertook was to be admired as glorious; what he performed, to be commended as profitable; and wherein he failed is to be excused as pardonable.[1]

Pierre Freneau resided in Frankfort Street after his marriage, and there his eldest son, Philip Morin Freneau, the poet, was born. In the year of Philip's birth, Pierre bought an estate of one thousand acres in Monmouth County, New Jersey, upon which he built a residence, naming it Mount Pleasant, after the residence of his grandfather in La Rochelle.

Here he removed when Philip was in his second year, and interested himself in the care of his increasing family and in the improvement of the estate. Some of the trees planted by him are still standing. Most of these were locusts, which formed a grove around the house. Here all his children except Philip were born, and their names were registered in his own handwriting, thus: —

Philip Morin Freneau	born	Jan. 2d O.S.	1752
Mary Freneau	"	Sept. 10th	1754
Peter Freneau	"	April 5th	1757
Andrew Freneau	"	April 3d	1759
Margaret Allaire Freneau	"	Feb. 27th	1761

Pierre died in the year 1767, and was buried in the family vault in Trinity churchyard, along with his

[1] Appleton.

parents and brothers and sisters. The vault has never since been opened for an interment.

It is most unfortunate that, owing, first, to the British occupancy of New York during the Revolution; secondly, to the disastrous fire of 1776 which destroyed Trinity Church; and thirdly, to the fact that a family burying-ground was laid out in Mount Pleasant,— the vaults of the family in the city were forgotten until it was too late to decipher the inscriptions.

Would that Old Mortality had lived in those days or that there had been some other to do his work!

"Aunt Allaire" dying in the year 1779, a burying-ground was selected in a grove of locust trees, and named from that fact "Locust Grove Cemetery;" and she was laid therein. Her death was not entered in the old Bible until some years later. It is in Philip's handwriting and runs thus:—

"1779 Aunt Allaire was the first buried in the Locust Grove, on the south side of my mother's grave."

Mrs. Freneau did not long remain a widow. A few years after Pierre's death she married Major James Kearny, a member of the New Jersey family of which General Philip Kearny is a descendant.

It is probably not universally known that Keyport, in the northern part of New Jersey, was named from that family. It was at first called K-port, then Kearnyport, and finally it was spelled in the way it is at present. It is a singular coincidence that Philip's stepfather should also be the grandfather of his granddaughter's husband.

Major Kearny died a few years after his marriage, and left Philip's mother again a widow. She did not marry again. Her death is thus registered in the old Bible: "Died on the 18th of October, 1817, Agnes Kearny in her ninety-first year, born of Richard and Margaret Watson in the year 1727 April the twenty-third. She survived her first husband, Pierre Freneau, fifty years and one day; her second, James Kearny, nearly forty-five years. She was interred in Locust Grove, the family burying-ground, on the twentieth of October. Her funeral sermon preached by Mr. Dubois from the words in Rev. chapt. 14th, verse 13."

Of Philip and Peter, we will speak later on. Mary, the eldest daughter, was said by her brother Philip to be "as pure as an angel." She was said to be beautiful and accomplished, for those days. James Madison, afterwards president of the United States, and in early days a college, class, and room mate, as well as confidential friend, of her brother Philip in Nassau Hall, Princeton, told the latter, confidentially, that he admired her more than any woman he had ever seen; and, during his vacation visits to Mount Pleasant, formed an acquaintanceship that ripened into something more on his part. He made proposals of marriage to her, but, although she admired and respected him, she preferred to lead a single life, and could never be induced to alter her decision.

Mary lived to an advanced age, spending most of her time with her dearly loved younger sister Margaret, whom she speedily followed to the grave. Her brother Philip recorded her death in these words: "Mary Freneau, eldest daughter of Peter Freneau and Agnes Watson, died at Newburgh, New York State, on Thursday evening, Jan. 22d, 1829. This truly worthy woman was born in her father's house at Mount Pleasant, near Middleton Point, on the 10th of September, 1754, and at the time of her decease was well advanced in her 75th year. She was virtuous and innocent as an angel, and if there is any happiness in another life for the upright she certainly enjoys it. Farewell.

"By the attention and care of her relative John S.

Hunn, her body was interred on Jan. 24th in the Newburgh burying ground adjacent to the grave of her sister Margaret A. Hunn, who died in 1828."

Andrew, the third and youngest son, died in infancy; and Margaret, the youngest daughter, having married Mr. John S. Hunn, a resident of Newburgh, was not buried in Locust Grove. Her sister, as we have seen, faithful to her during life, was laid by her side in death. Philip has entered only two of these deaths.

"My brother Andrew died of the small pox at Middletown Point in April, 1759, aged about one year. He was interred in the old burying ground near Mount Pleasant which Hendrick Schenk now owns."

Chapter Fifth

MONT PLEASANT, now called Freneau, is situated about ten miles north of Freehold, the seat of Monmouth County, New Jersey. There is no picture extant of the old mansion in its setting of locust trees; but most likely it was built in the usual style of country houses of that period. A writer[1] upon colonial times says that the country residences of the landed gentry of New York and New Jersey resembled those of the large planters of the South, in that they usually had the same wide hall running through the house, the same large porticos and detached kitchens for summer use; and that the condition of life was somewhat similar, for, although the broad acres of the former were usually farmed by tenants, the house was always filled with domestic slaves; and there was the same tendency to imitate the life of the English country families, as far as the surroundings would permit.

I am quite certain that in Pierre Freneau's case the latter paragraph did not hold good; for, although he probably conformed to the architectural style of his adopted country, he still retained the French manner of life that he had been accustomed to lead in his father's house.

To the northeast of the mansion rose the tree-crowned summit of what is now known as Beacon Hill; from whose heights may be seen, to the north, the blue waters of the lower bay, and eastward, the deeper blue of the broad Atlantic. From its foot toward the south, stretch the fertile lands of New Jersey, with the historic battle-field of Monmouth

1 Mr. Eggleston, in The Century Magazine.

in the foreground, — although at that time unstained by the nation's blood.

As a boy, it was Philip's delight to climb the rugged heights of the old hill, and feast his eyes upon the beauties of nature spread before him, and watch the white sails, which, like mammoth birds, hovered over the foam-crested waves. It is very probable that these early scenes made a lasting impression upon his youthful mind, and gave rise to his lifelong yearning for the perils of the deep.

Did the future ever cast its long shadows over the beauty of the scene, and cause the boy to draw his breath yet more quickly, as if to assure himself that the pure air of heaven was not wanting? Did it seem at times as if already the heavy fetters were pressing upon his freedom-loving hands and feet? Was there ever an idea of suffering connected with the flutter of those sails, as they passed and repassed upon the peaceful waters?

Probably not; yet the ancients believed that to the poet it is given to penetrate the mysteries of the future, and read the secrets written there. He turns away — perhaps 't is so; but shortly after, in a pleasanter mood, we see him bending over a new-found treasure, and inhaling the perfume of its pure sweet breath. He seats himself, and, drawing from his clothing a tiny tablet, he inscribes its perfections thereon. Let us look over his shoulder, — he will not heed us, so busily is he engaged, — and let us read what he is so rapidly writing.

THE WILD HONEYSUCKLE.

Fair flower, that dost so comely grow,
  Hid in this silent, dull retreat,
Untouched thy honied blossoms blow,
Unseen thy little branches greet:
  No roving foot shall crush thee here,
  No busy hand provoke a tear.

By nature's self in white arrayed,
  She bade thee shun the vulgar eye,
And planted here the guardian shade,
And sent soft waters murmuring by;
  Thus quietly thy summer goes,
  Thy days declining to repose.

Smit with those charms, that must decay,
  I grieve to see your future doom;
They died — nor were those flowers more gay,
The flowers that did in Eden bloom;
  Unpitying frosts, and autumn's power,
  Shall leave no vestige of this flower.

From morning's suns and evening's dews
  At first thy little being came;
If nothing once, you nothing lose,
For when you die you are the same;
  The space between is but an hour,
  The frail duration of a flower.

At what precise age the little poet began to compose, we know not; but we are told that verses flowed from his pen while he was yet a child.

Philip's mother was a woman of rare intelligence and exceptional education; and she superintended her son's studies until he had completed his tenth year; at which time he was placed, as customary in those days, under the care of a minister to learn the rudiments of the Greek and Latin languages, as a preparation for the higher course. His sensible mother knew that a boy of Philip's ardent temperament required sterner control than a loving mother could use; and she willingly consented that he should become an inmate of the household of the Reverend William Tennant, pastor of the old Tennant Church, which yet stands on Monmouth's battle-field, its floor still bearing the stains of blood shed by its country's martyrs. Perhaps, as a writer has remarked, the boy, playing about what afterwards became historic ground, was inspired by some unseen power to become the "Poet of the Revolution," as he has been styled.

Three years have passed away, and Philip has been booked for the opening term in the Penolopen Latin School, conducted by the Reverend Alexander Mitchell, for a preparatory course in college.

The boy is on his way for the last time to the residence of his tutor, having spent a short vacation at home. Changes are always sad, even when most desired; and as he trudges along, with his favorite Horace under his arm, the merry whistle at times takes a somewhat sadder strain, — for are not joyous natures ever the most capable of the deeper sentiments? He pauses on a slight eminence; the whistle dies upon his lips, and a dreamy look comes over his face. There are moments in the lives of most of us — I might say portions of seconds — in which the misty veil of the future is raised; and down the vista of years our mental vision has barely time to travel, and rest upon some object, when the veil is dropped again, and we are conscious only of an isolated impression, concerning which we would fain know more. Let us, too, look beyond the veil and read the secrets of the future.

Where the road forks, not far from the old Monmouth meeting-house stands a war-horse; and on it leans a person of majestic mien dressed as a soldier, — none such, however, as Philip had ever seen before. Anxiously he looks down the road, as if awaiting some one. A soldier on horseback rides up, and, throwing himself from his horse, makes a military salute, as if to a superior, and imparts some information of a seemingly unpleasant nature. The officer quickly throws himself into the saddle,

AGNES WATSON
Mother of Philip Freneau

and both riders disappear in the distance, from which the rolling of drums and rattle of musketry are heard.

The boy pursues his way wrapped in deep thought; a morass lies to one side of the roadway, over which comes the wailing of the wintry wind, and great storm-clouds veil the sun. The snow begins to fall — thicker and yet faster its great flakes come; and by the border of the morass lies an aged man as if asleep; the large flakes fall upon his upturned face, and play amongst his silvery locks — and the night falls — The boy shudders and passes his hand across his eyes to know if he is really awake. The wind has fallen and the sun is brightly shining; the aged sleeper has vanished, and with him the wintry storm. It is now what it was a moment ago, — a beautiful, bright morning in December, the eighteenth of the month.

On the fourteenth day of February in the year 1766, Philip's father left him in the care of the Reverend Mr. Mitchell, where he remained until November the seventh, of sixty-eight. His father had died the previous year, and, much as his widowed mother desired to retain Philip with her, she did not blind herself to the fact that his freedom-loving spirit needed the discipline that a set form of rules, enforced by a firm hand, alone could give. She also realized that, although there were many undesirable features in a college life, still the training of the intellectual capabilities received therein surpassed all other, and consequently his power of benefiting others would be enhanced. Therefore, in accordance with her late husband's views, Philip was harnessed into the routine of a collegiate course, in Nassau Hall, Princeton, New Jersey.

During Philip's course John Witherspoon was president of the college. He was Scotch by birth, but had thrown himself heart and soul into the fortunes of his adopted country; and his great desire was to see it free from the galling yoke of servitude. Just before Philip's entrance General Gage had marched with seven hundred troops into Boston; and the colonies were thrown into a state of excitement by an Act of Parliament which declared the people of Massachusetts rebels; it had also issued an order for those considered the most guilty to be sent to England for trial.

The young patriots of Princeton were not backward in denouncing this injustice; they kindled amongst themselves the fire of patriotism, that was never to be extinguished, and their efforts were encouraged by their patriotic president. Many of Philip's classmates took an active part in later troubles, and left their names inscribed in their country's annals.

Nearly all his college-mates obtained prominence in the paths they entered in after life. Amongst these were Hugh Henry Brackenridge, the talented author and judge; Brockholst Livingston,[1] future Justice of the Supreme Court of the United States; William Bradford, Attorney General during Washington's second term of office; Gunning Bedford, a framer of the Constitution; Samuel Spring, chaplain to the Revolutionary army; who, by a strange coincidence, carried wounded from the field another old classmate, Aaron Burr, afterwards Vice President of the United States; Aaron Ogden, afterwards Governor of New Jersey; Henry Lee, Light-Horse Harry; and James Madison, the fourth President, who was Philip's room-mate while in college, as well as his warm personal friend, and an aspirant, as we have already seen, for the hand of his sister.

Philip Fithian, class of 73, in a letter to his father,[2]

[1] This college-mate was afterwards related to Philip by marriage.
[2] Philip Vickers Fithian, Journal and Letters.

gives us an idea of the routine of college life in Nassau Hall during President Witherspoon's administration. He says the rules were exceedingly well formed "to check & restrain the vicious & to assist the studious, & to countenance & encourage the virtuous." The bell for rising was rung at five o'clock, and lest any one might oversleep themselves, the servant, after ringing the bell, knocked at each door until the sleeper awoke. Half an hour was allowed for them to dress, after which prayers were said in common. The grammar scholars, being mostly small boys, were excused during winter from morning prayers. On Sundays no student was allowed, except by reason of sickness, to be absent from public worship. Two sermons were preached, one in church in the morning, and another in the college hall in the afternoon. He styles Dr. Witherspoon's sermons almost inimitable. It is to be feared that some of the gifted preacher's moral lessons were lost upon a few of his hearers, as in a later letter Fithian writes: "I am sorry that I may inform you that two of our members were expelled from the college, not for Drunkenness, nor Fighting, nor for Swearing, nor Sabbath-Breaking. But they were sent from this Seminary, where the greatest Pains and Care are taken to cultivate and encourage Decency, & Honesty, & Honour, for stealing Hens!" In 1773, one Israel Evans mentions some delinquencies of a higher grade, in which the future Justice of the United States along with some others were fined for "stealing Turkies." In that year 1770 there were upward of one hundred students, including the grammar scholars. The Senior class contained ten, the Junior twenty-eight, the Sophomore twenty-five, and Freshman eighteen. Freneau was a Senior at the time.

During Philip's first year we are told he made such rapid progress as to cause the President to make his proficiency the subject-matter of a letter to his mother. It is said that in his early days, Philip gave such evidence of his satirical powers upon whatever gave him displeasure as to cause him to be as much dreaded as a foe as he was loved as a friend.

In his sophomore year he wrote a poem in four cantos, entitled "The Poetical History of the Prophet Jonah;" a rhythmical poem, or "versified paraphrase," to use his own expression. He likewise wrote other compositions in various metres, on classical and historical themes, during his collegiate course. Two years after depicting Jonah's sad fate, he wrote the "Pyramids of Egypt," a dramatic dialogue in blank verse. The scene of this poem is laid in Egypt, and the characters are a Traveller, a Genius, and Time; it contains one hundred and thirty-five lines, and was considered a remarkable poem for one so young. The plot of the poem we give.

The Traveller, who has visited Italy, arrives in Egypt, meets the Genius, and asks to be shown the Pyramids, saying that he thought the remnants of Rome he had lately seen were unrivalled. The Genius thus answers: —

"Talk not of Rome! before they lopt a bush
From the seven hills, where Rome, Earth's Empress, stood,
These Pyramids were old, their birthday is
Beyond tradition's reach, or history."

On seeing them, the Traveller asks how many generations, monarchies, and empires —

"had their rise and fall
While these remain and promise to remain,
As long as yonder sun shall gild their summits,
Or moon, or stars, their wonted circles run."

The Genius replies :—

" The time shall come
When these stupendous piles you deem immortal,
Worn out with age shall moulder on their bases,
And down, down, low to endless ruin verging,
O'er-whelmed by dust, be seen and known no more.

. . . .

'T was on this plain the ancient Memphis stood,
Her walls encircled these tall pyramids, —
But where is Pharao's palace, where the domes
Of Egypt's haughty lords? — All, all, are gone,
And like the phantom snows of a May morning
Left not a vestige to discover them!"

To the Traveller's question as to how the Pyramids were built, the Genius says :—

" What cannot tyrants do,
When they have nations subject to their will,
And the world's wealth to gratify ambition?
Millions of slaves beneath their labors fainted,
Who here were doomed to toil incessantly,
And years elapsed while groaning myriads strove
To raise this mighty tomb, — and but to hide
The worthless bones of an Egyptian king."

The poem closes with Time's address to the Traveller in these striking lines :—

" These piles are not immortal;
This earth, with all its balls of hills and mountains,
Shall perish by my hand. Then how can these,
These hoary-headed pyramids of Egypt,
That are but dwindled warts upon her body,
That on a little, little spot of ground
Extinguish the dull radiance of the sun,
Be proof to death and me! Traveler, return,
There 's naught but God immortal — He alone
Exists secure, when Man, and Death, and Time,

(Time not immortal, but a fancied point in the circle of eternity)
Are swallowed up, and like the pyramids,
Leave not an atom for their monument."

"Is not this true poetry?" Mr. Delancey adds. "Is it not extraordinary as the work of a youth of eighteen years? But one other American poet ever wrote anything to compare with it so early in life. Bryant wrote at nineteen his 'Thanatopsis,' and never later did he surpass that great poem."[1]

In the year 1770 the soldiers in New York City cut down a liberty pole that had been erected by the band of patriots called the "Sons of Liberty." A conflict ensued in which the latter won the day. Shortly after this event the Boston massacre occurred, which created a great sensation throughout the country. As we have already said, President Witherspoon was an ardent patriot, and he left no means untried to instil into the minds of his collegians the same fire of enthusiasm that burned within him; and his efforts met a ready response in the enthusiastic temperament of Philip, whose hatred of oppression and of England was equalled only by his passionate love of liberty and America. During his college days the young poet offered his pen on the shrine of Liberty, and vowed to ever use it in her sacred service. How well he used it, her enemies best can tell. His pen was his bayonet, and its wounds were mortal.

In 1771, the year of Philip's graduation, he composed, jointly with Hugh Henry Brackenridge, their commencement address, which they recited. It was entitled "The Rising Glory of America," and was written in

[1] I am indebted to Mr. Edward F. Delancey for permission to reprint this fragment of the poem along with his remarks which are taken from his lecture before the Huguenot Society of America entitled "Philip Freneau the Huguenot Patriot Poet of the Revolution and his Poetry."

blank verse in the form of a dialogue. It was in eulogy of the energy and progress of the colonies, and prophetic of the future glory of the United States. The poem was well received and appeared two years later in print in Philadelphia. Its motto, taken from Seneca, was afterwards adopted by Washington Irving as the heading to his "Life of Columbus."

I would call the attention of the reader to his eulogy of Washington in the poem which is used as the dedicatory poem of this work; his admiration of that illustrious man's character never waned, although in after years many and severe were his comments upon his policy.

This poem has been said by a reviewer[1] to possess "considerable merit in respect to the ease of its versification and beauty of its description; and although as a whole it bears the marks of youth, some points are worthy of a person of mature years, and will not suffer by comparison with similar productions of the present day." In it he has displayed his remarkable prophetic gift.

The ivy planted by the class of '71 still clasps in its embrace the old walls that supported it during the many varied and thrilling scenes through which it passed; but the hands that planted it have long since turned to dust.

Upon leaving college, Philip, to comply with the desire of his deceased father that he should study divinity, accepted an invitation from Hugh Henry Brackenridge, his former classmate and fellow-orator of '71, to take the second position in a seminary in Maryland, of which he, Brackenridge, was to be principal, and at the same time pursue his theological course.

It would seem from the letter to Madison while with Brackenridge, that in the interim of his leaving

[1] North American Review, v. xciii.

Princeton and beginning his course of teaching and study in the Maryland seminary, he had tried his hand at pedagogy in Flatbush, Long Island; we will let him describe his non-success in that occupation which he held some thirteen days.

SOMERSET COUNTY IN MARYLAND.

November 22, 1772.

SIR, — If I am not wrongly informed by my memory, I have not seen you since last April. You may recollect I was then undertaking a school at Flatbush on Long Island. I did enter upon the business, it is certain, and continued in it thirteen days — but Long Island I have bid adieu, with all its brainless crew. The youth of that detested place, are void of reason and of grace. From Flushing hills to Flatbush plains, Deep ignorance unrivall'd reigns. I am very poetical, but excuse it. 'Si fama non venit ad aures,' if you have not heard the rumour of this story (which, by the by, is told in various Taverns and eating houses), you must allow me to be a little prolix with it. Those who employed me were some gentlemen of New York; some of them were bullies, some merchants, and others Scoundrels. They sent me Eight children, the eldest of whom was 10 years. Some could read, others spell and a few stammer over a chapter of the Bible. These were my pupils and over these was I to preside. My Salary moreover was £40, — there is something else relating to that I shall not at present mention. After I forsook them they proscribed me for four days and swore that if I was caught in New York they would either Trounce or maim me, but I luckily escaped with my goods to Princetown, where I remained till commencement — so much for this affair. I have printed a poem in New York called "The American Village," containing about four hundred and fifty lines, also a few short pieces added; I would send you one if I had a proper opportunity — the additional poems are: 1. "A Poem to the Nymph I never saw," "The Miserable Life of a Pedagogue," and Stanzas on "An ancient Dutch House on Long Island." As to the main poem, it is damned by all good and judicious Judges. My name is in the title page; this is called vanity by some — but "who so fond as a youthful bard of fame?" I arrived at this Sommerset Academy the 18th of October and intend to remain here till next October. I am assistant to Mr. Brackenridge. This is the last time I shall enter into such a business; it worries me to death and by no means suits my "giddy, wandering brain." I would go over for the gown this time two years, but the old hag necessity has got such a prodigious gripe of me that I fear I shall never be able to accomplish it. I believe if I cannot make this out I must turn quack — and indeed I am now reading Physic at my leisure hours, that is, when I am neither sleeping, hearing classes, or writing Poetry. For these three take up all my time. It is now late at night; not an hour ago I finished a little poem of about 400 lines, entitled a Journey to Maryland, being the sum of my adventures. It begins: "From that fam'd town where Hudson's flood unites with streams perhaps as good, Muse, has your bard begun to roam" — & I intend to write a terrible Satire upon certain vicious persons of quality in N. Y. — who have also used me ill — and print it next fall; it shall contain 5 or 600 Lines. Sometimes I write pastorals to shew my Wit, —

> "Deep to the woods, I sing a Shepherd's care,
> Deep to the woods, Cyllenius calls me there,
> The last retreat of Love and Verse. I go.
> Verse made me mad at first and—will keep me so."

I should have been glad to have heard from you before now. While I was at College I had but a short participation of your agreeable friendship, and the few persons I converse with and yet fewer whose conversation I delight in, make me regret the Loss of it. I have met with a variety of rebuffs this year, which I forbear to mention. I look like an unmeaning Teague just turned out of the hold of an Irish ship. Coming down hither I met with a rare adventure at Annapolis. I was destitute even of a brass farthing. I got clear very handsomely. Could one expect even to see you again? if I travel through Virginia I shall stop and talk with you a day or two. I should be very glad to receive a Letter from you if it can be conveniently forwarded. In short, "Non sum qualis eram" as Partridge says in Tom Jones. My hair is grown like a mop and I have a huge tuft of Beard directly upon my chin. I want but five weeks of twenty-one years of age, and already feel stiff with age. We have about 30 students in this Academy, who prey upon me like Leaches. When shall I quit this whimpering Jack, and hide my head in Acomack? Shall I leave them and go "Where Pokomoke's long stream meandring flows"? Excuse this prodigious Scrawl — without stile or verse. I send this by Mr Luther Martin, who will forward it to Colonel Lee, and he to you, I hope. Mr Martin lives in Acomack in Virginia, this side the bay. Farewell, and be persuaded I remain your

truly humble Servt. and friend,

PH. F-R-E-N-E-A-U.

Finding in himself no signs of vocation to the ministry, Philip took up the study of law, but after a time he found it too dry for his poetic temperament, and instead he occupied the time left from his professional duties in writing for the press articles of such a nature as to stir up love and enthusiasm for liberty, and a detestation of Britain's galling yoke. "He was the poet of hatred, and he carefully trained himself for his function as a stern political satirist, by studying the Roman and French masterpieces in satire; he began his career at a fortunate moment when just such a satirist was needed and when the materials for such satire — sincere, wrathful, Juvenalian satire — were furnished to him in abundance by the conduct of the English government and its civil and military representatives in America."[1] Upon the breaking out of the war Philip returned to Philadelphia and threw himself heart and soul into the interests of his country, endeavoring by his pen to throw off at once and forever the yoke of foreign servitude.

The colonists were not desirous of severing all

[1] Professor Tyler.

connection with the mother country, and were quite willing to make any concessions to preserve their former relations with it; and therefore contented themselves with merely endeavoring to maintain the rights guaranteed them by their charters and ratified by the Constitution.

They acted solely on the defensive, hoping to gain redress for their grievances by another petition to the Crown.

Philip was no conservative; and, finding his countrymen too slow in making use of the golden opportunity now offered of making themselves independent, and fearing that further concessions from the Crown might adjust the present difficulty, he determined not to witness the total overthrow of all his cherished hopes; he therefore accepted an invitation from a West Indian gentleman by the name of Hanson, to visit him in his island home. This gentleman owned a large plantation in the island of Jamaica, and sailed as master of his own ship.

During the passage the mate died: and Philip's love of the sea led him to offer himself to fill his place, and also to study navigation; of which branch of science he soon made himself a master.

While in Jamaica he recorded his detestation of the cruelties of slavery in a poem addressed to Sir Tobey, a planter on that island:—

> "If there exists a Hell — the case is clear
> Sir Tobey's slaves enjoy that portion here."

It is probable that if Philip ever made a second visit to that island, Sir Tobey did not receive him as favorably as he did upon the first visit.

From Jamaica, Philip visited the Danish Island of Santa Cruz, where his poetic nature revelled in the natural beauties of the scenery, which he enjoyed to the fullest extent. He loved to watch the great soft waves folding themselves gently and noiselessly over beaches of the whitest sand; the brilliant water, now sparkling like sapphire in the sunlight, and again paling into the most delicate turquoise hue when shadowed by a passing cloud; the long sea-grasses of crimson and amber waving to and fro in the water, or tossed here and there when a slight breeze ruffled its bosom; the gauzy-winged fishes as they skimmed over the waves, reflecting the colors of the rainbow, —

"Some streak'd with burnish'd gold, resplendent glare,
Some cleave the limpid deep, all silver'd o'er,
Some clad in living green, delight the eye,
Some red, some blue; of mingled colors more."

He admired the vari-colored houses, of delicate tints of pink, yellow, and blue, nestling in a rich setting of different shades of green: —

"Among the shades of yonder whispering grove
The green palmettoes mingle, tall and fair,
That ever murmur, and forever move
Fanning with wavy bough the ambient air.

"Sweet orange groves in lovely vallies rise,
And drop their fruits, unnotic'd and unknown,
The cooling, acid limes in hedges grow,
The juicy lemons swell in shades their own."[1]

He admired the plantain and banana trees with their burdens of luscious fruit; the crimson pomegranates and golden pawpaws of the valleys, behind which towered the rugged peaks of the volcanic ridge clothed with forests of the "guava's stripling tree," the smooth white cedar, and the "bay tree with its aromatic green," and crowned with the graceful waving palm.

[1] The Beauties of Santa Cruz.

"Such were the isles which happy Flaccus sung
Where one tree blossoms while another bears,
Where Spring, forever gay, and ever young,
Walks her gay round through her unwearied years." [1]

All this was very delightful to the poetic side of Philip's nature; but like all that is beautiful on earth, it had its dark side in the detestable slavery that "cast a shadow over all. 'If you have tears to shed, prepare to shed them now,'" he writes: —

"A description of the cruelties the poor slaves endure would be too irksome and unpleasant to me; and to those who have not beheld it, would be incredible. Sufficient be it to say, that no class of mankind in the known world undergo so complete a servitude as the common negroes in the West Indies. It casts a pall over the natural charms of the country, it blots out the beauties of the eternal spring which providence has there ordained to reign; and amidst all the profusion of bounties which nature has scattered — the brightness of the heaven, the mildness of the air, and the luxuriancy of the vegetable kingdom — it leaves me melancholy and disconsolate, convinced that there is no pleasure in this world without its share of pain. And thus the earth, which, were it not for the lust of pride and dominion, might be an earthly paradise, is, by the ambition and overbearing nature of mankind rendered an eternal scene of desolation, woe, and horror; the weak goes to the wall, while the strong prevails; and after our ambitious frenzy has turned the world upside down we are contented with a narrow spot, and leave our follies and cruelties to be acted over again by every succeeding generation."

It was during his sojourn upon this island that he wrote his poems entitled, "The Beauties of Santa Cruz," and the "House of Night." The latter poem is a weird thing "founded upon the authority of the Scripture, inasmuch as these sacred books assert,

[1] The Beauties of Santa Cruz.

that *the last enemy that shall be conquered is Death.*" Death is herein personified and represented on his dying bed. This scene is in a solitary place, and the time midnight. An amiable, majestic youth who has but lately suffered from his aggression, Death having carried off his beloved wife, with a noble fortitude and humanity entertains him, although an enemy; thus carrying into practice the divine precept, "*If thine enemy hunger, feed him; if he thirst, give him drink.*" The poem concludes with some reflection on the impropriety of too great an attachment to this present life, and incentives to such moral virtue as may assist in conducting to a better one.

He describes it as a "fearful vision at the midnight hour."

"Such was the dream the sage Chaldean saw
Disclosed to him that felt heav'n's vengeful rod
Such was the ghost, who through deep silence cry'd,
'*Shall mortal man be Juster than his God?*'"

The poem contains one hundred and thirty-six stanzas, having been increased from the original seventy-three.

The latter stanzas contain the moral,—

"What is this Death, ye deep read sophists, say?
Death is no more than one unceasing change;
New forms arise, while other forms decay,
Yet all is Life throughout creation's range.

"The towering Alps, the haughty Appenine,
The Andes wrapped in everlasting snow,
The Appalachian and the Arrarat
Sooner or later must to ruin go.

"Hills sink to plains, and man returns to dust,
That dust supports a reptile or a flower;
Each changeful atom by some other nurs'd
Takes some new form, to perish in an hour.

"Too nearly join'd to sickness, toils and pains,
(Perhaps for former crimes imprison'd here)
True to itself the immortal soul remains,
And seeks new mansions in the starry sphere.

"When Nature bids thee from the world retire,
With Joy thy lodging leave, a fated guest,
In Paradise, the land of thy desire,
Existing always, always to be blest."

Both of these poems have been changed since originally written in Santa Cruz, and they have been lengthened considerably, the former being increased from fifty-two to one hundred and nine stanzas, and the latter, as we have already stated, from seventy-three to one hundred and thirty-six stanzas.

Most of Freneau's poems have been greatly changed in later editions of his works. He was given to reviewing, which exhibits the care he bestowed upon his productions; but which perhaps caused them to lose some of their original bouquet, if we may use this word in such connection.

It is doubtful if so much revision is beneficial to such spontaneous productions as poetry is supposed to be, and marked by more or less of inspiration. Revision usually being done in moments in which that fire burns low, if at all, it would not be surprising if the various parts of such a whole would seem to be somewhat lacking in harmony of sentiment.

In his "House of Night" Freneau has acknowledged this fact, although he was not alluding to reviewing: —

"Stranger, believe the truth experience tells, —
Poetic dreams are of a finer cast
Than those which o'er the sober brain diffus'd
Are but a repetition of some action past."

Returning northward, Philip stopped at the Bermudas; and remained there some six months as a guest of the governor. The reason of his prolonged stay in these islands may be accounted for by the numerous sonnets addressed to the fair Amanda, the amiable daughter of his host. And while Philip sipped the governor's wine and basked in the smiles of his fair daughter, his first pure love, fair Liberty, lay bleeding in the dust; and the pen he had vowed to her service was employed in depicting the charms of her rival.

Chapter Sixth

WHILE Philip was still a collegian, and even indeed a schoolboy, his cousin, John Morin Scott, whom we have already mentioned, was actively engaged in the affairs of the colony, and had already formed ideas of its future freedom. Perhaps, indeed, it was from him that Philip drew some of his enthusiasm on the subject, as, being considerably his senior in years, Scott's opinions would have great weight with his fatherless young cousin.

Morin Scott was in reality Philip's father's cousin, their mothers, Mrs. André Freneau and Mrs. Scott, being sisters. Both of these men were gifted with the enthusiastic nature of their French parentage; but Morin Scott was not so easily carried away by his feelings as was his young cousin, — whether it was from the fact of his early education having been in less exciting times, thus giving him time to learn self-control before the soul-stirring events that immediately preceded the Revolution, or from his habits of logical thought engendered by his steady application to his profession. It may have been partly due to the mixture of Scotch blood in his veins, — his father being a descendant of the ancient Scotch barons of Ancram.[1]

Morin Scott's birth antedated Philip's some twenty-two years; he was graduated from Yale College in the year 1746, and had finished his law course before Philip was born. His marriage took place about the time of his cousin's birth. Scott's wife was Helena, daughter

[1] Miss Scott of Ancram, whose name appears amongst the British poets, was a member of this family.

of Peter Rutger and Elizabeth Williams,[1] the daughter of a naval officer of the Port of New York; their children were: Mary, born July 17, 1753; Louis Allaire, afterwards Secretary of State, born February 11, 1754; John Morin, Jr., born May 9, 1755, and baptized by the Reverend Aaron Burr[2] June 15, 1755; and Peter Rutger born July 6, 1756.

Scott was a stanch whig in the ante-bellum days, and was devoted to the interests of his country; he was considered one of the most eminent lawyers of the time. We find his name in O'Callaghan's "Documentary History" as being retained by Jacob Daller, who arrived in New York in the year 1765 and invited himself into the pastorate of the French Church, threatening the Consistory to carry the matter into court if they did not receive him. Trouble ensuing, Morin Scott and William Smith[3] were retained by the aforesaid self-appointee, who was advised by them to submit his difference with the church to arbitration. The Consistory threatened the lawyers for the act and asked for an interview, which was held in the room of the Consistory. After a long and painful process of litigation and personal antagonism Mr. Daller set out for London the year following.

In 1754 we find Scott's name in the records of the French church, of which he does not seem to have been a member, as a witness, along with his cousin André Freneau, Jr., to the marriage of their mutual cousin Marie Allaire; the marriage being held at the house of the bride's parents.

As we have stated in a preceding chapter, Governor Dongan, upon assuming the administration, had given the colony its first Legislative Assembly; which con-

[1] This lady was step-daughter to Col. Fred. Philipse, the last proprietor of Philipse Manor of Philipseburgh.

[2] Father to Aaron Burr the vice-president.

[3] William Smith married a daughter of John Adams.

sisted of the governor, two counsellors, and representatives chosen by the people to represent each ward, who were elected annually. Scott had been for five years, or from 1757 to 1762 successively, chosen to represent the "Out-ward," which comprised Harlem and all that district outside of the city's wall.

During the second attempt made by Parliament in the year 1761 to enforce the Importation Act, the colonial courts were authorized to issue Writs of Assistance, or search-warrants, to constables to enable them to effect an entrance into any locality in which there was the slightest suspicion of goods that had evaded the duty being concealed; and such goods were liable to be seized by those officers. William Smith, William Livingston, and John Morin Scott, all three eminent lawyers, protested through the public print against these proceedings: they claimed that the judiciary was not dependent upon the king; and they protested against the search warrants being issued, denying the government the right of instituting the search.

In Boston, James Otis denounced the Act as unconstitutional, and in a masterly address pleaded the rights of the colonists,—which produced a great sensation throughout all the colonies; and hints of resistance even to arms were thrown out.

After the passage of the Stamp Act in the year 1765, although it was not in itself oppressive, Scott publicly resented its being carried into effect, as being illegal and unconstitutional. He, as well as all patriots, claimed that, as British subjects, the Constitution was as dear to them as to all those born in England; and it provided against all forced loans by the Crown, which was in reality taxation without representation. The Act was carried into effect, however, and the colonists divided themselves into two parties; the one upholding the king and styled Tories, and the Whigs, who deemed it but right to resent even to death all acts of tyranny. The contest between these parties was full of bitterness, and the members of one heaped abuse on those of the other without mercy. The public printers, Rivington on the one side, and Hugh Gaine on the other, tried their utmost to fan the flames, which spread in all directions.

The other colonies took up the matter, and finally James Otis, Massachusetts' eloquent orator, suggested that without leave of the king, each colony should appoint delegates to meet in a congress to discuss the affairs of the nation. To this proposition all the colonies agreed; the day set for it to convene was October 7, 1765, and by common consent New York City was chosen as the place in which it would be held. Nine of the thirteen States were represented, and the number of delegates was twenty-eight, John Morin Scott representing New York. Timothy Ruggles was elected president of the Congress, and two papers were drawn up; one of which was a Declaration of Rights, and the other an Address to the King. The former set forth that as English subjects the American colonists could not and would not consent to be taxed but by their own representatives. The paper to the king was a humble petition for a more just and humane course of action towards his loyal subjects in America. Memorials were also addressed to the two houses of Parliament. At the Congress it was decided to abandon the use of all such goods as were imported from England, and to stop all commerce between the mother country and the colonies, until she should desist from her illegal efforts to tax them.

A society was then formed called the "Sons of Liberty;" meetings were held during the summer months, and sharp eyes watched all proceedings. The paper at length arrived, no notice having been taken of their petition; therefore the first night after the night rattle had gone his rounds, billets were hastily posted on trees throughout the city which read —

PRO PATRIA!

The first man that distributes or makes use of stamped paper, let him take care of his house and effects.

VOX POPULI[1]

James McEvers had been appointed stamp collector for New York, but as he owned a handsome residence near Hanover Square, he thought it wiser to resign his office than his house; and no one being found to fill his vacated position, the paper found no "local habitation" and was relegated to the fort.

The Sons of Liberty held their meetings at what was then known as the Fields,— now City Hall Park; and here platforms wer rected, and the population met to listen to the exhortations of the tribunes, amongst whom were Oliver Delancy, John Jay, Alexander McDougall, Isaac Sears, Robert and Philip Livingston, John Morin Scott, John Lamb, Peter Curtentius, Alexander Hamilton, and others. On the opposite side were Cadwallader Colden, Thomas Gage, Revs. Myles Cooper and Auchmuchty, Samuel Bayard, S. H. Cruger, D. Harsmonden, and others.

The thirty-first of October, the day the governor was to take the oath to carry the Act into effect, was kept as a day of public mourning; and in the evening two hundred leading merchants met in the City Arms Coffee House, and passed a resolution to import no more goods from England until the Act was repealed. The following day a meeting was held in the Fields, after which the Sons of Liberty marched to the fort and gave the governor's house, in which the paper was stored, a house-warming.

The Act was repealed, and the following June, upon

[1] Todd.

the king's birthday, his loyal sons set up a liberty pole to commemorate the joyful event and also his great clemency in repealing the Act; but some way the soldiers did not see it quite in this light and they pulled it down. Again and again it was raised, and again and again it was levelled; until, to save time in future, the "Sons" braced it with iron to the height of seventy-three feet from the ground, and after that it was "let live."

When the news of Boston's tea party reached New York, the "Sons" met together and formed a resolution that no tea should land at the wharves of the city. The mayor tried to induce them to allow it to land and remain until it could be placed, but they decidedly refused it hospitality, not allowing it to remain for even one night in the fort, after which the meeting adjourned until the tea should arrive.

After a long delay the "Nancy,"[1] that was supposed to have the tea, hove in sight in a most pitiable condition: one mast was gone, an anchor had been lost, and she had met with various other mishaps. But the hearts of the "Sons" were not touched by her plight: they bade her remain at the length of the harbor, and a committee was appointed to watch her until she should be sufficiently repaired to make a return trip with her tea. The sailors were not allowed to land, lest they might not be ready when wanted; but her captain was escorted to the city and advised to make preparations for an early return, but was forbidden to enter the Custom House.

As soon as the "Nancy" was ready, the Committee of Safety, of which Morin Scott was a member, waited upon the captain at his lodgings, and a procession was formed to escort him to the sloop that was to bear him to his "Nancy," and he marched to the sound of martial music and the ringing of bells.

[1] The tea in reality was in another ship.

It was a veritable sight for the American small boy. Every ship in the harbor ran up its colors, and the liberty pole was graced with bunting; and with the roar of artillery the captain sailed away, and he and his "Nancy" were heard of no more.

About noon of Sunday, the twenty-third of April in the year 1775, four days after the Battle of Lexington, Scott, along with other members of the Committee of Safety, were assembled in the committee room on Broadway, when a rider hastily drew up and, dismounting, handed them a paper. It was to apprise them of the fact of the mother country having been the first to shed the blood of her children, and that all that was left for them was to defend themselves; therefore the Massachusetts Committee of Safety had resolved to enlist eight thousand men. After reading it the Committee endorsed it, and the rider started on his way southward.

The news was speedily made public, and there was a popular outbreak in the city. The keys of the arsenal were not to be found, but the door was forced open by the excited populace, and six hundred muskets and accoutrements were distributed amongst the citizens. The fort and magazines were seized and the citizens assumed the government of the city. They proceeded at once to elect a committee of one hundred of the most influential inhabitants, to take charge of the government; amongst these was Scott. It was called the "Committee of One Hundred."

The soldiery had been ordered to Boston to reinforce Gage, and the Committee permitted them to depart. They marched to the wharf at the foot of Broad Street, where lay the "Asia" ready to receive them. Six carts laden with arms and ammunition preceded them. At the foot of the street a member of the "One Hundred" stepped forward and said that the Committee requested them to leave the arms and ammunition behind, as they belonged to the colony and could not be taken out of it; then taking the bridle of the first horse he turned it off towards Beaver Street, and the other five followed. The soldiers were permitted to embark.

During the remainder of seventy-five and until the spring of seventy-six the state of affairs was sad enough. In a letter written by Morin Scott, dated November fifteenth, seventy-five, he describes the general feeling. He says: —

> "Every office shut up almost but Sam Jones', who will work for six a day and live accordingly. All business stagnated; the city half deserted for fear of a bombardment. A new Congress elected. Those for New York you will see by the papers, changed for the better. All staunch Whigs now. . . . Nothing from t' other side of the water but a fearful looking for of wrath. Our Continental petition most probably condemned — the bulk of the nation, it is said are against us and a bloody campaign next summer. But let us be prepared for the worst. Who can prize life without liberty! it is a bauble only fit to be thrown away."

The spring and summer of seventy-six were spent in equipping and drilling the hastily formed troops and in fortifying the city. On the ninth of May the Continental Congress met in Philadelphia, in which a last appeal was made to the king; and he was informed that the colonists had chosen war instead of slavery. John Adams, in an address to the assembled patriots, spoke of the necessity of having a commander for the army, and proposed George Washington as Commander-in-Chief of the American army. Congress confirmed the nomination on the fifteenth of June, and Washington at once repaired to New York and met the new Provincial Congress, of which Scott was a member, and which was then sitting in the city. The Continental Congress had put the quota for New

York at three thousand men, and the new commander conferred with the New York Congress upon their equipment and officering, also upon other military matters.

Four regiments were immediately raised, and Scott's old companion tribune, and also fellow-member of the Committee of One Hundred, Alexander McDougall, was appointed to command one. Another old fellow-tribune, John Lamb, was ordered by the Provincial Congress to remove some of the guns from Fort George to the passes by the Hudson. While fulfilling the order on the night of August twenty-third, a launch belonging to the "Asia," a British ship, fired upon his men. Lamb returned fire, and killed one man and wounded several other men; the "Asia" then opened a broadside into the city, and some of Lamb's men were wounded, and most of the inhabitants fled. The Committee of One Hundred ordered that as the ship had fired upon New York she should have no more communication with it, and that in future all communications should be with Governor's Island.

After the British had evacuated Boston and Washington had formally taken possession, the latter brought his army to New York, where he was met by Lee with his Connecticut forces, who had come just in time to baffle the plans of Sir Henry Clinton, who had arrived off Sandy Hook for a descent upon the city, but instead sailed southward.

The mother country now levied twenty-five thousand English troops and seventeen thousand Hessians, and ordered an immense squadron to attempt the reduction of her colonies; and they, seeing no more hope of an amicable settlement, urged their general assemblies to take some definite step toward their independence of Great Britain. Morin Scott, being a member of assembly, met with the other members in council, and they urged Congress to declare formally the independence of the United Colonies. Congress responded by recommending the different colonies to adopt such government as might best conduce to the safety and welfare of the people; and the result, after much deliberation, was the Declaration of Independence, which was adopted by Congress July fourth, seventy-six.

On the ninth of the month, at six o'clock in the evening, the troops assembled in the Fields, and formed in a hollow square at the lower end, the Commander-in-Chief on horseback being in the centre, and the Declaration of Independence was read aloud by one of his aids. At the conclusion three hearty cheers were given. The following morning it was read at White Plains, and after it the Provincial Congress pledged themselves to "sustain it at the risk of their lives and fortunes." The Provincial Congress then despatched a messenger to their delegates in the Continental Congress convened in Philadelphia, empowering them to vote in the name of the New York colony for its adoption, and ordered it to be proclaimed in the city of New York by beat of drum, and to be read publicly from the City Hall in Wall Street.

All efforts were now directed to preparing for war. Scott was appointed to assist in sustaining Washington, with the rank of brigadier-general, and was appointed to hold and fortify Long Island. Powerful works were constructed on Brooklyn Heights to command New York, this point being the key of the whole position. The army was divided into five divisions under Generals Putnam, Sullivan, Greene, Knox, and Stirling. Aaron Burr, then aged twenty years, was on Putnam's staff, and Alexander Hamilton, a youth of nineteen, held the position of captain of battery.

I find by comparison of dates that Morin Scott held several positions at the same time, one overlapping two or more others; but as I have the facts from public records, it may be accounted for in this way: "It is common," a writer[1] has said in speaking of the times, "to see several offices in the hands of a single person who perhaps was a colonel, a judge of probate, justice of the peace, member of the legislature," etc.

The British had now concentrated their forces, amounting to thirty thousand men, nearly half of whom were Hessians, in the vicinity of New York. Washington's army was greatly inferior to them in numbers as well as in equipment and discipline.

On the twenty-second of August ten thousand British troops landed on Long Island under Howe, Tryon, Clinton, and Cornwallis. The American army, being only eight thousand strong, was posted around Brooklyn. On the twenty-seventh of August General Grant's division of the British army proceeded as far as Greenwood Cemetery, where General Stirling met him with fifteen hundred men, and hostilities commenced, with no decisive result. General Heister, in command of the British centre, advanced beyond Flatbush and engaged the main body of the Americans under Sullivan; but they gained little until the latter was made aware that a battle was going on at his left.

Along the length of the island extended a ridge over which no army could pass except at the regular passes of Flatbush and Jamaica, and at these points videttes had been stationed to give warning of any attempt on the part of the British to cross. Putnam, towards the north, held the fortified camps. Howe, by some strategy, induced the young officers appointed to guard the Flatbush pass to advance to meet him; when a portion of his army making a détour captured the pass, and only waited for the morning to fold around our army. Sullivan's division had been literally cut to pieces. Nothing was now left for the

1 Henry W. Frost.

patriots but to yield the position; and Washington, with his wonderful tact, that caused his retreats to rank next to victories, collected all the boats possible. A motley assembly, surely, and I doubt if ever such a fleet was seen before; sloops, schooners, whale-boats, periaugers, and rowing-galleys worked all night, and morning gave to the enemy only a few worthless guns. Sullivan, Stirling, and Woodhull, with nearly one thousand patriots, were missing from the day's battle. The English hastily crossed in pursuit, and the patriots tried to escape across the island, having landed at different points in New York. Scott's brigade crossed at Fifteenth Street, and making a détour of the city reached Harlem Plains, where he met the other stragglers. Too much praise cannot be awarded to Mrs. Murray,[1] whose large farm-house stood at the junction of the present Thirty-fourth Street and Lexington Avenue, then a large farm. Here by her tact she entertained Howe's men with her good cheer, and himself and officers by her gracious hospitality, till the Americans had crossed the island and were safely intrenched on Harlem Heights.

The American army was now obliged to leave New York, and Washington wrote to Governor Turnbull that the Provincial Congress had resolved not to injure the city; but a fire broke out, no one knew how it originated, and the greater part of the city was destroyed. This fire consumed the Huguenot church.

In this year Captain Nathan Hale was arrested by the British, who now held the city, and was executed in the orchard belonging to the family of Scott's wife, Helena Rutger. It took place on what is now East Broadway, a little above Franklin Square.

On the fourth of June, 1777, the New York convention met at Windsor; and the inhabitants of the grant known as New Connecticut elected some depu-

[1] Mother of Lindley Murray, the grammarian.

ties to "sitt" at the said convention, at which it was declared that the grant should thenceforth be known as an independent State, and be called Vermont. A certain Williams, writing to the Secretary of the New York convention, mentions the affair, and says in regard to the pending election for Governor: —

I believe we have been pretty unanimous in the Election for governor and Lieutenant Governor, to witt, Genl. Morin Scott & Clinton [1] but there were very few that voted. The Lott number 68 in Argyle belonging to Genl Scott, I must beg you'll procure for me in behalf of Capn. Martin, I'm informed som other people are after it. However I am of opinion Genl Scott will not Lett any one have it without giving Capt. Martin the refusal.

I am dear Sir your very Huml. Servt.

JOHN WILLIAMS.[2]

Morin Scott's name appears in the State Senate from the year 1777 to 1782; as a member of Congress from the year 1779 to 1781; as member of the Continental Congress, 1782–1783; as Secretary of State of New York from 1778 to 1789; and as member of Congress, 1780–1783.

After the battle of White Plains the Americans were driven from position after position, and finally through the Jerseys to Princeton, Trenton, and into Pennsylvania. Then came the battle of Princeton, after which the greater part of New Jersey was recovered by the patriots. War was raging all around the old homestead, and while our modern Telemachus was enjoying his life of *dolce far niente* in the isles of the Atlantic, the courageous Penelope was guarding the lares and penates of her hearthstone.

On the twenty-third of July Howe sailed from New

[1] Clinton was nominee for Governor and Scott for Lieutenant-Governor, although from the letter it would appear *vice versa*.

[2] Doc. Hist.

York to attack Philadelphia, then the seat of the Continental Congress, and succeeded in reducing it by the twenty-sixth of September. Then came the defeat of Germantown and the long and dreary winter at Valley Forge, and at the close of 1777 the patriot cause was nearly ended. Then came the treaty with France, and D'Estaing's fleet approached the capital, and on the eighteenth of June, 1778, Howe's army evacuated Philadelphia and retreated across New Jersey. At Monmouth the British were overtaken.

Sunday the twenty-eighth was an intensely hot day. Clinton was moving cautiously and Knyphausen was hastening forward on the Middletown road; the left wing, following, had passed a mile or more beyond the Court House. On the north, outflanking the British, were the American columns. Lee advanced from the old Monmouth church by the main road, crossing two deep ravines upon causeways; his left wing was folding around Cornwallis on the north, occupying superior ground; his centre, under Wayne, was close behind; and his right wing, under Lafayette, was already past the Court House, threatening the other end of the British lines, whose position was one of extreme danger, and there was every prospect of a glorious victory for the American army. Wayne had just begun a vigorous attack, but a halt was ordered by Lee. The British troops came down the road to separate Wayne and Lafayette; but it was an easy matter to check them, and the Marquis started to do so, but a halt was again ordered by Lee, who commanded, instead, a retreat across a marshy ravine. On the verge of a victory they were compelled to flee, but from what no one knew; and bitter disappointment took the place of their exultant ardor of the morning. The enemy began to pursue them, and as they crowded over the causeway the ranks began to fall into disorder and many sank exhausted by the heat, and some were slain by the enemy. The Marquis ordered an aid to seek the Commander-in-Chief and report the strange conduct of Lee. The soldier met him just where the road forks not far from the old Monmouth church and delivered his message. Washington hastily sprang to his horse and soon found himself in the midst of the disorder. A halt was ordered, and the retreating soldiers immediately wheeled and formed under the firing with as much calmness and precision as they could have shown on parade. And while they stopped the evening's progress Washington rode back and brought up the main body of his army, — Greene with his battery from the heights, and Wayne from the front; and the British were driven back upon the second ravine which Lee had crossed in the morning's advance. The gallant Steuben brought up from the rear, and night fell. Morning found the British troops withdrawn, and America claimed a victory. Lord Stanhope saw a drawn battle.[1]

This battle of Monmouth was partly fought on the land which fell to Philip's wife as her portion, and on which they resided after the flames had destroyed their residence at Mount Pleasant, from which the battle could be easily heard at the time, and in which were assembled his mother and her little family — all but Philip.

[1] Gen. John Morin Scott took part in this battle, also Gen. David Forman.

Chapter Seventh

NEWS travelled slowly in the days of our ancestors, and for several reasons that of the Declaration of Independence was delayed in reaching Philip. First, the distance was great, the nearest point of land being Cape Hatteras, some six hundred and fifty miles distant; but on account of the war between Great Britain, to whom the Bermudas belonged, and the colonies, no American ship landed in her ports, and the trading vessels were few and far between. When at last the word, so delightful to Philip's ears, reached him, that the colonies had really declared themselves free, he quickly roused himself from the poetic languor that had taken possession of him, and embraced the first opportunity that presented of returning to his native land. The voyage was roundabout, and consumed considerable time; consequently he did not reach home until after the battle that had been fought so close to his doors.

The fate of the "amiable Amanda" we have never learned. Whether, like Sappho, she took a fatal leap from the heights of one of the Bermuda peaks, or, like a sensible woman of the eighteenth century, bade her poet good-bye, with a promise to remember him in her orisons, is unknown; and, as Philip's sonnets ceased to flow, her fate is buried in oblivion.

Upon arriving in his native land Philip probably paid his respects to his mother. It is most likely, and then he buckled on his sword in his country's cause. This phrase is certainly figurative, for Philip could never buckle himself into anything that looked like a harness; but he did what lay in his power, he took out letters of marque and reprisal from the Continental Congress, and sailed far out on the deep blue sea to catch all the British ships he could find. We learn from the public print that he played sad havoc with the English merchantmen, capturing and destroying many.

But after a time poor Philip came to grief, and the way it happened runneth thus.

Whether he had purchased the ship he commanded or only used it for the time being we know not, but we do know that he had one building in the Philadelphia yards, which was his own, his very own — the dream of his life. Philadelphia was famous in those days for her shipbuilding capabilities; her harbor favoring it, she could easily bring from the Southern and New England States the best of woods for the purpose; and we are told that at one time might be seen some twenty ships in her stocks in progress of construction. Those she turned out were swift sailers, highly finished, and even considerably ornamented; so much so, indeed, that her figure-heads were praised by foreign artists. In fact the colonies had developed such talent in naval architecture that many of the English trading vessels were built in their yards.[1]

Although Philip's description of the building of his ship may not equal that of Schiller's, it may bear criticism: —

> "Assist me, Clio! while in verse I tell
> The dire misfortunes that a ship befell,
> Which outward bound, to St. Eustatia's shore,
> Death and disaster through the billows bore.
> From Philadelphia's happy port she came;
> (And there the builder plann'd her lofty frame,)
> With wonderous skill, and excellence of art
> He form'd, dispos'd and order'd every part,
> With joy, beheld the stately fabric rise

[1] Mr. Eggleston, in The Century Magazine.

To a stout bulwark, of stupendous size,
'Till launch'd at last, capacious of the freight,
He left her to the pilots, and her fate.
First, from her depths the tapering masts ascend,
On whose tall bulk the transverse yards depend,
By shrouds and stays secur'd from side to side
Trees grew on trees, suspended o'er the tide:
Firm to the yards extended, broad and vast,
They hung the sails, susceptive of the blast,
Far o'er the prow the lengthy bowsprit lay,
Supporting on the extreme the taut fore-stay,
Twice ten six pounder, at their port holes plac'd,
And rang'd in rows, stood hostile in the waist:
Thus all prepar'd, impatient for the seas,
She left her station with an adverse breeze,
This her first outset from her native shore,
To seas a stranger, and untry'd before."

The ship finished, Philip named her "The Aurora," and on her broad prow she carried for a figurehead the rising sun, so brightly gilded as, quoting his words, to "throw over the water a mimic blaze." Poor sun, destined to set before it ran its course!

Delaware Bay, although admitting the largest vessels to its head, and even into the river beyond, had a very tortuous and intricate channel, occasioned by the numerous shoals formed by long, narrow sandbanks stretching northwest and southeast, which nearly filled the central portion. It was therefore something of a feat to guide a good-sized vessel through it and round the cape, — the shelving ground around the latter causing it to be fatal to those unacquainted with its peculiarities. It was renowned for shipwrecks; so much so that captains felt greatly relieved when they had safely left it behind them.

On the 25th of May the "Aurora," "daughter of the sun," with all sails spread to catch the breeze, which at starting was adverse, passed gaily down the river, and through the sixty miles of Delaware Bay, and waited for morning to round the point called by the old Swede settlers the "Point of Paradise," by the more prosaic modern Americans, Cape Henlopen. During her progress down the bay an event occurred which was considered by the crew a prognostic of future success, but which was, in reality, the cause of the "Aurora's" disaster. Overtaking a small sloop belonging to the enemy and laden with corn, the details incident to its capture prevented the "Aurora" from rounding the point the same evening, and thus caused the delay so fatal to her.

The morning was beautiful; and, assisted by a favorable breeze, the cape was successfully passed, and the "Aurora" made her début on the broad ocean, where "a sea unruffled and a sky serene" awaited her All seemed propitious; and spreading the sails, her prow was turned eastward, then to the southeast.

The sun crossed the meridian, and a gale springing up it bore the light-hearted master and crew out of the sight of the misty line of hilltops, which seemed to sink beneath the waves. Toward afternoon, a seaman was ordered to go aloft, to see peradventure if any prey, in the form of an English merchantman, might be in sight.

The tar returned and reported a ship approaching very rapidly from the east; which soon became visible to all. The master used his glass, and from her top-gallant spied the English Jack; and soon after he recognized her to be the "Iris," once the "Hancock," one of the swiftest ships on the American station, and one that had made the fortunes of every one that had ever commanded her save the last;[1] he had lost her in consequence of having put her out of trim, by starting her water while chased by the "Rainbow," commanded by Sir George Collier, who finally captured her.

[1] Captain Manly.

"Her lofty masts stood bending to the gale,
Close to the wind was brac'd each shivering sail;
Her spangled bottom seem'd in flames to glow.
. . . . . .
With all her might she strove to gain our tack,
Nor strove in vain — with pride and power elate,
Wing'd on by winds, she drove us to our fate.
No stop, no stay her bloody crew intends.
So flies a comet with its host of fiends,
Nor oaths, nor prayers arrest her swift career,
Death in her front, and ruin in her rear."

Knowing the futility of attempting to hold their own against such odds, — the vessel carrying guns double the size of theirs, — the officer gave orders to change the course of the "Aurora" and steer for the land, their only safety lying in flight.

"Struck at the sight, the master gave command
To change our course, and steer toward the land —
Straight to the task the ready sailors run,
And while the word was utter'd, half was done;
As, from the south, the fiercer breezes rise
Swift from her foe alarm'd Aurora flies,
With every sail extended to the wind
She fled the unequal foe that chas'd behind.
Along her decks, dispos'd in close array,
Each at its port, the grim artillery lay,
Soon on the foe with brazen throat to roar;
But, small their size, and narrow was their bore;
Yet, faithful, they their destin'd station keep
To guard the barque that wafts them o'er the deep,
Who now must bend to steer a homeward course
And trust her swiftness rather than her force,
Unfit to combat with a powerful foe, —
Her decks too open and her waist too low."

Land appears, most welcome sight! The Point of Paradise looms up before them; but near and nearer presses on the foe, intent upon the "Aurora's" ruin. Listen to the boatswain's prayer — it, like most such prayers, fell back upon the head of its maker: —

"List, all ye powers that rule the skies and seas!
Shower down perdition on such thieves as these,
Winds, daunt their hearts with terror and dismay,
And sprinkle on their powder salt sea spray!
May bursting cannon, while his aim he tries,
Distract the gunner, and confound his eyes —
May they who rule the round-top's giddy height
Be canted headlong to perpetual night;
May fiends torment them on a leeward coast,
And help forsake them when they want it most."

Freneau, in his poem entitled "The Prison Ship," from which we have been quoting, beautifully compares the flight of the "Aurora," and the pursuit of the "Iris," to the flight of Hector pursued by Achilles round the walls of Troy: —

"The Frigate, now, had every sail unfurl'd,
And rush'd tremendous o'er the watery world;
Thus fierce Pelides, eager to destroy,
Chas'd the proud Trojan to the gates of Troy —
Swift o'er the wave while, hostile, they pursue,
As swiftly from their fangs Aurora flew."

The Point of Paradise gained, all efforts to take the ill-fated vessel ashore were vain; a sudden calm caused the sails to droop. Meanwhile the foe had advanced within range of shot, and pointed her guns.

"Rang'd her black cannon, pointed on our lee,
Then up she luff'd, and blaz'd her entrails dire,
Bearing destruction, terror, death and fire.
Vext at our fate, we prim'd a piece, and then
Return'd the shot, to show them we were men."

Night fell; even the shoals in this sad extremity would have been a welcome risk, but—

> "Fate stood between, and barr'd us from the land."

Already becalmed and helpless, the ebbing current bore the doomed "Aurora" into the power of her enemy, who—

> "Flash'd her red lightnings o'er the trembling flood."

At every flash untold mischief ensued, and—

> "Mad for revenge, our breasts with fury glow
> To wreak returns of vengeance on the foe;
> Full at his hull our pointed guns we rais'd,
> His hull resounded as the cannon blaz'd;
> Through his broad sails while some a passage tore,
> His sides re-echo'd to the dreadful roar,
> Alternate fires dispell'd the shades of night—
> But how unequal was this daring fight!"

While shouting defiance to the foe, Laboyteaux, the captain of the marines, fell staining the deck with his heart's blood. Another blast tore the shrouds, stays. and braces away; while through the air flew the fragments of sails, blocks, and oars, and the "Aurora" shook from stem to stern. The elements seemed to vie with each other in working the doom of the ill-fated vessel; earth receded from her grasp; and the wind, rising, filled the sails of the "Iris" and blew it close and closer upon her prey; the fire tore open her sides, into whose wounds the water gurgled to complete the work of destruction; and slowly the doomed vessel began to sink, and there was naught left but to submit or die.

> "'T was then the Master trembled for his crew,
> And bade thy shores, O Delaware, adieu!—
> And must we yield to yon' destructive ball,
> And must our colors to these ruffians fall!—

They fall! — his thunders forc'd our strength to bend,
The lofty topsails with their yards descend,
And the proud foe, such leagues of ocean pass'd,
His wish completed in our woe at last."

According to Freneau's log-book it would seem that on this voyage he was merely a passenger, and bore no active part in the ship's management. As this account has been given to the public by Mr. Weymer Jay Mills[1] great-grandnephew of Agnes Freneau's husband, we give the account of the capture as found in Freneau's poem, "The Prison Ship." In the log-book Freneau states that when first pursued by the "Iris" his advice to the officers had been to stand for Egg Harbor or any part of the Jersey shore, and to run the ship upon the flats rather than allow it to be taken. Why his advice was not followed, or why he was only a passenger on his own ship, it does not appear.

Let the reader imagine for himself the sentiments with which the freedom-loving Freneau passed from the deck of the "Aurora" to that of the victor, and those with which he watched the waters closing over the wreckage of his ship, — for that which was left of her was but the ghost of her former self, — until the darkness covered all things with its pall.

Owners of fair ships have expressed their love for them as greater far than for anything on land; and the "Aurora" was his very own, the creation of his love, which he had dreamed of day by day as she grew into her fair proportions; whose birth he had sung, and to whom finally he had confided his life and fortunes. Too late he regretted, for his own part, that he had not chosen death when it could honorably have been courted.

In passing through the lower bay in his transfer to New York, Freneau gazed across the waters and de-

[1] Revolutionary Americana, published by Wessels & Co.

scried in the distance the crest of the old hill from whose heights, as a child, he had so oftentimes watched the white-sailed vessels flitting to and fro, and longed so ardently to be in one of them; and was it thus his desires had been fulfilled? In one he was indeed; but the shackles of the captive were weighing on his hands and feet, and these he had not longed for.

Arrived at the port of New York, then in the hands of the British, he was condemned to breathe the foul, infected air of the sickly hulks which were moored within sight of the very residence in which, in former years, his ancestor had resided, and in which his father had been born. Imagine all this and then blame him if you can for that spirit of acrimony that many perhaps have wondered at, thinking it far exceeded its cause.

An exile from the land of his fathers through the merciless tyranny of one monarch, and in fetters by that of another, is it to be wondered at that in after years he fought so strenuously against all tendency to a monarchical form of government, or the least thing that savored of it?

The "Scorpion," the hulk in which he was confined, was one of the old transport vessels in which the British troops had been brought to the city. It was moored at first off the Battery, along with the "Jersey," a sixty-four-gun ship formerly employed as a store ship, the "Hunter," and others, and afterwards taken to Wallabout Bay, on the Long Island shore. These vessels were all unseaworthy and had been dismantled.

"No masts or sails these crowded ships adorn,
Dismal to view, neglected and forlorn.

. . . . . .

From morn to eve along the decks we lay
Scorch'd into fevers by the solar ray;

No friendly awning cast a welcome shade,
Once it was promis'd, and was never made;
No favours could these sons of death bestow,
'T was endless vengeance, and unceasing woe."

As Freneau has described the treatment of the captives on the prison ships in the poem mentioned above, we will quote a few portions of it relative to his sufferings while on board the "Scorpion," and the "Hunter," the hospital ship, to which he was afterwards taken. It is an admitted fact that the sailors captured by the British during the war suffered even more than the soldiers who fell into their hands, if such a thing were possible. They were crowded together so closely, and their accommodations were so wretched, that diseases broke out and swept them off in such numbers as to arouse compassion in hearts the least sensible to woe.[1]

It has been asserted that, as near as could be estimated, in the last six years of the war more than eleven thousand captives died on board the "Jersey" alone. Besides the three ships already mentioned, there were the "Provost," the "Strombolo," and the "Good Hope." The prisoners on the latter set fire to it, hoping to gain their freedom in that way, preferring to meet a speedy death in the dark waters rather than a lingering one in its hold; but the chief incendiaries were removed to the "Provost," and the others to the "Jersey." The latter, being freed from her living freight at the close of the war, was shunned as a nest of pestilence. The worms destroyed her already half-

[1] "Thus wrote JohnMorin Scott, an illustrious statesman and soldier of those days: —

'Let the dark Scorpion's hull narrate
The dismal tale of English hate;
Her horrid tales let Jersey tell,
And mock the shades where demons dwell,
Their shriek of pain and dying groan
Unheeded fell on hearts of stone.' "

decayed bottom, and she sank, bearing inscribed on her planks the names of thousands of American prisoners. For more than twenty years the ebbing tide exposed her bare ribs, but this evidence of British barbarity was at length buried beneath the United States navy yard.[1] The precise number of deaths that occurred from ill treatment and starvation on these hulks will never be known till the day of doom. Many of these victims never had the rites of sepulture; and others were so imperfectly covered that for some time after the war their bones were found uncovered on the shores of Long Island.

To return to Freneau's description: —

"Thou, Scorpion, fatal to thy crowded throng,
Dire theme of horror and Plutonian song,
Requir'st my lay — thy sultry decks I know,
And all the torments that exist below!
The briny wave that Hudson's bosom fills
Drain'd through her bottom in a thousand rills:
Rotten and old, replete with sighs and groans,
Scarce on the waters she sustain'd her bones;
Here, doom'd to toil, or founder in the tide,
At the moist pumps incessantly we ply'd,
Here, doom'd to starve, like famish'd dogs, we tore
The scant allowance that our tyrants bore.

. . . . . .

When to the ocean sinks the western sun,
And the scorch'd Tories fire their evening gun,
'Down, rebels, down!' the angry Scotchmen cry,
'Base dogs, descend, or by our broad swords die!'
Hail, dark abode! what can with thee compare? —
Heat, sickness, famine, death, and stagnant air —
Swift from the guarded decks we rush'd along,
And vainly sought repose, so vast our throng;
Four hundred wretches here, denied all light,
In crowded mansions pass the infernal night,

[1] History of New York, by Miss Booth.

Some for a bed their tatter'd vestments join,
And some on chests, and some on floors recline;
Shut from the blessings of the evening air
Pensive we lay with mingled corpses there,
Meagre and wan, and scorch'd with heat below,
We look'd like ghosts, ere death had made us so—
How could we else, where heat and hunger joined,
Thus to debase the body and the mind,—
No waters laded from the bubbling spring
To these dire ships these little tyrants bring—
By planks and ponderous beams completely wall'd
In vain for water and in vain we call'd—
No drop was granted to the midnight prayer,
To *rebels* in these regions of despair!—
The loathsome cask a deadly dose contains,
Its poison circling through the languid veins.

. . . .

Sweet morn dispell'd the horrors of the shade;
On every side dire objects met the sight,
And pallid forms, and murders of the night,—
The dead were past their pain, the living groan,
Nor dare to hope another morn their own;
But what to them is morn's delightful ray?
Sad and distrestful as the close of day;
O'er distant streams appears the dewy green,
And leafy trees on mountain tops are seen,
But they no groves nor grassy mountains tread
Mark'd for a longer journey to the dead."

The freedom-loving and freedom-craving spirit of Freneau, like the caged eagle, vainly beat its wings against the bars of its cage; and what wonder that it finally succumbed to the horrors of his situation, and that he was borne in a half-dying condition from that infected hulk to the even more loathsome one of the hospital ship, the "Hunter"?

"Joyful we left the Scorpion's dire abode;
Some tears we shed for the remaining crew,
Then curs'd the hulk, and from her sides withdrew."

Philip Freneau

The Hospital Prison Ship.

" Now tow'rds the Hunter's gloomy decks we came,
A slaughter-house, yet *hospital* in name;
We were so pale! — that we were thought by some
A freight of ghosts, from death's dominions come —
Down to the gloom we took our pensive way,
Along the decks the dying captives lay;
Some struck with madness, some with scurvy pain'd,
But still of putrid fevers most complain'd!
On the hard floors these wasted objects laid,
There toss'd and tumbled in the dismal shade,
There no soft voice their bitter fate bemoan'd,
And death trode stately, while the victims groan'd;
Of leaky decks I heard them long complain,
Drown'd as they were in deluges of rain,
Deny'd the comforts of a dying bed,
And not a pillow to support the head —
How could they else but pine, and grieve, and sigh,
Detest a wretched life — and wish to die?
Scarce had I mingled with this dismal band
When a thin victim seiz'd me by the hand —
'And art thou come,' (death heavy on his eyes)
'And art thou come to these abodes?' he cries.
'Why didst thou leave the Scorpion's dark retreat,
And hither haste, a surer death to meet?
Why didst thou leave thy damp infected cell? —
If *that* was purgatory, this is hell.'

. . . . . .

From Brooklyn heights a Hessian doctor came,
Not great his skill, nor greater much his fame;
Fair Science never call'd the wretch her son,
And Art disdain'd the stupid man to own; —
Can you admire that Science was so coy,
Or Art refus'd his genius to employ? —
Do men with brutes an equal dullness share,
Or cuts yon grovelling mole the midway air?
In polar worlds can Eden's blossoms blow?
Do trees of God in barren deserts grow?
Are loaded vines to Etna's summit known,
Or swells the peach beneath the frozen zone?

He on his charge the healing work begun
With antimonial mixtures by the tun,
Ten minutes was the time he deign'd to stay,
The time of grace allotted once a day. —
He drench'd us well with bitter draughts, 't is true,
Nostrums from hell, and cortex from Peru —
Some with his pills he sent to Pluto's reign,
And some he blister'd with his flies of Spain;
And Tartar doses walk'd their deadly round.

. . . . . .

Here, uncontroul'd, he exercis'd his trade,
And grew experienc'd by the deaths he made,
By frequent blows we from his cane endur'd
He kill'd at least as many as he cur'd,
On our lost comrades built his future fame,
And scatter'd fate where'er his footsteps came.
Knave though he was, yet candour must confess
Not chief Physician was this man of Hesse —
One master o'er the murdering tribe was plac'd,
By him the rest were honour'd or disgrac'd;
Once, and but once, by some strange fortune led
He came to see the dying and the dead —
He came — but anger so deform'd his eye,
And such a faulchion glitter'd on his thigh,
And such a gloom his visage darken'd o'er,
And two such pistols in his hands he bore!
That by the gods! — with such a load of steel,
He came, we thought, to murder, not to heal —
All were astonish'd at the oaths he swore;
He swore till every prisoner stood aghast,
And thought him Satan in a brimstone blast;
He wish'd us banish'd from the public light,
And wish'd us shrouded in perpetual night!
That were he king, no mercy would he show,
But drive all rebels to the world below.

. . . . . .

Each day, at least six carcasses we bore
And scratch'd them graves along the sandy shore.
By feeble hands the shallow graves were made,
No stone, memorial, o'er the corpses laid;

In barren sands, and far from home, they lie,
No friend to shed a tear, when passing by;
O'er the mean tombs the insulting Britons tread,
Spurn at the sand, and curse the rebel dead.
When to your arms these fatal islands fall,
(For first, or last, they must be conquer'd all)
Americans! to rites sepulchral just,
With gentlest footstep press this kindred dust,
And o'er the tombs, if tombs can then be found,
Place the green turf, and plant the myrtle round.
These all in Freedom's sacred cause allied
For Freedom ventur'd and for Freedom died."

Sixty long days and nights Freneau passed between the deck and the hold of the "Scorpion;" how many more he remained in the "Hunter," we do not know exactly; but the capture occurred in May, and he was released in July of the same year, 1780.

It had been agreed between the British government and the United Colonies that all privateers sailing with letters of marque should be subject to the same rules of exchange as officers in the army. Boudinot had been appointed commissioner for the exchange of prisoners, and his father and André Freneau having been old friends as well as compatriots, he, as may be supposed, lost no time in setting Philip at liberty. Pintard, Boudinot's secretary, was a warm friend of Freneau's, and frequently spoke of the sufferings of his friend and his fellow-captives. A very romantic story in regard to the supposed escape of Freneau from the prison ship has been published, but we have the reality of his exchange in his own words:—

"On the 12th of July, the flag came alongside and cleared the hospital ship. But the miseries we endured in getting to Elizabeth Town were many; those that were very bad, of which the proportion was great, naturally took possession of the hold. No prisoner was allowed to go in the cabin, so that I, with twenty or thirty others, was obliged to sleep out all the night, which was uncommonly cold for the season. About ten next morning we arrived at Elizabeth Town Point, where we were kept in the burning sun several hours till the Commissary came to discharge us. I was afflicted with such pains in my joints I could scarcely walk, and besides was weakened with a raging fever; nevertheless, I walked the two miles to Elizabeth Town; here I got a passage on a wagon to within a mile of Crow's Ferry, which I walked; got a passage over the ferry, and walked on as far as Molly Budleigh's, where I stayed all night; next morning, having breakfasted on some bread and milk, I set homeward; when I came to Obadiah Budleigh's corner, I turned to the right and came home through the woods, for fear of terrifying the neighbors with my ghastly looks had I gone thro Mount Pleasant. July 14, 1780. I forgot to mention that as soon as we came to New York, and things were a little adjusted, Mr. Chatham, our first mate, went on board the "Aurora" and found his desk with mine and several books open and everything taken out; so much for English honor and honesty.[1] N. B. Wrote a letter by Hulings to Mr. G., but received no answer. Two days before I was exchanged got a letter from Mr. G. offering me anything I wanted, pretending he did not know what ship I was in. I returned him a letter of thanks, letting him know that if he could get me a parole it would be the greatest favor he could do me. The same day Mr. Robins came alongside in a small boat with fish, offering me what money I wanted. I begged him to lay the money out in wine, oranges, and lemons, and send them to me. He promised to be alongside in three hours, but I never saw him after-

[1] In leaving the "Aurora" Freneau had been assured by the commander of the "Iris" that his personal effects would be carefully cared for and would be turned over to him later on.

ward; in short I met with nothing but disappointment among this people, and cannot sufficiently congratulate myself upon having got from among them."

Among some papers belonging to Freneau's daughter, Mrs. Agnes Leadbeater, was a clipping from a newspaper yellow with age; it bore no date and read as follows: "At Big Flats, Steuben Co., N. Y., the 4th inst., Hon. Wm. Steele, æt. ninety-five years. Mr. Steele was born in the city of New York, and took an active part in the revolutionary struggle. In the spring of 1780 he sailed from Philadelphia on board the 'Aurora,' a twenty-gun ship, which was shortly after captured by the British frigate 'Iris' bearing despatches of the surrender of Charleston to the British. In the running fight which ensued he was severely wounded, taken prisoner, and detained between four or five months when he was exchanged in the exchange of prisoners."

It was a singular coincidence that the "Iris" that captured Freneau should be the bearer of despatches containing news of the defeat of an afterwards intimate friend, Charles Cotesworth Pinckney of South Carolina, who commanded Fort Moultrie, but was obliged to abandon the fort to help with the defence of the city of Charleston; but not, however, until he had inflicted great injury upon the British, whose force was greatly superior to his.

Chapter Eighth

THE exchange of prisoners occurring in the summer of 1780, Philip returned to his mother's house to recuperate; his health having been quite shattered by the rigors of his captivity. It is unnecessary to add that he carried with him a burning resentment for the ignominious and cruel treatment he had undergone. It was during these months of rest and a mother's care that he wrote the poem from which we have so largely drawn in the preceding chapter. Originally, the poem contained four cantos, and was thus printed by Francis Bailey in Philadelphia in the year 1781, entitled "Cantos from a Prison Ship." Later on, the author recast it, as was his wont with his productions, and it appeared in the Monmouth edition in three cantos, and was entitled, "The British Prison Ship;" it runs to about six hundred and fifty lines. Mr. Edward Delancey, having quoted a few lines of this poem in his "Proceedings of the Huguenot Society of America,"[1] says: "The poem was intended to rouse up American feeling, then—in 1780—excessively depressed; and it serves to show Freneau's power to arrest public attention, as well as the variety, beauty, and force of different characteristics of his verse;" and he continues: "Of course, the poem is exaggerated in its statements, but in this the skill of the true poet shows itself, for in all appeals of this kind exaggeration is a necessity if an effect is to be produced—just as the sculptor is obliged to make the figure of his hero larger than life, if his statue is to be impressive." In the accounts given by persons who were

[1] Vol. ii. No. 2.

not poets, and therefore without any poetical license to exaggerate, the description falls very little, if at all, short of Freneau's. Nearly half of the British force in the vicinity of New York was Hessian, and we learn from history that in such contempt were the Hessians held on account of their brutal force and hireling character, that Frederick the Great, disgusted at the thought of any sovereign employing such a force to reduce his colonies, charged *so much* a head for permitting them to cross his territory; saying, satirically, that was the rate he charged for driving *live stock* across his kingdom. The boot now exhibited at Washington's Headquarters in Newburg on the Hudson as belonging to one of these troops, speaks volumes as to the owner of such a machine.

The year of Freneau's capture and imprisonment, as well as the succeeding one, was dreary enough for the patriots. In the north, military operations were mostly suspended; and in the south the army had met with many reverses. As we have seen in the last chapter, Charles Cotesworth Pinckney had been compelled to yield Fort Moultrie to greatly superior forces, and to reinforce General Lincoln, who was trying to hold Charleston with fourteen hundred men against Sir Henry Clinton with five thousand. South Carolina was at last obliged to surrender, and the garrison, including Pinckney, were made prisoners of war. The latter was not released until peace was declared. Meanwhile, the nation's credit was at its lowest ebb; the continental bills fell in value to two cents on the dollar, and business was paralyzed. Had not Robert Morris and a few wealthy patriots come forward and laid their private fortunes on their country's shrine, its sun would have sunk then and there. The condition of the army was desperate; no food, no pay, no clothing. The American women came forward and did their best to provide the latter, still the army suffered. To add to all this misery, Benedict Arnold had turned traitor. Dismissed from Virginia, where he had held supreme command after General Phillips' death, he returned to New York; and, receiving from Clinton a second detachment, he entered the sound, landing at New London, and captured the town. Colonel William Ledyard,[1] who was doubly related to Philip's wife, held command of forts Griswold and Trumbull which protected the city, but finding his force inadequate to hold them both, he withdrew all his force, amounting to one hundred and fifty militia, to the former, and held it for about an hour against eight hundred British troops. The works were carried after severe fighting, but not until the two superior officers and two hundred men had been killed or disabled on the British side. Upon its surrender, Major Bromfield, upon whom the command now devolved, asked who commanded the garrison. Ledyard replied, "I did command it, but you do now," and handed him his sword. Bromfield, taking it, ran it through the body of Colonel Ledyard up to the hilt, and a general massacre ensued. About one hundred men were killed and wounded. A monument has been erected near the spot to commemorate the massacre.

Miss Fannie Ledyard, a niece of Colonel Ledyard, was on a visit to Groton, Conn., while Arnold was carrying on his butcheries there, and she devoted her whole time to caring for the wounded and dying. She became quite a heroine during the war, and her name is honorably mentioned amongst the devoted and self-sacrificing women of the Revolution. She afterwards married R. L. Peters of Southold, and her remains rest in the old cemetery near the historic home of her ancestors. This family, being so nearly related to Philip, and its history a romantic one, it will not do to pass over.

[1] Colonel Ledyard was at the time thirty-one years of age.

Philip Freneau

At the eastern extremity of Long Island is a quaint old town called Southold; and one of the oldest and most interesting landmarks of the place is the Case House, which was erected in the year 1647, at which time the only communication with it was by water. A writer, in speaking of the house, has said: "Around this old building cluster many romantic legends and quaint stories, interwoven with the names of men and women who have figured in the early history of Suffolk County."

In those early times this house was considered quite an aristocratic affair. It stands about a mile south of Horton's Point, where the settlers of Suffolk landed in 1640. In 1673 the Dutch commissioners, supposing themselves, like Crusoe, monarchs of all they surveyed, paid a visit to this town for the purpose of making Thomas Moore high-sheriff; but, unlike Crusoe, they found they were not so, for the settlers, indignant at the idea of being made Dutch whether they would or not, protested against this aggressive measure and desired the authority of the commissioners to act in their regard; and they immediately voted to connect themselves with the commonwealth of Connecticut.

John Ledyard, a son of this old house, married the daughter of Judge Young, and afterwards removed to the township of New London, Conn.; the place near Groton is named Ledyard after him. His eldest son, also named John, returned to Southold and married the famous beauty of the time, Abigail, the daughter of Robert Hempstead.[1] Mr. Ledyard engaged in the West Indian trade, but died at the early age of thirty-five years; Mrs. Ledyard retained much of her former beauty, and afterward married Dr. Micah Moore, the beloved physician of that section.

Her eldest son, John, afterwards known as Ledyard

[1] The city of Hempstead is named after this family.

the Traveller, upon the second marriage of his mother, went to reside with his paternal grandfather in Connecticut. After making his studies he attempted law, but his mother, desirous of having him become a missionary to the Indians, had him placed at Dartmouth College with that intention. During his stay there he absented himself for several months, and upon his return he excused his absence as arising from a desire to visit the Six Nations and study Indian life. Whether it was the experience he had with them or a disinclination for the ministry that caused him to abandon the project, is not known; but he soon after presented himself at his mother's house, having sailed down the Connecticut River and across the sound, master of his own vessel; this original affair being a dug-out, or canoe made from the trunks of a tree hollowed out in Indian fashion. Soon after, his adventurous spirit caused him to run away from home and embark on a ship bound for the Mediterranean.[1] Arriving in London as Captain Cook was preparing for his third voyage around the world, Ledyard was introduced to him and produced such a favorable impression upon the bold navigator that he readily accepted him as an assistant. Ledyard was with Captain Cook when he was killed by the cannibals. Although Ledyard remained in the British service, he refused to bear arms against his native country. In 1782 the man-of-war to which he belonged arrived off Huntington, and, obtaining leave of absence, he paid a visit to his mother. Finding some British officers in her parlor, he did not make himself known; and he had changed so much during his eight years of absence that he was not recognized. During the visit some familiar ex-

[1] According to the Records of the Genealogical Society, Ledyard had "just cause" for leaving his relatives. A commentator remarks that the fact that people sometimes retain the property belonging to others is not calculated to keep those who are wronged around the ancestral home.

pression attracted the lady's attention; and, after scrutinizing him for a moment, she pressed him to her heart, forgetting the presence of strangers, so great was her joy; their astonishment was considerable until the matter was explained. In 1785 Ledyard visited Paris, and was received most kindly by Mr. Jefferson, United States minister at the time, and also by Lafayette. Desirous of fitting out an exploring expedition, he found Captain Paul Jones a ready co-operator in his plan; but circumstances prevented their carrying it into effect. During one of his journeys he attempted to cross the Gulf of Bothnia on the ice, but upon reaching the middle he found open water, and was obliged to alter his course and walk around the whole coast of the gulf, although it was the dead of winter. By the time he reached St. Petersburg he had journeyed upwards of fourteen hundred miles in seven weeks. At Irkootsk he was arrested as a spy, and thought he got off very easily when the empress ordered two guards to accompany him to the frontiers of Poland, and there dismiss him with the threat of being hanged if he ever entered Russia again. It is most probable that he did not. After travelling over the most of the then known part of the world, he died at Cairo, as he was preparing to cross the African continent westerly from Sennaar. It is said of him that he was adventurous beyond the conception of ordinary men, yet wary and considerate; and he appeared to be formed by nature for achievements of hardihood and peril; for capacity of endurance, resolution, and physical vigor, he was one of the most remarkable of modern travellers; and had he possessed means equal to his zeal, his name would doubtless have been associated with important discoveries, as it now is with wonderful and romantic, but unprofitable adventures. Writing to Mr. Jefferson, he utters a beautiful and refined compliment. Expressing his appreciation of the former's kindness while in Paris, he writes: "I shall never think my letter an indifferent one when it contains the declaration of my gratitude and my affection for you; and this, notwithstanding you thought hard of me for being employed by an English association, which hurt me while I was in Paris. You know your own heart; and if my suspicions are groundless, forgive them, since they proceed from the jealousy I have, not to lose the regard you have in times past been pleased to honor me with. You are not obliged to esteem me, but I am obliged to esteem you, or take leave of my senses and confront the opinions of the greatest and best characters I know. If I cannot therefore address myself to you as a man you regard, I must do it as one that regards you, for your own sake and for the sake of my country, which has set me the example." [1]

His relative, Freneau's wife, used to tell an amusing story of an unexpected visit from him upon his return from one of his perilous adventures. She was seated by a window in Middleton Point engaged in reading, when she heard the hasty galloping of a horse, and suddenly felt herself embraced most warmly, and then heard the retreating gallop of the same down the street; and all in shorter time than it takes to tell it. Her feeling of indignation cooled down later on, upon learning that the author of the affair was her wild, fun-loving relative; for no one could be angry with Jack Ledyard.

After the battle of Long Island, in which, as we

[1] A biographer of Ledyard has written, "Ledyard gave Jefferson a great deal of valuable information, which, for political reasons, Jefferson did not publish, but which was of great benefit to him in the conduct of foreign affairs when he became president." He likewise says that the success of the administration in pushing forward the contest which made the Pacific the western boundary, in opposition to the Hudson Bay Co., and also in opposition to a great many American Congressmen, was partly due to information given by Ledyard in the early days.

have seen, the patriots were defeated, the British occupied the eastern extremity of the island, making their headquarters at the Vail[1] house, which was not far from Mrs. Moore's residence. The officers frequently visited that lady, probably attracted by her charming daughters. Mrs. Moore was a thorough patriot, but nevertheless entertained her guests most hospitably; keeping, however, a sharp eye on her young people. A ship lay at anchor in the sound in sight of the house, whose commander very frequently was a guest of the lady. Her third and last child by the name of Ledyard, Jerusia, looked favorably on her suitor, although he wore the uniform of a British naval officer, and was fighting against her country; but her mother looked less favorably upon his suit. One day Jerusia was missing, and the ship gave tokens of a sudden departure. Summoning some men, the determined mother had herself taken in a boat alongside the ship, and demanded her daughter; but gave her consent to the nuptials, provided the ceremony was performed in the little Puritan church in the village, which was done.

The oldest daughter by Mrs. Ledyard's second marriage, Rebecca, married Captain Jonathan Landon, who commanded the brig "Georgia" of historic fame; and Julia, the youngest, became the wife of Matthias Case and succeeded her mother as mistress of the Ledyard-Moore-Case house. The latter name it bears at the present day. For years the town meetings were held at this house; and whenever there was a question of a vote it was taken on the lawn in front, the voters being drawn up in lines.[2]

[1] Both this house and the Case house are yet standing.

[2] Connected with this family are: Rev. Theodore Ledyard Cuyler, D.D., Lewis Cass Ledyard, Horatio Seymour, John Seymour, Ex-Gov. E. D. Morgan, Thomas Seymour of Connecticut, Governor and Congressman, Senator George Ledyard, and the Baroness von Kettler.

The Poet of the Revolution

When Arnold left New York with his family for England in 1781, Freneau celebrated his departure by an ode which is in imitation of Horace.

Duyckinck says Freneau's rendering is quite skilful, and shows his scholar's appreciation of the original.

ARNOLD'S DEPARTURE.

Mala soluta navis exit aliter
Ferens olentem Mævium.

Imitated from HORACE.

With evil omens from the harbour sails
  The ill-fated ship that worthless Arnold bears,
God of the southern winds, call up thy gales,
  And whistle in rude fury round his ears.

With horrid waves insult his vessel's sides,
  And may the east wind on a leeward shore
Her cables snap, while she in tumult rides,
  And shatter into shivers every oar.

And let the north wind to her ruin haste,
  With such a rage, as when from mountains high
He rends the tall oak with his weighty blast,
  And ruin spreads, where'er his forces fly.

May not one friendly star that night be seen;
  No Moon, attendant, dart one glimmering ray,
Nor may she ride on oceans more serene
  Than Greece, triumphant, found that stormy day,

When angry Pallas spent her rage no more
  On vanquish'd Ilium, then in ashes laid,
But turn'd it on the barque that Ajax bore
  Avenging thus her temple and the maid.

When toss'd upon the vast Atlantic main
  Your groaning ship the southern gales shall tear,
How will your sailors sweat, and you complain
  And meanly howl to Jove, that will not hear!

But if at last, upon some winding shore
  A prey to hungry cormorants you lie,
A wanton goat to every stormy power,[1]
  And a fat lamb in sacrifice, shall die.

Of this poem, Professor Murray says some parts are unequalled.

In this year, 1781 Freneau published his poem commemorating the naval victory of Paul Jones. It was entitled "On the Memorable Victory," which the same professor says is a genuine specimen of the national ballad. One beautiful phase of Freneau's character was his freedom from all sentiment of jealousy. Probably no one was ever found more willing to bestow praise, when deserved, than he. Although the entire poem is a panegyric, I select a few stanzas to exemplify what I have already stated: —

"'T was Jones, brave Jones, to battle led
As bold a crew as ever bled
    Upon the sky surrounded main;
The standards of the western world
Were to the willing winds unfurl'd,
    Denying Britain's tyrant reign."

And again: —

"But thou, brave Jones, no blame shalt bear;
The rights of men demand your care:
    For *these* you dare the greedy waves —
No tyrant, on destruction bent,
Has plann'd thy conquests — thou art sent
    To humble tyrants and their slaves."

The poem contains twenty-one stanzas descriptive of the battle. The concluding stanzas run thus: —

"Go on, great man, to scourge the foe,
And bid these haughty Britons know

[1] The tempests were goddesses among the Romans.

They to our *Thirteen Stars* shall bend;
The *Stars* that, veil'd in dark attire,
Long glimmer'd with a feeble fire,
But radiant now ascend.

"Bend to the stars that flaming rise
On western worlds, more brilliant skies,
Fair Freedom's reign restor'd —
So when the Magi, come from far,
Beheld the God-attending Star,
They trembled and ador'd." [1]

During the year 1781 and till peace was declared, Freneau strove to animate his countrymen with his pen, as indeed he had ever done since the outbreak of hostilities. From Concord to Yorktown, during the bleak winter at Valley Forge, and round the camp-fires on Temple Hill, his verses encouraged the desponding soldiers. The newspapers widely published them, and they were written on slips of paper and distributed throughout the army, or posted in some conspicuous place to be memorized. And not alone by the camp-fire did they accomplish their work, but even on the field; his earnestness and zeal encouraged the patriots to greater efforts, or urged them on at the point of his bayonet (the pen) when he saw any signs of their lagging behind; and afterwards he immortalized the victories they won. Not a memorable incident either by land or by water escaped his ever watchful and unwearied pen.

Conscious that ridicule best kills a cause, every vain exploit of the enemy was depicted in a ludicrous light; and so successfully did he attack those that still adhered to the crown that he gained to his side many who through indifference had given their adherence to

[1] This action was fought off Flamborough Head the 23d of September, 1779. Few naval battles have made a greater popular impression. The history of Jones has an air of romance and gallantry, of courage and adventure. His ability as an officer and seaman cannot be disputed.

neither party. This was too serious a time to think of future fame; the stern realities of the present were to be met, and by a supreme effort everything was to be gained or all lost. His country's fortunes were his, and he threw himself heart and soul into the task. Exquisite melodies could hardly touch the hearts of the half-clothed barefooted soldiers. It would be like the mockery of pouring a wineglass of Tokay or Johannisberg into the poor empty canteens of half-famished soldiers. No, he wrote to arouse, to inspire, to encourage the rough, illiterate men of whom the army was mostly composed. And as no two natures are precisely alike, he enlisted all his talents in his work; burlesque, satire, imprecation, — nothing was neglected that might touch an answering chord in their hearts. Now he would ring a note of victory, now one of defiance, again that of denunciation in answer to some Tory gibe.

Some writer has said, "Was it not as grand and true a spirit that would belittle itself to cheer the down-hearted patriots, or give their unrefined ears some jingle to sing or some praise to cheer, as issued from the lips of the officers on the field? — it was all for the same cause." It has also been truthfully said that among the poets of the Revolution that contributed the most effectually to animate the colonists in their struggles with England, Freneau holds the chief place; and that during the war, and for several years afterwards, his efforts were so much appreciated that he enjoyed a large measure of popularity: and even since that time many of his productions have received high praise abroad and at home. His real strength lay in his earnestness, and it was this quality that made his revolutionary verses popular, and contributed to their real merit.

During the war he satirized Tryon, Gage, Burgoyne, Vaughan, Knyphausen, and Lords Percy, North, and Jeffries, also the blundering of the British troops by land, and their losses by sea; and, above all, the crown in its representative, George, whom he called a "royal coward." In fact, as Professor Tyler has said, "a running commentary on his Revolutionary satires would be an almost complete commentary on the whole Revolutionary struggle; nearly every important emergency and phase of which are photographed in his keen, merciless, and often brilliant lines."

The war ending in 1783, Freneau dropped his bloodless warfare and turned his satirical powers upon the rival printers Rivington and Gaine; who had changed their signs as well as their coats to suit each power that held the ascendency; and which he thought called rather for ridicule than eloquence. And in this, Dr. Witherspoon, Francis Hopkinson, and Trumbull joined him, opening their batteries of severity and ridicule upon these unfortunate remnants of Toryism. James Rivington was a London bookseller who had established himself in New York, and commenced, in 1773, the publication of the "New York Gazetteer," a Tory organ. In 1775, Isaac Sears, a "Son of Liberty," destroyed his office and ran his type into bullets; Rivington repaired to England, obtained the appointment of king's printer, and returned with new type to New York. Although he seemed to do his best to fan the flame of Toryism before and during the war, after it was over he escaped deserved punishment by having acted as a spy for Washington. Nevertheless, Freneau, who detested insincerity, commemorated his turncoat propensities in several poems; but Rivington, a supple courtier, stood the fire, took down the royal arms of which Freneau made sport, and continued his paper under the title of "New York Gazette and Universal Advertiser." This latter quality drew upon him Freneau's ridicule; it is said that his advertisements supplied no small amount of amusement to all his readers. The poet caricatures them thus in his verses entitled, "Rivington's last Will and Testament," of which I will only quote an occasional verse: —

"To the king, my dear master, I give a full sett,
In volumes bound up, of the Royal Gazette,
In which he will find the vast records contain'd
Of provinces conquer'd, and victories gain'd.

"As to Arnold, the traitor, and Satan his brother,
I beg they will also accept of another;
And this shall be bound in morocco red leather,
Provided they 'll read it, like brothers, together.

"But if Arnold should die, 't is another affair,
Then Satan, surviving, shall be the sole heir;
He often has told me he thought it quite clever,
So to him and his heirs, I bequeath it forever.

"I know there are some, that would fain be thought wise
Who say my Gazette is a record of lies;
In answer to this I shall only reply —
All the choice that I had was, to starve or to lie.

"My fiddles, my flutes, French horns and guitars,[1]
I leave to our Heroes, now weary of wars —
To the wars of the stage they more boldly advance,[2]
The captains shall play and the soldiers shall dance.

"To Sir Henry Clinton his use and behoof,
I leave my French brandy, of very good proof;
It will give him fresh spirits for battle and slaughter
And make him feel bolder by land and by water:

"To Baron Knyphausen, his heirs and assigns,
I bequeath my old Hock, and my Burgundy wines,

[1] Rivington seems to have prided himself on his supply of "good fiddles."

[2] "It became fashionable at this period with the British officers to assume the business of the drama, to the no small mortification of those who had been holding them up as the conquerors of North America."

To a true Hessian drunkard, no liquors are sweeter,
And I know the old man is no foe to the creature.

"To a General, my namesake, I give and dispose
Of a purse full of clipp'd, *light*, *sweated* half Joes:
I hereby desire him to take back his trash,
And return me my Hannay's infallible Wash.

"My chessmen and tables, and other such chattels
I give to Cornwallis, renowned in battles:
By moving of these, not tracing the map,
He'll explain to the king how he got in a trap."

The type of the "Gazette" being rather delicate through age, Freneau commemorates the fact in an epigram entitled "Epigram. *Occasioned by the Title of Mr. Rivington's New York Royal Gazette being scarcely legible.*"

Undoubtedly *to please* Freneau, the editor of the "Gazette" got new types, and this fact called for some "Lines. *Occasioned by Mr. Rivington's new Titular types to his Royal Gazette of February* 17, 1782."

Then his arms fell under Freneau's fire and the editor had new ones engraved, which called for another set of verses: —

ON MR. RIVINGTON'S NEW ENGRAVED KING'S ARMS TO HIS ROYAL GAZETTE.

From the regions of night, with his head in a sack,
Ascended a person accoutred in black,
And upward directing his circular eye whites;
(Like the Jure-divino political Levites)
And leaning his elbow on Rivington's shelf,
While the printer was busy thus mus'd with himself:
"My mandates are fully complied with at last,
New Arms are engrav'd, and new letters are cast;
I therefore determine and freely accord,
This servant of mine shall receive his reward."

Then turning about, to the printer he said,
"Who late was my *servant* shall now be my *aid;*
Since under my banner so bravely you fight,
Kneel down! — for your merits I dubb you a *knight,*
From a passive *subaltern* I bid you to rise
The Inventor, as well as the Printer of Lies."

Freneau's other victim, Hugh Gaine , an Irishman by birth, had settled in New York as a printer in 1750; and two years later established a newspaper called the "New York Mercury." His sign was a Bible and a crown; his politics, whichever side was uppermost. After the war he was allowed to continue his book store, striking the crown from his sign; but his paper was discontinued. At the beginning of the war he sided with the patriots, and when the British seized New York, he retired to New Jersey and published his paper there for a few weeks, but returned to New York and continued his printing, under the protection of the royal army. Freneau has written a Poetical Biography, of Gaine , in which he depicts his retreat to New Jersey, and in which occurs an image to which Mr. Delancey draws attention as being an "exceedingly fine one — one of the striking creations of the true poet."

"IV.

"From this very day 'till the *British* came in,
We liv'd I may say, in the *Desert of Sin;* —
Such beating, and bruising, and *scratching, and tearing;*
Such kicking, and cuffing, and cursing and swearing!
But when *they* advanc'd with *their numerous fleet,*
And Washington made his *nocturnal retreat,*[1]
(And which *they permitted,* I say to *their* shame,
Or else *your* New Empire had been but a name).
We townsmen, like women, of *Britons* in *dread,*
Mistrusted *their* meaning, and foolishly fled;

[1] Retreat from Long Island.

Like the *rest* of the dunces I mounted my steed,
And gallop'd away with *incredible* speed,
To Newark I hastened — but trouble and care
Got up on the crupper and followed me there."[1]

Before the war Gaine had published some of Freneau's satires against Great Britain, and the poet puts these words in Gaine' mouth in apology for the act: —

"I first was a whig with an honest intent;
Not a Rebel among them talk'd louder or bolder,
With his sword by his side, or his gun on his shoulder,
Yes, I was a whig, and a whig from my heart,
But still was unwilling with Britain to part —
I thought to oppose her was foolish and vain,
I thought she would turn and embrace us again,
And make us as happy as happy could be,
By renewing the aera of mild Sixty-three;
And yet, like a cruel undutiful son,
Who evil returns for the good *to be done*,
Unmerited odium on Britain to throw,
I printed some treason for Philip Freneau,
Some damnable poems reflecting on Gage,
The King and his Council, and writ with such rage,
So full of invective, and loaded with spleen,
So sneeringly smart, and so hellishly keen,
That, at least in the judgment of half our wise men,
Alecto herself put the nib to his pen."

Dr. Francis, in his reminiscences, relates the meeting of Freneau and his victim after the war. The former was quietly looking at some books in the store of the latter, when a friend entered; and in saluting Freneau, called him by name quite distinctly. The name arrested the attention of the old printer, who, lifting up his eyes, said, —

[1] Probably adapted from Horace: —

"Post equitem sedet atra Cura."

"Is your name Freneau ?"

"Yes," replied the poet, "Philip Freneau."

"Philip Freneau ?" repeated Gaine .

"Yes, sir, the same."

"Then, sir," warmly returned the latter, "you are a clever fellow; let me have the pleasure of taking you by the hand. Will you join me in my parlor around the corner and we will have a glass of wine together. You have given me and my friend Rivington a wide and lasting reputation."

In 1784 we find Freneau dating a poem from Port Royal; and from another, dated Charleston, 1786, we learn that he was visiting his brother in that year. From a note in a very old book we find that he made two voyages to Madeira as commander of the brig "Washington," which was owned and freighted by his brother.

Pierre, or Peter Freneau, as he was usually called, was the younger and only living brother of the poet. It has been stated that he was graduated at Princeton College, but his name is not found upon their records. This may be satisfactorily accounted for by the fact of his being a student at the time the British took possession of Nassau Hall, and the rolls then in use may have been destroyed, while the earlier records were, probably, safe by having been stored away, and have thus been handed down. Some years after his graduation, and in the year 1782, Peter took up his residence in Charleston.

South Carolina was a favorite location for the Huguenot refugees; consequently their numbers in that State exceeded that of any other. They founded large plantations on the banks of the Cooper River, and to them it is said the State is indebted for the introduction of the olive and mulberry. In the city of Charleston they added many new streets, and their merchants were distinguished as being the most active and thrifty in the provinces; and many of the most distinguished families of later days are descended from the Huguenot settlers. Charleston was a very aristocratic city, and it has been said to have had its nobility in everything but titles. Among its residents at that time were the Right Hon. Richard Beresford, brother to the Premier; Pierce Butler, cousin to the Duke of Ormond; Lady Mary Middleton, and others. All these circumstances may have combined to cause Peter to choose that city for a permanent residence. It is said that from the first he attracted general and favorable notice from those the best qualified as judges, and that he became a prominent and influential citizen of his adopted city.

Peter was renowned throughout the State for his personal beauty; and his manners were such as to endear him to all and render him popular in the extreme.[1] It is most probable, if he married, that his wife died early, as Mr. Thomas in his Reminiscences, to which I am indebted for most of these facts, says that although he kept up an establishment, he had no family but his slaves. It has also been stated that he never married. This, we think, is a mistake, as Philip's daughter Agnes remembered, as a child, seeing his wife frequently at Mt. Pleasant, and that upon one of Mr. and Mrs. Pierre Freneau's visits they drove by easy stages from Charleston, and presented her father with the handsome span of horses, carriage, and slave coachman. Peter was noted for his handsome presents and generous liberality. Mrs. Agnes Leadbeater also states that her elder sister Helen went to Charleston with her uncle and aunt and remained there some time, for the purpose of attending an excellent school conducted by a daughter of Admiral

[1] It is said that, when visiting Mr. and Mrs. Philip Freneau in Philadelphia while that city was the seat of government, he became one of the greatest social favorites and one of the most talked-of men at the assemblies.

de Grasse,[1] as schools for females were few and poor near her home. Pierre never married again, but he enjoyed in his home the friendship of many who were not friends alone in name, but in the deepest sentiments of the heart. His conversational powers, we are told, were unequalled; and what enhanced the charm was his utter unconsciousness of possessing such in any eminent degree; he communicated the most interesting truths in a manner all the more agreeable, as he was not conscious of saying anything not already familiar to his hearers.

Sometimes he would entertain his friends by rendering into English the famous Paris editions of Voltaire's plays. He was an admirable reader, and his translations were ready and unequalled, so that it was considered a great treat to listen to him. He was well versed in ancient, as well as modern languages, reading the Old Testament in Hebrew, and the New in Greek. His Latin was said to be good, but he took greater pleasure in the living languages and translated well from the Italian, French, Spanish, and Portuguese. Napoleon is said to have remarked to Berthier, the Minister of War, that Freneau's translations of his bulletins were the only correct ones. Berthier communicated this fact to the French minister. Pierre's reading was extensive; he devoted most of his time to it, taking a book into his hand almost as soon as he entered the house.

In his early life he had started a paper called the "Charleston City Gazette," which obtained a vast controlling influence throughout the entire State; and it continued to increase until it was a complete political lever, he himself being a host. Pierre was peculiarly fitted for the position of editor, as he had a wide range of general knowledge and information; and

[1] This lady afterwards married Mr. de Pau of New York.

he wrote with the greatest ease and facility, being seldom obliged to make an erasure. His style of composition is said to have combined the smoothness and beauty of Addison with the simplicity of Cobbett; his wit was ready, and he occasionally indulged in versification.

Decided in advancing his own opinions, he was nevertheless just, and even liberal, to those that thought differently from him; and no difference in political opinion ever caused a loss of his many warm-hearted and devoted friends. In politics he maintained the Republican-Democratic party, and remained ever identified with it. His paper was, even before Jefferson's administration, the journal of the State as well as of the city, but after the nomination of the latter for the presidency, the patronage of the general government was added. Jefferson was warmly attached to Pierre, and kept up a correspondence with him, as did many other prominent men. Unfortunately, many of his letters and papers were burned in the fire which consumed Philip's residence at Mount Pleasant. Of one of these letters we are fortunate enough to have a copy. It reads as follows: —

WASHINGTON, May 20, 1803.

DEAR SIR, — I received last night from Paris the enclosed small parcel of Egyptian rice. I am not informed of its merits, but your's being the State where that can be best tried, I take the liberty of consigning it to your care, that we may be availed of whatever good it may offer.

The New York election no doubt attracted your attention from the inflated hopes of the Federalists. From a concurrence of circumstances they had been out with all their boldness. One source of their delusion was that they were so desirous of war themselves that they really believed the nation desired it. Never was defeat more complete; in Jersey it is confidently believed we shall have 29 members out of 52 which constitute both houses; in Massachusetts we have gained two senators more than we had last year, and it is believed that in the election of representatives now going on, we shall gain also. In Connecticut we have lost greatly in their house of representatives, yet in the whole body of the people we have unquestionably gained, as is proved by the votes for Governor. Last year the votes for Trumbull and Kirby were 10,000 to 4523; this year they are 14,300 to 7848; so that the last year of 100 parts of the whole voters, the Federalists had 71 and the Republicans 29; this year, of 100 parts of the whole voters the Federalists had 65, and the Republicans 35. We have advanced then from 29 to 35, or $\frac{1}{6}$, while they have fallen from 71 to 65, or $\frac{1}{11}$. In New Hampshire they appear to have been more stationary. Delaware is entirely equivocal and uncertain. On the whole there is no doubt of republicanism gaining the entire ascendency in New England within a moderate time and consolidating the union into one homogeneous mass. In Philadelphia some heats have been excited against the leaving any Federalists in office, but these are softening down to moderation, while in the other states generally the course which has been pursued, altho' thought to have gone too far into removal, is acquiesced in and on the whole approved. We laid it down as a principal, in the beginning, that the Federalists had a right to a participation of office proportioned to their numbers; they in fact professed all. We removed a few in marked cases; we determined to remove all others who should take an active and bitter part against the order of things established by the public bill. Removals for this cause and for other delinquencies, resignations, and deaths have nearly given us our full proportion of office in all the States except Massachusetts. I speak of these offices only which are given by the President himself; the subordinate ones are left to their principals. At present, therefore, as from an early period of the administration, political principle, unless producing active opposition, is not a ground for removal, altho' it is as yet a bar to appointment, until the just proportion is fully restored.

A letter begun with a view to cover a few deeds, and to say a word about elections, has led to a length not at first contemplated. Desirous, however, that the principles of our proceedings should be understood, I explain them to no one more willingly than yourself, because I am sure you will use them with prudence and sincerity for the information and satisfaction of others when occasions may lead you to an expression of sentiment. Should it be the means of giving me the advantage of receiving communications sometimes from you on the political state of things in your quarter, it will contribute to that information so desirable to myself, and so necessary to enable me to do what is best for the public interest. I pray you to accept my salutations, and utterances of esteem and respect.

TH. JEFFERSON.

Peter's influence was extended and widely felt; and had he any personal ambition, there is no position in the power of the State to give that he could not have obtained, if he had manifested any desire for it. Although Freneau was so well fitted for the position of an editor, he was not so well qualified for that of a proprietor, as he was nothing of a business man; and his friend adds that it would be difficult to say, at times which was in the greatest confusion, his private affairs or those of the establishment. Over two hundred more papers than were needed were printed daily, and made way with by the slaves attached to the office. In the year 1810 he gave the paper into the hands of his friend Mr. Thomas, and was after that time Director of the State Bank. After the paper had passed from his hands, his intimate friend Charles Cotesworth Pinckney and Colonel Lehre met at his house, as they were accustomed to do pending election, but this time it was for a special purpose. Knowing how impossible it was for Peter ever to say no, they asked him to request Mr. Thomas, the acting editor of the paper, to uphold a certain candidate they were desirous of having elected; and they took this way of accomplishing their end, conscious of the unwillingness of the editor to further the candidacy, yet also knowing that he could never refuse his friend anything that he asked of him.

Freneau for some years held the office of Commissioner of Loans for the State of South Carolina; and was several times member of the State Legislature, in which his services were said to be alike creditable to himself and useful to the State. Desirous of knowing how long he filled the position of Secretary of State, we applied to the corresponding secretary of the South Carolina Historical Society, and received in reply: "Concerning Peter Freneau, once an honored citizen of this State, I gather that he was Secretary of State in the years from 1788 to 94 inclusive;[1] there is no list of State officers for 1795, and a new name appears in the office for 1796. So long a tenure of office as was that of your honored relative Peter Freneau is very uncommon," etc.

Peter's inability to say no, and his readiness to oblige his friends, frequently got him into serious difficulties, as he too often went security for them and was thereby the loser. It was owing to this virtue, or fault, according to the different ways of viewing it, that he for the first time in his life was known to lose his wonted cheerfulness. An old and dear friend had indorsed his paper, and he became alarmed lest this friend should suffer on his account. He called upon an intimate acquaintance and informed him that the note would go to protest that day, as he was unable to meet it unless the former could loan him the money for the present. His friend, not having the amount on hand, promised it the next day and invited Peter to dine with him, which invitation Freneau refused. Something in his manner attracted the attention of the other, and he shortly after called at Freneau's office. Entering softly, he was not perceived until he laid his hand upon Peter's shoulder. The latter was absorbed in his writing, and, starting, looked up into his visitor's face. Four notes lay folded upon the desk, the upper

[1] Freneau held the office eight years altogether.

one being addressed to the visitor. In a moment the intention of Freneau flashed upon his friend, but he pretended not to notice anything, saying quietly, "Freneau, give me your word of honor that I shall find you here one hour hence," adding, "I am on my way to the notary's." Peter's face evinced how a mighty mind could be shaken and even overcome by the tempest of adversity, but he gave the desired promise. The friend hastened to the bank and had the note delayed until the next day, and hurried back to Freneau's office. The note had disappeared, and in a slight degree the old cheerfulness had returned. His friend remained with him till late, avoiding any allusion to what had happened, merely saying that all would be satisfactorily arranged in the morning; and the serious danger with which his friend was threatened was never known, and he adds, "he lived to be the delight of his friends for several years."

With talents fitted for any station, his friend tells us, he nevertheless wished to retire from active life that he might be able to enjoy seclusion and the society of his books and friends in peace; consequently he began to build a cottage in the interior of the State, intending to spend there the remainder of his days. Desirous of visiting the workmen, although dissuaded by his friends, he went there, trusting to the perfect condition of his health to insure him against the dangers of the miasma, so fatal at that time of the year. He remained there over a week, and returned apparently in perfect health, and with his usual flow of spirits, but was soon after taken very ill. The devoted attention of his friends and the best medical advice were of no avail; he was constantly watched by the daughter of one of his old friends, but Death had marked him for his prey, and on the fifth day he succumbed. His strong constitution was so completely exhausted that for some time before his death he did not utter a groan or even sigh, and scarcely seemed to breathe; and "thus ended the life of a man, who, to transcendent talents united that amiability of temper and benevolence of heart that made him the friend of his race."

"This all who knew him know,
This all who loved him tell,
Whose like we ne'er shall look upon again."

In appearance, Freneau resembled to such a remarkable degree the great British statesman Fox that a friend purposely brought a portrait of the latter with him on his return from England to deceive his acquaintances; who, knowing Freneau's aversion to sitting for his portrait, would exclaim upon seeing it on the mantelpiece, "How did you come by Freneau's portrait?" and not alone in physique did Peter resemble the great statesman, but in his mental calibre also. In height he was six feet two inches, and of such perfect proportions and beauty of countenance that one would say "every god did seem to set his seal to give the world assurance of a man."

Mr. Thomas, his devoted friend, took charge of his funeral, which was largely attended, and he was buried in the French Huguenot church in Charleston. His epitaph reads: —

"*Whatever Omnipotence decides is right.*

"Below this marble are deposited the remains of Peter Freneau, Esq. A native of New Jersey, but for more than thirty years past a citizen of South Carolina. He was the second son of Peter Freneau and Agnes Watson, born April 5th, 1757. Died Nov. 9th, A. D. 1813, æ. fifty-six years seven months and four days. His upright and benevolent character is in the memory of many, and will remain when this inscription is no longer legible. He was Secretary of State of South Carolina eight years."

Chapter Ninth

THE year 1789 was an important one in Freneau's life, as during that period there occurred two events that covered the entire course of his future, — the one shaping his private, and the other his political life.

The first of these events was that of his marriage with Eleanor, daughter of Samuel and Helen Denise Forman, a prominent and wealthy family of New Jersey, which had, and has since that time, given to the country a galaxy of names which have reflected honor on the land of their birth, and occupied prominent places on its roll of honor, in military as well as civil affairs.

Eleanor's two brothers and cousin served in the Revolutionary War, — the latter, General David Forman, being familiarly known as " Black David," on account of his excessive severity towards those who did not favor the Revolution. This officer ably commanded the New Jersey militia in the battle of Germantown, which engagement, in reality a defeat, was considered as advantageous to the Americans as a victory. In it the genius of Washington and the bravery and discipline of the army showed to such advantage as to rank it in the eyes of all Europe as nearly on an equality with the surrender of Burgoyne, and as to cause Frederic of Prussia to acknowledge the formidable power the American army might become, as well as to decide the French Court to consider us as allies.[1] After the war General Forman

[1] John Fiske, in Atlantic Monthly.

was a member of the Council of State, and Judge of the County Court. He was also one of the original members of the Order of The Cincinnati.

Eleanor's eldest brother, Colonel Jonathan Forman, married a sister of Colonel William Ledyard, of whom we have spoken in the preceding chapter; their grandchildren were Horatio Seymour, who married into the Bleecker family, and was several times Governor of New York State, and a candidate for the Presidency,[1] and John Seymour, who married in the Tappan family; his granddaughters married, the one, Judge Miller of Utica; another, Roscoe Conkling; and, a third her cousin, Ledyard Lincklaen, whose daughter married Charles S. Fairchild, Secretary of the Treasury during Cleveland's first administration.

Eleanor Freneau's second brother, Captain Denise Forman, married into the Kearny family to which Philip's step-father belonged. This family, trebly related to Freneau, gave Major-General Philip Kearny[2] to the country. The daughter of Eleanor's third brother, Major Samuel Forman, married General Rensselaer Van Rensselaer, and her eldest sister, Catherine, married Colonel William Ledyard, thus forming a double connection with that family. Catherine's eldest son, Major Benjamin Ledyard, married the daughter of Freneau's old college-mate, Brockholst Livingston, and consequently the niece of John Jay's wife; and his son[3] married a daughter of General Cass. Catherine's other grandchildren formed double rela-

[1] Governor Thomas Seymour of Connecticut was also a relative.

[2] Philip Kearny married Susan, daughter of John Watts and Jane Colden a sister of Cadwallader Colden. This John Watts was son of John Watts senior and Ann Delancey; Philip was father of General Philip Kearny.

[3] A son of this gentleman is now President of the Michigan Central Railroad, viz., Mr. Henry Ledyard, father of the Baroness Von Kettler, whose husband was killed in China, when minister to that country from Germany.

tionships with the families of Seymour and Fairchild; and another of them married into the Fitzhugh family; and through their child, a triple connection was formed with the Seymour family.

Eleanor's second sister, Margaret, married Major Burrows. Major Gordon, a graduate of Princeton College of the class of 1786, was likewise a relative of hers. Eleanor is said to have been distinguished for her well informed mind, sprightliness of disposition, elegance of manner, affability, and excellent conversational powers; and she is said to have retained these qualities, as well as much of her personal beauty, to her old age. She was intimately acquainted with many distinguished personages, and was a charming hostess, in her husband's residence at Mount Pleasant as well as in Philadelphia. Mrs. Freneau had a poetic taste and wrote with ease; her compositions are said to have been distinguished by character and intelligence. She corresponded for some time before her marriage with Freneau in verse. An amusing anecdote is told of her sprightliness before her marriage. In one of Freneau's visits she left him to entertain the other members of the family, and, slipping from the room while he was thus engaged, she dexterously sheared off some of the superfluous capes attached to his outer garment, such as we have already spoken of as having been in vogue; whether they were displeasing to her as being old-fashioned, or for some other reason, she probably stated in the verses in which she commemorated the feat, and which she enclosed to him. Her writings were consumed in the conflagration at Mount Pleasant, but in a paper of the day [1] is found an extract from a letter of hers to her brother Samuel, he having removed with his family, consisting of his wife and one child who afterwards married General Van Rensselaer, to central New York.

[1] Evening Post.

"I am forever thinking of you and our other dear friends in that new country.[1] Had you and they been situated nearer together, and nearer to me, I should then care more for the world than I do. My two little girls and books are my chief comforters. I wish it was in my power to send you out as good a collection of the latter as we have here. You would not feel the loss of friendship and the want of company as much as you do. We must endeavor to make ourselves as independent of the world as possible, and let our own minds furnish us with that pleasure which too many are in search of abroad. . . . I know you will make the best use of your solitude. Mr. Freneau joins me in much love to you."[2]

The second great event of the year 1789 was the adoption of the Constitution, and its consequence, the inauguration of Washington as the first President of the United States. In one of the centennial publications in the year 1809, it was said that the President elect was met at Elizabethtown by a joint committee of Congress and escorted to New York, and that Philip Freneau, who afterward, as editor of the "National Gazette," made it hot for the Washington administration, accompanied the party across the bay, and in the excitement of the occasion probably huzzahed with the loudest. Another version is that he came up the bay from Charleston on the day of the procession, but he would not run up his colors in honor of the event. As the subject is an open one, we leave our readers to believe which they choose; we prefer the former. Upon the attendant ceremony it was Freneau's relative, the Right Reverend Samuel Provost, that conducted the religious services in old Saint Paul's Church.[3]

[1] Cayuga and Cazenovia Lakes.

[2] This brother died in Syracuse, New York, in 1862.

[3] It is said that when the question of holding services on the day of the inauguration was agitated and Bishop Provost was appealed to on the subject, he said that he had always been used to look up to the Government upon such occasions, and he thought it prudent not to do anything till

Although the oath of office was administered, and the Constitution went into operation the last day of April, it was not until the fall of the year that any important step was taken. After the Cabinet and judges of the Supreme Court were chosen, the next matter was to decide upon the location of the future capital of the nation. New York was not willing to cede the amount of territory required, therefore it was decided to remove to Philadelphia for the period of ten years.

A certain writer,[1] in praising Philadelphia, and after enumerating all the various ports at which she traded, her schools, and other advantages, adds: "In fact, there may be obtained the knowledge of the arts and sciences, and here may be had, on any day of the week, tarts, pies, cake, etc.; and no jealousy amongst men, and no old maids." It seems quite evident, after this panegyric, why Congress selected this favored city in which to hold its sessions. Undoubtedly the anticipation of regaling themselves in their recesses upon the tarts, pies, etc., had great weight with those upon whom the selection devolved; and does not the fact go to prove that in reality woman was the factor that transformed this charming city of "Brotherly Love" into the city of Brotherly Discord it eventually became, and of introducing some jealous men into it? for a writer has said, "Man is what he eats, and woman is the caterer." Tarts, pies, and cake were the modern apple, the fair caterer the modern Eve; and, tempting the modern Adam, "he did eat;" and the modern Eden became a modern Babel.

However it was, Congress in removing itself to other quarters greatly discomfited the residents of

they knew what Government would direct. Eben Hazard, hearing this, said: "If the good bishop never prays without an order from Government it is not probable that the kingdom of heaven will suffer much from his violence." (Bowen, in Century Magazine.)

[1] Gabriel Thomas.

New York City. No more public fêtes and court balls; no more state pageants and processions; no more president, senators, or legislature. Freneau, too, was disappointed, as he had made arrangements to edit a paper in New York, called "The Daily Advertiser," but it would seem from a letter written by him to Madison, dated July 25, 1791, that the latter had offered him some inducements to go to Philadelphia. Freneau writes from Middletown Point, New Jersey, saying that he is detained there by some pressing business, but that if he should meet Madison upon his return to New York, which would be in a few days, he would then give him a definite answer relative to printing his paper at the seat of government, instead of in New York as he had intended. Freneau eventually succeeded in exchanging the "Advertiser" for the "National Gazette" of Philadelphia, and the first number appeared under his direction in October of the year 1791.

The revenues of the country had been well drained for the expenses of the war, and the indebtedness of the States amounted to eighty million dollars, — an immense debt for an impoverished country. The princely fortune of Robert Morris had gone to pay his country's debts, and the fortunes of many others had gone in the same way. Affairs were bordering on bankruptcy, the colonial currency had depreciated to a few cents on the dollar, and the treasury existed only in name. Literary work, not being an absolute necessity, was below par; and, as we know, the loss of his fine ship, the "Aurora," had sadly crippled the resources of Freneau, who had now a family to support, and an estate and slaves to maintain. It may have been to add something to his small editorial revenue that he accepted the proposition to become foreign translator to the Department of State, with the paltry salary of two hundred and fifty dollars per annum. It may have been, as some thought, that he accepted the position through some political motive. Amongst the Jefferson papers one may find the proposal made Freneau in the handwriting of, and signed by, the Secretary of State; it runneth thus:—

PHILADELPHIA, Feb. 28, 1791.

SIR,—The clerkship for foreign languages in my office is vacant; the salary, indeed, is very low, being but two hundred and fifty dollars a year; but also it gives so little to do as not to interfere with any other calling one may chuse, which would not absent him from the seat of government. I was told a few days ago that it might, perhaps, be convenient to you to accept it,—if so, it is at your service. It requires no other qualification than a moderate knowledge of French. Should anything better turn up within my department that might suit you, I should be very happy to bestow it as well. Should you conclude to accept the position, you may consider it as engaged to you, only be so good as to drop me a line informing me of your resolution.

I am, with great esteem, sir,
Your very humble servt.
TH. JEFFERSON.

Freneau's appointment appears amongst the State papers, dated August 16, 1791, signed by Jefferson; below which, in Freneau's handwriting, appear these significative words: "I hereby resign the same appointment from October first, 1793." He had held the office two years, one month, and fifteen days.

In a Philadelphia paper of the times appeared the following paragraph: "Thomas Jefferson Esq., Secretary of State for the United States, has appointed Captain Philip Freneau, interpreter of the French language for the Department of State." It seems that Philadelphia no longer lacked "jealousy amongst men," for an outcry was raised immediately. "A combination between an editor of a journal and the Secretary of State!" And they did not let any time pass without letting Freneau feel the weight of their displeasure.

"The circumstance of your having come *from another state* to set up and conduct a *state paper;* the circumstance of the *editor* of that *new paper* being appointed a clerk in the Department of State; the *coincidence* in point of time of that appointment with the *commencement* of your paper, or to speak more correctly its precedency — the conformity between the complexion of your paper and the known politics of the head of the department who employed you — these circumstances, collectively, leave no doubt of your true situation; the connection arising from them is too strong to be weakened by any of those bold or even solemn declarations which are among the hackneyed tricks employed by the *purists* in politics of every country and age to cheat the people into a belief of their superior sanctity, integrity, and virtue. If you had been previously the conductor of a newspaper in this city — if your appointment had been any considerable time subsequent to the institution of your paper — there might have been some reason for subterfuge, but as matters stand, you have no possible escape."

We all know that at the time of the framing of the Constitution the political world was divided into two antagonistic parties: the one calling themselves Federalists, who believed in centralization, and the other, anti-Federalists or Republicans (the name of Democrat then being given only by way of reproach), who believed in decentralization.

The former party had adopted as their platform the principles of a close and lasting union between the States, and a compact form of government invested with authority by the State, and not by the individuals of which it was composed. The English Constitution being in their opinion the nearest to perfect ever planned, they deemed it the most desirable one upon which to form the Constitution of the United States. They desired that the President should be elected for life upon good behavior; and that the senators and the governors of the different States should be selected by the Senate. They wished the Senate and House of Representatives to make the laws, and the President to execute them, and that the latter should have the power to veto the Acts of the State Legislatures. They desired restricted suffrage, the encouragement of foreign commerce and domestic manufacture, the latter protected by tariff. They deemed it necessary to have a powerful standing army, and desired a diplomatic service like that of Europe, and that there should be great formality along with the etiquette of the foreign courts, which they thought necessary to insure respect for authority. This party comprised those who inclined to England through kinship, language, and hatred of France.

The anti-Federalists, or Republicans, desired to preserve the independence of the several States, and advocated unity in regard to foreign matters, but plurality in home affairs. They wished to retain the Plan of Confederation, altering it to suit the present state of affairs and present needs. They thought such a centralization of power as the Federalists desired would rob the individual States of their sovereignty, and clothe the President with too much power, leaving the people too unprotected. They advocated the extension of suffrage, and the encouragement of agriculture and internal trade, rather than foreign commerce. They preferred the employment of well drilled militia instead of standing armies, and advocated simplicity and economy in the government, and the doing away with all monarchial forms; also open sessions of Congress. They charged the Federals with the design of establishing a monarchy on the ruins of the republican form of government, and they even thought to see embodied in their plan certain principles which might sustain this charge. They inclined to France, as having come to our assistance in time of need, and hated England because of her injustice and unnatural conduct towards her colonies, and harsh treatment of her colonial subjects.

The Federalists were in the majority and were defended by Alexander Hamilton, who was of foreign birth, and, although free from State prejudices in a considerable degree, still evinced a repugnance to a republican form of government. His sympathies were pre-eminently with England.

Franklin had been the originator of the Plan of Confederation; it had been his ruling idea for a republican form of government since before the Revolution, and he desired its continuance in a modified form.

The strife between the two parties for the shaping of the Constitution ran high, and very probably there has been nothing equal to it in the history of America.

From this strife arose a third party; for many feared that such a vast amount of power centralized in one person might lead to despotism, yet they were desirous of having a closer bond of union between the States than would exist under the Plan of Confederation. Of this party Madison was the founder, and his plan combined the views of the other parties, and is the basis of our present Constitution.

All three parties felt the truth expressed in these words of James Wilson, although their several applications of them differed somewhat: —

"We are laying the foundation of a building in which millions are interested, and which is to last for ages. In laying one stone amiss we may injure the superstructure, and what will be the consequences if the corner-stone should be loosely placed?"

Jefferson was in France at the time, and had no

part in the framing of the Constitution; but he was known to have opposed it in its origin, and his adversaries did not hesitate to make known the fact at the time of his supposed coalition with the editor of the "National Gazette."

> "It is a fact," they wrote, "which the debates in the Virginia Convention will testify, that Mr. Jefferson was, in the origin, opposed to the present Constitution of the United States. It is a fact known to every man who approaches that officer (for he takes no pains to conceal it and will not thank you to deny it), that he arraigns the principal measures of the government and it may be added with *indecent* if not *indiscreet* warmth."

And he was brought to task pretty severely for conferring an office in his department upon an editor of a paper. It was said to be "an experiment somewhat new in the history of political manœuvre in the country;" and again, that "a connection between the *editor of a paper* and a head of a department of the government is *indelicate* and *unfit*, and consequently of a nature to justify suspicion."

In his reply to a letter from Washington, in which the latter seems to have reproached him for this connection, Jefferson makes some very sarcastic allusions to the Secretary of the Treasury, whom he seems to hold accountable for the reproach, and then goes on to say: —

> "When we removed to Philadelphia, Mr. Pintard, the translating clerk, did not choose to remove with us; his office then became vacant. I was applied to there, for Freneau, and had no hesitation to promise the clerkship for him. I cannot recollect whether it was at the time or afterwards, that I was told he had a thought of setting up a newspaper there; but whether then or afterwards, I considered it a circumstance of some value, as it might enable me to do what I had long

wished to have done; that is, to have the material parts of the 'Leyden Gazette' brought under your eye and that of the public, in order to possess yourself and them of a juster view of the affairs of Europe than could be obtained from any other public source. This I had ineffectually attempted through the press of Mr. Fenno while in New York, selecting and translating passages myself at first, then having it done by Mr. Pintard, the translating clerk. But they found their way too slowly into Freneau's papers.

"Mr. Bache essayed it for me in Philadelphia; but his, being a daily paper, did not circulate sufficiently in the other States. He even tried, at my request, the plan of a weekly paper of recapitulation, from his daily paper, in hopes that that might go into the other States; but in this too we failed. Mr. Freneau as translator, and the editor of a periodical paper likely to circulate through the States (uniting in one person the parts of Pintard and Fenno), served my hopes that the thing could at length be effected.

"On the establishment of his paper, therefore, I furnished him with the 'Leyden Gazettes,' with an expression of my own wish that he would always translate and publish the material intelligence they contained; and I have continued to furnish them from time to time, as regularly as I received them. But as to any other direction or indication of my wish, — how his press should be conducted, what sort of intelligence he should give, what essays encourage, — I can protest in the presence of Heaven, that I never did, by myself or through any other, directly or indirectly, say a syllable nor attempt any kind of influence. I can further protest in the same awful presence, that I never did, by myself or any other, directly or indirectly, write, dictate, or procure any one sentiment or sentence to be inserted *in his or any other gazette*, to which my name was not affixed, or that of my office.[1]

"I surely need not except here a thing so foreign to the present subject as a little paragraph about our Algerine captives, which I put once into Fenno's paper. Freneau's proposition to publish a paper having been about the time that the writings of 'Publicola,' and the discourses on 'Davila' had

[1] This letter was written in 1792, a year before Freneau retired from the editorship of the paper.

National Gazette.

By P. FRENEAU: (at No. 209, Market Street) *Published* WEDNESDAYS *and* SATURDAYS, [THREE DOLLARS *per annum*.]

NUMB. 72 of VOL II] SATURDAY, July 6, 1793. [Total NUMB. 176.]

PHILADELPHIA

JULY 1st 1793

I A PICHON, a French Citizen at Philadelphia, to M. COTELLE.

SIR,

AS it is more than probable that your letter* to Citizen GENET will remain unanswered, I conceive it to be the duty of such French citizens as are acquainted with our West India affairs, to point out to the public the sycophantic intimations it contains, and to warn American citizens to pay as little attention to calumniators from the West Indies as they have done to the slanderous reports of the emigrants from Europe.

I am sensible, sir, that a full and thorough investigation of facts should be subjoined, to support such a preliminary injunction, and this I have *every* means in my power to do. At the same time, I am altogether unwilling to call out of their peaceful tomb of oblivion, the bloody proceedings which for three years past have disgraced your country; and it is with the greatest reluctance that I take a painful review of those horrid scenes, some of which I have been an eye-witness to. Indeed, sir, I have been so unfortunate as to reside in your island, and in that very town from whence you came. Thanks to the obscurity in which I lived, I was allowed to look at the *epidermocratical* tyranny when it was at its zenith. Yes—I have witnessed the murderous and doleful consequences of a system nonsensical in the extreme. Documents of these transactions are now in my hands, and possibly the time may come when I shall let the world know that *our* white people of the West Indies have out done the Spaniards in absurd and ridiculous systems, and at least equalled them in baseness and ferocity.

You seem to affect a very sincere concern for the national laws, which, you pretend, have been trampled upon by the national civil commissioners.—Sir, your meaning must be, beyond all doubt, that they enforced the execution of those laws against which you have waged war these three years past. Nobody but YOU (your colour I mean) has been guilty of an infringement of those very laws you had sworn to support. Nobody but *you* opposed the sovereignty of the people, and the DECREES of their representatives.

If the name of FRENCHMAN had become burdensome to you, if after an examination of your principles and situation you had discovered that a political regeneration would never suit men of your cast; then a fair and open conduct was to be preferred: you ought to have declared to the world that you never meant to have a share in the glorious toils of France, and that the feast of FREEDOM was a species of entertainment illy adapted to your degenerate stomachs.

You ought not, however, to advocate our laws and oppose them afterwards. Whenever a colony becomes weary of its mother country, it is no more than just that they should shake off its yoke, and, if its independence is opposed, wage war against it. But you add insult to injury. You called for a separate constitution, and in the mean time set yourselves up for reformers of OUR OWN!

For three years past your conduct has been little else than a series of unprincipled pride, unsettled schemes, and unbounded ferocity . . . . You have entered the field in defence of the bloody, but childish prejudices of *your females*—you have waged war against the people of colour [mulattoes] with poignard, wheel and gallows, while bearing the Olive Branch of PEACE, they proffered you their prayers and intreaties!—Your manœuvres have been constantly in the dark, and the wound given under the veil of secrecy. CONVINCED, at length, of the absurdity of your claims, you were still too obstinate to part with them. No less than four different *colours* had been displayed in your towns: internal divisions have given you up, hands and feet tied, to the citizens of colour who, steady to the principles they set out upon, and, strongly encamped on inassailable mountains, have pursued a fixt and energetic line of conduct, from which neither success or calamity have prevailed on them to deviate.

This being the case, was it not high time for the representatives of the French nation to put an effectual stop to such fatal intestine dissentions, particularly when they were threatened by an external foe, whose invasion it was more than probable the whites had a mind to facilitate in order to crush those citizens of colour whom, by their own confession, they were always by themselves too weak to subdue. In such circumstances was it not the true interest of the nation to secure in the island that class of steady citizens who would defend it to death; and to favour it rather than a class of an other description, who, always divided among themselves, could never furnish one fourth part of their number, as men to be depended on. That part of the white people who were patriots were always floating between the interest of the country and that of their own pride. The first power that would have pledged itself to re-instate them in their unnatural rights would have gained them over to their side; while the citizens of colour would not have hesitated between a revolution which allotted them their true place, and a counter-revolution by means of which, supposing it to have been successful, they would have been sunk lower in political consequence than at any former period.

From what has been said it is not at all surprizing to see here certain COCKADED-GENTLEMEN from the French West Indies. It is true, they were patriots, but on condition of their pride being spared; and although they apparently submitted to the laws, still they had sworn in their hearts and before the great god of their pride, that when ever opportunity should offer they would take a signal and memorable retaliation. The national commissioners having therefore divided all opposers into two classes; the first including all those guilty of *Lese nation*; the second, such as had caught the *epidermocratical* mania. The former were embarked for France, for trial; the latter have been sent over to this continent to cool their raging blood by the respiration of the wholsome air of liberty and equality.

Colonists of the *French West Indies*, I accuse you before the whole world of having sullied the name of Frenchmen. I do accuse you of having opposed the execution of the mandate† for convoking the states general, so far as it regarded the people of colour. I accuse you of having trampled under foot the decree of the eighth of March, and the 4th article of the annexed instructions. You loudly opposed the law of the 15th of May, before it came into existence, and you proclaimed open war against it after it passed into a decree; and, thro' the influence of your agents at Paris, you opposed its being sent to the islands, till you had time to kindle the flames of dissention and frighten the national assembly from its first resolutions. I accuse you of having put arms into the hands of your slaves. When the aristocrats were planning a counter revolution, you were always unwilling to unite yourselves with the citizens of colour in order to oppose them, & the daily increasing torrent of insurrections. I accuse you of having cut off all hopes of union by practicing cruelties‡ contrary to the laws of war, and by threatening an independency which you were neither strong nor hardy enough to undertake. I accuse you of having signed treaties and *concordats*, sword in hand, and of having meditated murders and devastations at the moment you were giving the cordial embraces of reconciliation.—In short, so loaded are you with crimes, that there is scarcely any thing of which I might not justly accuse you.—Take this then as a warning, sir, and rest assured that there are men here sufficiently acquainted with your affairs to prevent any imposition on the people of the United States, on that score.

* See National Gazette, No 174

† It is certain that the committee of recognition of the constituent assembly had acknowledged the deputies from the people of colour, but by what measure they were afterwards rejected, time will shew.—See Mirabeau's letter to his constituents—and Verbal Proces of the constituent assembly.

‡ Mr Cotelle has probably not forgot that venerable old man whom they burnt alive in a slow fire at Aux Cayes, for having made a gallant defence at the camp *Mercy*.

Extract of a letter from a gentleman in Philadelphia, to his Correspondent in New-York dated 20th of June, 1793.

"There seems to be a strong inclination in some of our executive officers of the United States to keep most of their proceedings secret from the public; and this suspicion is still gaining more force, from their late conduct in regard to the prize ship William, which was captured by the French privateer Citizen Genet, at more than 30 miles from the American coast; although some sailors aboard offered to swear that she was only at 2 or 3 miles distance.

"Be this as it may, it has not been brought in evidence into the late trial before the admiralty court for the Pennsylvania district—the court would only hear the arguments on the single question of its own jurisdiction; and by the decree of judge *Peters* it appears, as was expected, that the court has no jurisdiction or powers to interfere in the condemnation or restoration of prizes taken by the French, &c. So soon as this decree was known, the captors were about to take the ship into their own charge, when a very unexpected order issued from the Executive of the United States, addressed to Governor Mifflin, directing him to call out the militia and put a strong guard aboard the prize, in order to prevent the captors from taking possession of her. The light infantry were accordingly called out, and performed duty for two or three days without knowing for what purpose, except from the reports of the town, which were, "that it was to preserve the prize from being burnt or ran away with by the British sailors." And the infantry were so far imposed on by public report, as well as their own conjectures. But how great was their astonishment when the truth was at length discovered, viz. that they had been guarding the ship *from* the captors and *for* the British!—They then solemnly declared, at least I have heard many of them say so, that had they known the real cause of being called out, they would not have obeyed the governor's orders.

"The reason of the Executive of the United States imposing this duty on Governor Mifflin, for he only acted under that authority, is alledged to be this, viz. that as the admiralty court had declared its own incapacity to judge of the limits of its own [illegible] it was [illegible] necessary for the President to step forward and seize the prize, and detain it in custody of the United States until such time as it could be determined, whether she was captured within the bounds of the protection of the United States.

"This, however, is only surmise; for granting it to have been the real motive which urged the President to the step he took, still it would have been but satisfactory to the public to have had some explanation of the business, without making such a mysterious piece of work of it. The consequence has been, as I am informed, that governor Mifflin felt himself in rather an aukward situation; and as he had been ordered on the duty of guarding the French prize, he wished to be discharged by the same authority. But the President left town on a visit to Mount Vernon, in the midst of this dispute, and the French Consul entered a warm protest against the whole proceedings, declaring, "that no power on earth has a right to interfere between the French republic and its enemies—that this principle was acknowledged in the late decision of the admiralty court, and the present arrest and detention by a guard, of the prize, was an outrage against the authority of the official functions of the minister, &c. of the republic." A copy of the protest was sent by Mr Dupont, the French Consul, to governor Mifflin; but before it had reached him, he had dispatched a letter to Mr Dupont, informing him that the ship William, now in custody of a party of the militia of Philadelphia, would be delivered to him whenever he should please to apply, in consequence of an arrangement between the Secretary of State and the minister of France, by which it was agreed, (as the secretary at war informed governor Mifflin,) that the ship William shall be placed in his, the Consul's, possession, until it is determined, whether she was taken within the limits of the protection of the United States.

"The guard was consequently dismissed, and the Consul took possession of the William, and soon after delivered her to the owner who purchased her at public auction some time ago.

"From this it must be conjectured, that the secretaries of state, war, &c must have discharged governor Mifflin from the duty, in the absence of the President, and it also appears, that they only consented to restore the prize conditionally, which by some is thought to be taking into their hands a power of construing the law, or rather of no law, for there is no law yet existing which defines "the limits of the protection of the United States," whatever Congress may hereafter do to enact one; and thus we are led to think that both the arrest of the vessel, and the restoring her were unauthorised proceedings. I would be sorry to think they should be stiled pusillanimous.

"Indeed if NEUTRALITY be the GREAT and WISE aim of our executive, it seems strange that any offence should have been committed against the French of such consequence as to force the Consul to enter a protest against it; and that this is the case, as well as that I have stated the whole business tolerably accurate—you may rely on my information. I have read the protest and also the governor's letter.

"Other conjectures have taken place, that Mr. Genet has had a negociation with our secretaries, and that he has consented to take back the prize, on the conditions, rather too tamely. It is also said that he is too accommodating for sake of the peace of the United States.

"That there is strong reason to believe this last assertion, I agree, but that he will act with the utmost firmness and dignity I have not a doubt, for I firmly believe him to be one of the best men upon earth, independent of his great talents and true republicanism.

"It would be but poor and pitiful conduct in our executive to attempt treating such a man, and such a cause as that of liberty itself, with the coolness, that has been suspected, I hope without foundation; besides it would be acting diametrically in opposition to the GENERAL SENTIMENT of AMERICA, and we are not yet, God be praised, under the command of such an arbitrary government, as to have the laws dictated to us, and the execution of them managed contrary to our solemn and declared principles. Surely, if there be some among us who are SOLOMONS for their wisdom in preserving peace with Britain and Spain, &c. they ought not to be less so in their conduct towards France; and yet some things of late wear a strong appearance of fear or favoritism to one or other of the hostile powers. May prudence, justice and honor, guide us through the storm.

In the pleadings before judge Peters on this subject, Mr Lewis, counsel for the British, amongst other arguments to prove that the court of admiralty ought to have jurisdiction in the case observed, that were we under an arbitrary government the chief magistrate might lay hands on the prize and detain it until a proper decision could be had. But as the executive of the United States had no such power therefore there was the greatest reason for the courts interference. This was the substance of what Mr Lewis declared. Yet we find that the executive did afterwards exercise this power, which Mr Lewis denied them a right to do. Nay, they seized the prize twice, first by their marshal, and secondly, by a guard of militia. The result is already known, viz the court discharged the first arrest, and the guard was discharged, *the Lord knows how*—by negociation, we are told! and in the absence of the President of the United States.—It is rather humiliating, however, to think that our government should shew its own weakness in grasping twice at a power which it was not able to maintain."

Extract from a pamphlet just published entitled "LETTERS *to the* YEOMANRY *of the* UNITED STATES.

On whatever side we turn our eyes we see nothing in nature that is not governed by laws proper to its existence, & which is not organized in a manner to obey such laws to acquire every succour which is agreeable to the nature of its being, or necessary to the mode of its existence. Man is not neglected by his Creator—the gifts which to him are particular, and which give him the empire of the world shew that happiness and prosperity are designed for him, and an order proper to ensure him the enjoyment of them. That heaven-born French philanthropy which regards all mankind as brethren, is so far superior to the understandings of modern statesmen and financiers, as to be the object rather of derision than of imitation but which every government must adopt in order to become prosperous and happy.

The period of man's active life is too short, and his powers too weak to afford him more than a comfortable supply of necessaries of life, therefore the superfluities of some men, whether acquired by actual plunder or by unjust laws, must infringe on the rights of others: this being actually

FACSIMILE OF NATIONAL GAZETTE

a good deal excited the public attention, I took for granted from Freneau's character, which had been marked as that of a good Whig, that he would give free place to pieces written against the aristocratical and monarchical principles these papers had inculcated.

"This having been in my mind, it is likely enough I may have expressed it in conversation with others, though I do not recollect that I did; to Freneau I think I could not, because I had still seen him but once, and that was at a public table at breakfast at Mrs. Ellsworth's, as I passed through New York the last year; and I can safely declare that my expectations looked only to the chastisement of the aristocratical and monarchical writers, and not to any criticisms on the proceedings of the government. Colonel Hamilton can see no motive for any appointment but that of making a convenient partisan; but you, Sir, who have received from me recommendations of a Rittenhouse, Barlow, Paine, will believe that talent and science are sufficient motives with me in appointments to which they are fitted, and that Freneau, as a man of genius, might find a preference in my eye to be a translating clerk, and make good title, moreover, to the little aids I could give him as the editor of a gazette, by procuring subscriptions to his paper as I did,—some before it appeared,—and as I have with pleasure done for the labors of men of genius. As to the merits or demerits of his paper, they certainly concern me not. He and Fenno are rivals for the public favor. The latter courts them by flattery, the former by censure, and I believe it will be admitted that the latter has been as servile as the former severe. But is not the dignity and even decency of government committed when one of its principal ministers enlists himself as an anonymous writer, or paragraphist, for either the one or the other of them? No government ought to be without censors; and where the press is free, no one ever will. If virtuous it need not fear the fair operation of attack and defence; nature has given to man no other means of sifting out the truth, either in religion, law, or politics. I think it as honorable to the government neither to know nor notice its sycophants or censors as it would be undignified and criminal to pamper the former and persecute the latter."

It was a time of fierce political excitement; the new Constitution not being in fair working order, was consequently exposed in its weakest point, that of its infancy, to the attack of its adversaries. The "National Gazette" is said to have been, under Freneau, a powerful political paper; and for Jefferson to have such a powerful machine with which to fling his weapons at the heads of the government did not appear a very agreeable prospect to the opposite party. In speaking of the keenness and readiness of these weapons, Mr. Benjamin says, "What Tyrtæus was to the Spartans, was Freneau to the Republicans or anti-Federalists." Certainly he did a work, and a great one in his own way, for often what can be accomplished by no other means may be by ridicule, wit, and irony; and these Freneau could always bring to his aid. The first, a German critic has compared to a blow of the fist, the second to the irritating prick of a needle, and the third to the prick of a thorn.

In 1791 the Secretary of the Treasury proposed a "Bank of the United States," but this plan Jefferson violently opposed, deeming it unconstitutional and of a dangerous character, considering the feeling then existing in the Southern States; but Hamilton carried his point, and the bank was chartered in the same year, with ten million dollars as capital. The anti-Federalists were much opposed to this bank, and Freneau, who was always able, when pressed, to bring his muse to his aid, composed some doggerel for the occasion; it probably served to let off a little of his surplus steam:—

"George, on thy virtues often have I dwelt,
And still the theme is grateful to mine ear.
Thy gold let chemists ten times over smelt,
From dross and base alloy they 'll find it clear.

Yet thou 'rt a man, although perhaps the first,
But man at best is but a being frail;
And since with error human nature 's curst,
I marvel not that thou shouldst sometimes fail.
That thou hast *long* and *nobly* served the state,
The nation *owns* and *freely* gives thee thanks;
But Sir! whatever speculators prate —
She gave thee not the power to 'stablish banks."

Nevertheless, the "Bank of the United States" continued until President Jackson's time; but he, having always been its implacable enemy, vetoed the renewal of the charter in 1831; and at its expiration in 1836 it died the death, involving many interested in it. This act of Jackson's was considered a stroke of wisdom, but Freneau did not live to see it accomplished; he died the year before the renewal of the charter was vetoed.

One of the criticisms to which the newly framed Constitution was subjected was that of developing as much of a monarchical form of government, as well as its etiquette, as was possible. It was well known that the Secretary of the Treasury was in favor of curtailing State sovereignty and investing the federal authority with as great an amount of prestige as was consistent with a republican form of government; and that the Vice-President, according to his own words, considered the "love of superiority and desire of distinction, admiration, and applause the great springs of human activity, at least in all that related to politics, and that no government could be secure or permanent which did not provide for the reasonable gratification as well as for the due restraint of this principal passion; and that therefore a certain mixture of aristocracy and monarchy was necessary to that balance of interests and sentiments without which free governments could not exist." It was also well known that the chief magistrate inclined to English etiquette, as well as towards government ceremonial. His intercourse with Congress was modelled upon that of the English kings, being in person, — a committee having first perfected all the attendant ceremonies.

Washington has given us a description of the ceremonial. He drove there, he writes, —

"in a coach drawn by six horses preceded by Colonel Humphrey and Major Johnson, in uniform, on my two white horses, and followed by Messrs. Lear and Nelson in my chariot, Mr. Lewis on horseback following them. In their rear was the Chief Justice of the United States and the secretaries of the Treasury and War Department (Hamilton and Knox) in their respective carriages, and in the order they are named. At the outer door I was met by the doorkeepers of the Senate and House and was conducted to the door of the Senate chamber, and passing from thence to the chair, through the Senate on the right and the House on the left, I took my seat.

"The gentlemen who attended me followed and took their stand behind the senators, the whole rising as I entered. After being seated, at which time the members of both Houses also sat, I rose, as they also did, and made my speech, delivering one copy to the President of the Senate and another to the speaker of the House of Representatives, after which and being a few minutes seated, I retired, bowing on each side to the assembly (who stood) as I passed, and, descending to the lower hall, attended as before, I returned with them to my house."

Mr. Peter Gerard Stuyvesant, at a banquet in 1839, said that Washington seldom walked in the street; his public recreation was in riding. When accompanied by Mrs. Washington, he rode in a carriage drawn by six Virginia bays with two outriders, who wore rich livery, cocked hats with cockades, and powder. When he rode on horseback he was accompanied by one or more of the gentlemen of his family, and attended by his outriders. The state carriage was of English make, — a very large cream-colored chariot of globular form, surrounded by cupids supporting festoons of flowers emblematically arranged around the panel-work; the whole being covered with best coach-glass.

This display, it has been remarked, had the effect of repressing the spirits of those who approached the chief magistrate, and many comments were passed upon it, as it seemed to savor too much of the royalty which had been banished from the land. Mr. Joseph Dennie, the editor, remarked that "although the genius of our government is republican, yet our conversation partakes much of the old leaven of monarchy." The presidential levees and Mrs. Washington's parties people thought "imitated too much the pomps and maxims of the Court." Freneau held that Americans embracing the new and republican form of government should leave behind all that savored of the maxims and prejudices of the old régime, and become identified with the manner of life they profess to embrace; he therefore attacked all this ceremonial most unsparingly, going, it is said, sometimes beyond all bounds, and consequently drawing upon himself the attacks of the opposite party.

In 1792 Washington was a second time unanimously elected president; and he had scarcely entered upon his second term of office in the spring of '93, when France declared war with Holland; and in April Washington announced his intention of maintaining strict neutrality; his proclamation to that effect provoked great discussion. The French government, desirous of gaining the Americans to espouse its cause, appointed Citizen Edmund Charles Genest, written in America Genet, as ambassador to the United States; for, although his father was attached to the Court of France, and his sister, Madame Campan, was in the service of Marie Antoinette, he had espoused the cause of the republican party. Young Genet was already skilled in the art of diplomacy, having studied it in the school of his father; and he began to put it in practice immediately upon his landing. He was received in Charleston, at which port he landed, with the greatest enthusiasm. His journey to the capital consumed an entire month, and his progress was a complete ovation.

Upon reaching Gray's Ferry at Philadelphia, a large portion of the population went out to meet and welcome Genet, and he was conducted in triumph to the city, where he was tendered an address congratulating France upon obtaining the freedom she had helped the United States to secure. In the evening a banquet was given in his honor, during the course of which Freneau was requested to translate the French ode written by Duponceau, the singing of which is said to have been one of the items of the festival.

The French republic was looking anxiously to this country for aid in its conflict with Europe, and especially upon the ocean, where it was conducting an unequal fight with Great Britain, whom it looked upon as a mutual enemy; it therefore confidently expected from the United States the assistance it had rendered her in her time of need. Freneau, along with others, was desirous of a coalition with France; therefore, declaring himself in favor of Genet, he threw himself heart and soul into the projected plan of uniting the two republics in a bond of brotherhood. To this plan, however, Washington lent a deaf ear, and finding him inflexible, Genet formed the audacious design of appealing from the President to the people.

Encouraged by his warm reception in the country, Genet strove to arouse sentiments of enthusiasm towards France, notwithstanding the refusal of the President; how he succeeded, the chaos into which he threw the country can best describe. A sort of insanity seemed to have taken possession of the most serious minds, and even in the Cabinet there were warm and violent discussions. Jefferson, fearing it impossible to preserve neutrality considering the ill-concealed bad will of England, thought it well to secure a union with France, that in case of a rupture we might look upon her as an ally.

Genet now audaciously empowered the French consuls throughout the States to hold courts of admiralty, and try and condemn prizes brought to port. He also fitted out privateers, and commissioned officers, and enlisted men in the interests of France. He organized Jacobin clubs, and introduced the red cockade, and liberty-caps, in which Dr. Francis says he himself delighted as an urchin to appear; and not alone did urchins like him delight in them, but sedate men like "Robert Goodloe Harper[1] appeared in the *bonnet rouge*, with grace and dignity." Liberty-poles crowned with red liberty-caps were also raised in the public places.

The popular dislike to England now seemed determined to assert itself. All that savored of that country was ostracized, and in proportion arose an affection for the struggling French republic. When the French officers made their appearance, or their marines were met in the streets, the boys would cry, "Vive la République!" At night the streets were musical with La Marseillaise and La Carmagnole. Dr. Francis says that he delighted to shout the latter at the top of his voice while wearing the *bonnet rouge*.

I have never heard that Freneau donned one of these caps, but the thing is not in the least improbable.

Many French people now came from their colonies, and gave a new impetus to American simplicity. Dress, manners, and customs were *à la française*. Jewelry, ornaments, perfumes, and bonbons were of French designs and make. French boarding-houses hung out their signs, and French restaurants were all the style; they introduced the use of soups, salads, ragouts, fricassées and olive oil; and none but French

[1] Son-in-law to Charles Carroll, of Carrollton.

bread could be tolerated. Even the English dances were no longer in vogue, and the stately minuet gave way to the lively cotillon, and public fêtes were organized. "In fact, it required," as John Fanning Watson remarked, "all the prudence of Washington to stem the torrent of passion that flowed in favor of France to the prejudice of our nationality."

Party spirit rose during this French period to such a degree that intimate friends became the bitterest enemies, and those who had formerly always exchanged friendly greetings now crossed the street to avoid a meeting.

In the midst of all this confusion, and in the heated month of August, that dreadful scourge the yellow fever broke out, and its malignancy spread terror in all directions. The consternation which seized the already highly excited population is said to be beyond powers of description. Many fled from the city, and those who remained shut themselves up in their houses; and when obliged to go into the streets they walked in the middle of them to avoid, as much as possible, the infected air of the houses; a cold nod of recognition was all that friends vouchsafed to each other. Pedestrians carried in their hands tarred ropes or kept them in their pockets; some wore bags of camphor on their persons; others chewed garlic, or held handkerchiefs steeped in vinegar to their faces. In the houses either gunpowder, tobacco, nitre, or vinegar was kept burning, and men, women, and children puffed at cigars continually. The outdoor air was rendered lurid and heavy by the burning of tar and tar-barrels in every street.

Dead bodies were constantly met with as they were borne to some open grave, into which they were dumped as quickly as possible, the graves or holes being left open for the next body. The bodies of most respectable persons were taken on the shafts of a one-horse chaise, driven by a negro, to be dumped like the rest. Those fortunate enough to be taken in hearses were unattended, and at their sight every one fled in consternation. Masters sent their servants away on the first suspicion of the dreaded disease, and servants abandoned their masters; many persons died from lack of care, and frequently dead bodies were found in the streets. This dreadful state of affairs lasted from the latter part of August till some time in September.

Notwithstanding this terrible scourge, there was no mitigation of party animosity; and Greenleaf with his "Argus," and Freneau with his "National Gazette," only increased the general consternation.

Genet, by his imprudent measures, obliged Washington to request his recall; but he decided not to return to France, and instead become a naturalized citizen of the United States. He eventually married the daughter of Governor Clinton, the anti-Federalist Governor of New York State. This marriage was celebrated in the Walton Mansion, as we stated in a previous chapter. An article on Genet, which we are not able to place, it being a fragment written in pencil, but undoubtedly copied, runs: "I have spoken of Genet with severity; he labors under reproach by every historian who has recorded his deeds, and by none is he more chastised than by Judge Marshall; yet, withal, Genet possessed a kindly nature, was exuberant in speech, of lively parts, and surcharged with anecdotes. His intellectual culture was considerable; he was master of several living languages, a proficient in music, as well as a skilful performer. To remarks I made to him, touching his execution on the piano, he subjoined: 'I have given many hours daily for twelve years to this instrument, and I now reach some effective sounds.' He had a genius for mechanics, and after he had become an agriculturist in this country, wrote on machinery and on husbandry. He assured me (in 1812) the time would arrive when his official conduct as minister would be cleared of its dark shades. 'To other shoulders,' said he, 'will be transferred the odium I now bear.' In a conversation with him on the vicissitudes and events of the French Revolution, he said: 'Their leaders were novices; had they been versed in Albany politics but for three months, we would have escaped many trials, and our patriotism been crowned with better results.' It is to be regretted that the papers of Genet have not yet seen the light; they embrace letters from Voltaire and Rousseau, and years of correspondence with eminent American statesmen, down to the close of his eventful life. He died at Jamaica, Long Island, in 1834, aged seventy-one years."

The troubles that grew out of this unhappy season caused a rupture between Hamilton and Jefferson that never died out, and was the origin of the two political parties of Federalists and Republicans, which were headed by their respective founders.

Washington was greatly annoyed at the course the "National Gazette" had pursued throughout, and Hamilton attacked Jefferson for his official support of the troublesome editor, to which attack Jefferson replied that a man should not be ostracized for his political opinions, or for freedom of speech, and that his paper had saved the Constitution which was galloping fast into monarchy and had been stopped by no means so powerful as by that paper, which had checked the career of the monocrats.

Towards the close of this eventful year Jefferson resigned his position in the Cabinet, and Freneau retired from the editorship of the Gazette. His work had been of a pretty hot character, but it was directed to the end for which he had, from the first, toiled and struggled. Mr. Benjamin, in speaking of his efforts, has said: "Amid all the excitement and warfare of words which attended the adoption of the new Constitution, we observe one figure who, next to Washington, Jefferson, and Hamilton, appears to assume a prominence superior to that of all others engaged in the political contest, — not so much by the weight of his intellect, as by his versatility and vivacity, and the readiness and keenness of the weapons he brought to the warfare; and in all the history of American letters or of the United States press, there is no figure more interesting or remarkable, no career more versatile and varied than that of Philip Freneau; his mind was highly original and independent, and his paper spoke its mind without fear or favor, and even criticised the father of his country, whom many suspected of monarchical tendencies. Jefferson declared that the paper had saved the Constitution. In the 'Gazette' the administration was arraigned in bitterest terms. The paper was an immense political one under him. Some thought it all for good, others all for evil."

It does not seem that there was any personal feeling against Freneau; even his adversaries said: "The charges which have been brought against the editor of the 'National Gazette,' as he himself states them to be, are no otherwise personal charges than as they designate the person against whom they are made. In their application to Mr. Freneau, they affect him solely in his capacity of editor of a public paper which may justly be condemned in a public capacity and in relation to matters of public or national concern."

In the American Encyclopædia it is stated that in later life Freneau had admitted that Jefferson was the author of some violent articles against the government under Washington. It has also been stated that Freneau had made an affidavit to the same effect as Jefferson's letter to Washington in which he calls upon Heaven to witness that he had never written, suggested, nor dictated any articles against the government that had not borne his signature. That letter was dated 1792, and an article attacking Freneau's affidavit was also dated the same year. Freneau's affidavit and Jefferson's strong denial may have covered the time up to which they were made, yet after that event Jefferson may have written articles for the paper, as it continued under Freneau until the end of October, 1793. It is not at all probable that Freneau would perjure himself even to save a friend dearer than Jefferson. Through all Freneau's writings there seems to be the greatest respect and veneration for the name of the Almighty; and his hatred of untruth or insincerity in any form is well known; it breathes forth in almost every line of his poetry, and often to his own prejudice. He could hardly have expressed his open disgust of Rivington's duplicity, were he guilty of false swearing.

It is pleasing to know that although Freneau bitterly arraigned the government, and Washington's policy, there was no personal feeling between himself and Washington. Freneau always admired and praised the latter's character, and he has dedicated several poems to him; he has mentioned him in highest terms in others.[1] Even during the fierce times we have related there appears one headed, —

On Washington, a Truly Good Man.

"Justum et tenacem propositi virum."

Freneau's daughter Agnes, Mrs. Edward Leadbeater, over a decade of years deceased, remembered having seen Washington at her father's house, and has several

[1] Some satirical verses against Washington, signed, "Jonathan Pindar," have been credited to Freneau, although it was proved that they were written by George Tucker, editor of "Blackstone's Commentaries," first Am. edition. These verses unfortunately appeared in the "Gazette." Tucker is well known as an author.

times, when a child, sat upon his lap. She related an amusing story of an old slave in her father's family, named Aunt Stine, who boasted of having been addressed by Washington upon opening the door for him, when calling upon her master. Mrs. Leadbeater's oldest child having been born in Philadelphia, she was returning with it to Mount Pleasant, Aunt Stine accompanying her to carry the infant. They had taken their seats in the public coach, when the postilion called out that there was "a nigger inside," which was probably contrary to custom. Mrs. Leadbeater turned to her stage companions, strangers to her, and said that if her maid would not be allowed to ride inside she herself would be obliged to leave the coach, as she was not strong enough to carry the infant. Her companions at once expressed their perfect willingness to enjoy Aunt Stine's company, and the latter, triumphant in her victory, turned to the postilion, and said: "Guess she 'd rode in better carriages than that old coach; guess she had ridden in General Washington's carriage too." In telling the story her mistress added, she supposed Aunt Stine had climbed into the General's carriage upon one of his calls upon her father. The same lady always resented it when any one spoke of her father as being an enemy of Washington. She said, on the contrary, he admired and respected him, and always spoke of him in the highest terms. It was only towards his policy that he was inimical.

The same year as the withdrawal of Jefferson and Freneau from political life, saw another excitement before its close. George III. had given instructions to British privateers to seize all neutral vessels found trading in the French West Indies, but gave no notification of the fact to the United States, and American commerce was swept from the seas, to the great loss of the Government, as well as private individuals. Chief-Justice Jay was sent as envoy to demand redress of the British Government, and made a treaty with Lord Granville the following year, which was ratified by the United States; but it gave great umbrage to many Americans, as they thought too much had been conceded to the demands of Great Britain.

Washington having refused a third nomination, Adams and Jefferson were nominated by the two opposite parties; Adams, having the greater number of votes, took the presidential oath, and Jefferson, as was then customary, became Vice-President. This election was the outcome of the question whether the United States should enter into intimate relations with France. The President refused the offers of alliance, but the Directory demanded it and the American minister, Charles Cotesworth Pinckney, was ordered to leave the country. John Marshall and Elbridge Gerry were directed to join Mr. Pinckney abroad, and along with him endeavor to adjust matters peaceably; but the Directory refused to receive the ambassadors save upon the payment of a quarter of a million dollars into the treasury of France. To this demand Mr. Pinckney replied that the United States had millions for defence but not a cent for tribute; consequently they were all ordered to leave the country.

The adoption of the Alien and Sedition Acts, the first authorizing the President to send foreigners out of the country, threatened to lead to a great abuse of such unlimited power in the hands of one man; and the second, which punished with imprisonment and fine the freedom of speech of the press, savored of despotism, and caused the administration to become very unpopular; so that in the following election party spirit ran very high. Adams and Pinckney were nominated by the Federals, and Jefferson and Aaron Burr, Freneau's old classmate, by the Republicans.

The election being thrown on the House of Representatives, the choice fell upon Jefferson. Upon assuming his position the President sent for Freneau to come to the capital on "important business," and like the philosopher of old the latter sent the verbal reply: "Tell Thomas Jefferson that he knows where Philip Freneau lives, and if he has important business with him, let him come to Philip Freneau's house and transact it." Jefferson then tendered him an office, but Freneau declined. He had no ambition for offices, his work was done; he asked for no recompense, and he cared not for thanks; he had done what he thought was his duty to his country, and all he asked of it was to allow him to live and die in peace.

In studying the character of Thomas Jefferson, it would seem to be composed of two elements continually opposed to each other,—and rather unpleasant ones to be united in the same person. By birth and education he was certainly fitted to enjoy the first society in America; endowed with tastes excessively refined for those days, and with the instincts of a European nobleman, he nevertheless discarded every advantage his birthright gave, for the sake of his conviction that no man was better than his neighbor; and he mingled with common people as their equal. At an early age the head of a large family, the ruling mind of all he came in contact with, ceded the highest place in school, college, home, and society, he was, notwithstanding, an ardent lover of solitude. The cherished member of a large circle of friends, welcomed from his youth at the tables of the great, considered an ornament to the exceptionally brilliant society of Williamsburg (Virginia), cultivated and shrinking from all that savored of roughness, he nevertheless shocked the sensibility of others by his ultra simplicity. Never allowing himself to deal with the imagination, entering into the minutest detail of domestic life, calculating to a brick the amount needed for a building, yet a poetic and artistic temperament dominated his life. Popular with companions, courteous, cheerful, and of a sanguine temperament, his society said to have been delightful to all classes, yet, in spite of himself, making many enemies. Hating visitors and letter-writing, he had an almost feminine yearning for sympathy. Strong in physical vitality, yet of a feminine mould of character. Sensitive and peculiarly vulnerable, yet sharp and caustic in disposition. Limiting the individual powers of others, and believing sincerely in the opinion of the multitude, yet given to stretch his own powers whenever vested with authority. Without reverence, and even lacking in respect for authority, he resented it extremely when others resisted him. Never at ease in the atmosphere that surrounded him in his political life, and tortured by its manners, he was constantly immured in it. As a leader of democracy he appeared singularly out of place, resembling in many things the Duc de Liancourt, and building for himself a château at Monticello to be above the contact with men; yet his fears of a monarchy and aristocracy reached almost to fanaticism; with popular manners he never showed himself in a crowd. In the midst of the world he led a life entirely his own.

Why such a man should have entered the arena of political life was as much of a puzzle as was his entire character. He is said to have been no orator, and owed nothing to personal magnetism. According to the received standard of greatness he certainly ranked among the great men. He is said to have had a penetrating mind, looking deeply into events, and a clear judgment; he was well read in books, but better in mankind; master over his passions, a philosopher, experienced in diplomacy, a master in intrigue. He is said to have been double and vindictive, and insincerity is said to have been his predominant trait. It may have been these latter characteristics that caused Freneau, while upholding him politically, to avoid him when the political strife was over.

Chapter Tenth

TOWARDS the close of this stormy year, Jefferson and Freneau both retired from political life; the one returning to his home at Monticello, Virginia, the other to the home of his childhood, Mount Pleasant, New Jersey, — leaving a seat in the Cabinet and the editorship of the "Gazette" vacant. The paper was discontinued, as Freneau, it seems, owned the press and type; and he had them removed to Mount Pleasant, where he had a small building erected about two hundred yards from the house; there he amused himself by putting in print the various inspirations that visited him. It is said that when any incident of moment occurred, he would retire to the shelter of a favorite old tree, and indite his lyric; and would then repair to his press, set up the types, and issue his production.

He now became a contributor to the "Freeman's Journal," published in Philadelphia; and in 1793 published a translation of the travels of M. l'Abbé Robin, chaplain to Count Rochambeau, giving an account of the progress of the French army from Newport to Yorktown. In 1795 he published a new and complete edition of his poems, in an octavo volume of four hundred and fifty-six pages, of which we give the titlepage. The fifteen stars have their significance, as we may see from his translation of the Latin verses dedicated to the then existing fifteen States.

This year an almanac was ushered into existence, a copy of which, yellowed with use and age, is now in the possession of Mr. Weymer Jay Mills. It measures seven inches by four, and contains forty-two pages. On the reverse of the titlepage are the zodiacal signs;

POEMS

WRITTEN BETWEEN THE YEARS 1768 & 1794

BY

PHILIP FRENEAU

OF

NEW JERSEY

A NEW EDITION REVISED AND CORRECTED BY THE AUTHOR, INCLUDING a considerable number of Pieces never before PUBLISHED.

*

* *

* * *

* * * *

* * * * *

Audax inde cohors stellis e pluribus unum
Ardua pyramidos tollit ad astra caput.

MONMOUTH
[N. J.]

Printed
At the Press of the AUTHOR, at MOUNT-PLEASANT, near MIDDLETOWN-POINT, DCCXCV: and of American Independence
XIX.

then follows a page devoted to eclipses, movable feasts, and the cardinal points; after which is a tide-table with an execrable bit of — poetry; it certainly may not be called rhyme: —

THE NAMES, AND ORDER OF THE TWELVE SIGNS.

The Ram, the Bull, the heavenly Twins,
And near the Crab the Lion Shines,
The Virgin and the Scales;
The Scorpion, Archer and Sea-Goat,
The man that holds the Water-Pot,
And Fish with glittering tails.

An article on the Planetary system follows, with an account of Herculaneum and Pompeii. A description of the Prussian armies, a history of the Ugly Club in Charleston, S. C., "A Philosophical Speculation," a dissertation on Barbers' Poles, a receipt for the destruction of weevils in wheat, an article on the advantages of using oxen on farms instead of horses, a method of preserving peach-trees from a destructive species of worm, a Swedish method of breeding turkeys, an article on northeast storms, one on Indian corn, a scale of the ages of animal creation, an account of the Bastille of France, a remarkable imposition, and several anecdotes respectively of the King of Prussia, George Whitfield, and Dogs follow. One page is devoted to the apochryphal chapter of the Book of Genesis by Franklin, another to the calendar of the French republic. Some lines by a young prisoner before his execution, and a remarkable method of finding the body of a drowned person fill its pages.

THE

MONMOUTH

ALMANAC,

FOR THE

YEAR M,DCC,XCV:

Being the third after LEAP YEAR; and the XIXth *of* AMERICAN INDEPENDENCE

(*'Till the* FOURTH *of July*)

CALCULATED *for the* MERIDIAN *of* NEW JERSEY (Longitude 35 Minutes East from PHILADELPHIA,) AND LATITUDE of 40 DEGREES, 20 MINUTES NORTH

NUMBER I.

* * * * * * * * * * * * * * * * *

MIDDLETOWN-POINT.

Printed and sold by P. FRENEAU, near the above place and may be had of most of the Store-keepers in MONMOUTH and the adjacent Counties.

Original size of almanac.

Philip Freneau

THE PYRAMID OF THE FIFTEEN AMERICAN STATES.

*
* *
* * *
* * * *
* * * * *

Barbara Pyramidum fileat miracula Memphis ; [1]
Heu, male servili marmora structa manu!
Libera jam, ruptis, Atlantias ora, catenis,
Jactat opus Phari marmore nobilius :
Namque Columbiadæ, facti monumenta parantes,
Vulgarem spernunt sumere materiam ;
Magnanimi cœlum scandunt, perituraque saxa
Quod vincat, celsa de Jovis arce petunt.
Audax inde cohors stellis E Pluribus Unum
Ardua Pyramidos tollit ad astra caput.
Ergo, Tempus edax, quamvis durissima sævo
Saxa domas morsu, nil ibi juris habes.
Dumque polo solitis cognata nitoribus ardent,
Sidera fulgebit Pyramis illa suis!

(Translation)

No more let barbarous Memphis boast
Huge structures rear'd by servile hands —
A nation on the Atlantic coast
Fetter'd no more in foreign bands,
A nobler Pyramid displays,
Than Egypt's marble e'er could raise.

Columbia's sons, to extend the fame
Of their bold deeds to future years,
No marble from the quarry claim,
But soaring to the starry spheres,
Materials seek in Jove's blue sky
To endure when brass and marble die!

[1] The Latin verses were written by Mr. John Cary, formerly of Philadelphia.

Arriv'd among the shining host,
  Fearless, the proud invaders spoil
From countless gems, in æther lost,
  These stars, to crown their mighty toil:
To heaven a Pyramid they rear
And point the summit with a star.

Old wasteful Time! though still you gain
  Dominion o'er the brazen tower,
On this your teeth shall gnaw in vain,
  Finding its strength beyond their power:
While kindred stars in æther glow
This Pyramid will shine below!

In the Madison papers we find a letter from Freneau, dated Monmouth, New Jersey, November 2d, 1794, in which he requests the favor of having Mr. Francis Bailey appointed to the post of printer for the House of Representatives, — he having heard that in all probability such a person would be wanted. He assures Mr. Madison that Mr. Bailey "is an old, tried Republican, and has stood forth in the worst of times, both as a printer and soldier, a friend to the rights, liberties, and interests of the country. Such characters," he adds, "merit consideration;" and he concludes his letter with some probably experimental and very practical advice. "Permit me to tell you that, in my opinion, it would be preferable that the *whole* of the work were entrusted to his care; dividing the business, I never could persuade myself, answered any good purpose; and if one such person as Mr. Bailey were made responsible for the whole, considering his attention and abilities, and the *capital* printing apparatus he is furnished with, I am convinced the House would find their account in having the work done by him."

Among the very few letters to Freneau in possession of the family, we find Madison's reply to his request, which runs as follows: —

PHILAD^A, April 6, 1795.

DEAR SIR, — I delayed acknowledging your favor long ago rec^d, until I could inform you of the prospects of Mr. Bailey in whose favor it was written. I have now the pleasure to tell you that altho' his wishes are not to be immediately fulfilled, he is looking to obtain, under the auspices of Mr. Buckley and Mr. Randolph, a share of employment hereafter which may be very valuable to him. I congratulate you on the public intelligence just rec^d from Holland which gives joy to all true Republicans, and wish you all the private happiness which an exchange of your former troubled services for the shade & tranquillity of your present life can afford. Remember, however, that as you have not chosen any longer to labour in the field of politics, it will be expected by your friends that you cultivate with the more industry your inheritance on Parnassus. With my best respects to Mrs. Freneau, I remain, Dear Sir,

Your friend and your S.,

JS. MADISON, JR.

It seems the old leaven yet remained in Freneau, and the republishing of his patriotic verses caused it to effervesce in the form of a diminutive production, printed in his own little office at Mount Pleasant. It was called "The Jersey Chronicle," and its first copy appeared on the second of May, 1795. It comprised eight quarto pages, seven inches by eight, and was headed by a quotation from the editor's favorite poet, Horace: —

"Inter sylvas Academi quærere verum."

This journal was issued weekly, and was, as the editor assured his readers, "intended to review foreign and domestic politics of the times, and mark the general character of the age and country."

During the same month in which it first saw the light as a complete thing, Freneau combined gratitude, business, and courtesy in a letter to Mr. Madison. The former sentiment was awakened by the appointment of his friend, Mr. Francis Bailey, to the position he had solicited Mr. Madison to interest himself in procuring for him; the second was to announce the nativity of the seven by eight; and thirdly and *lastly*, he congratulates him on his marriage, which had taken place a good part of a year before. This letter is so characteristic of the man that we will insert it in full.

MONMOUTH, May, 20th, 1795.

MY RESPECTED FRIEND, — By some accident your kind letter of April 6th was a long time in finding its way hither, having not come to hand till the 17th. inst. I sincerely thank you for the interest you have taken in Mr. Bailey — He is a good Republican and a worthy honest man, which qualifications, I have thought, entitled him to some notice from the Government, in his line of business — I was heartily laughed at, however, a few weeks ago in N. York, by some Aristocrats, for having in my Letter to you or Mr. Buckley, I forget which, extolled his Military Services in the late war. I am sensible he never cut off the heads of Giants or drove hosts before him, as some have done; at the same time it ought to be remembered that he was an officer in the Pennsylvania Militia in the season that tried Men's Souls (as Paine says) and I believe never acted otherwise than became the character in which he acted —

I meet you at least half way in your congratulations on the public intelligence received from Holland. It is but another step toward the advancement and completion of that great and Philanthropic System which I have been anticipating for many years, and which you as well as myself, I hope, will live to see realized. When I first went to reside in Philad[a] in 1791, I wished to be one of those who would have the honour and happiness of announcing these great events to the public through the medium of a newspaper. A variety of circumstances however, needless to trouble you with, urged my departure from that city after completing a two years publication. — As I mean to pass the remainder of my days on a couple of hundred of acres of an old sandy patrimony, I have, by way of filling up the vacuities of time set on foot a small weekly newspaper calculated for the part of the country in which I am — Should you have any curiosity to see it I will forward it to you free of all expense except that of postage. I will not make high promises in regard to what it may contain. It will scarcely be expected that in a rude, barbarous part of the country I should calculate it for the polite taste of Philadelphia. — Should your fixed residence be in Philad[a] I can transmit the Papers to you once a week by the Public Post, who stops every Wednesday at my door. A Letter put into the Post Office at Philadelphia on Saturday morning, will be sure to reach me on Wednesday. — The public papers some time ago announced your marriage — I wish you all possible happiness with the lady whom you have chosen for your Companion through life — Mrs. Freneau joins me in the same, and desires me to present her best respects to your lady and yourself — and should you ever take an excursion to these parts of Jersey, we will endeavour to give Mrs. Madison and yourself — "if not a costly welcome, yet a kind — "

I am, Sir,
With Great Esteem
Your friend and humble Serv[t]

PHILIP FRENEAU.

Freneau was an original thinker; he combined the quickness and brilliancy of mind of the French with the firmness of belief in his own opinions for which his Huguenot ancestors were noted; and his natural frankness of disposition caused him to feel the necessity of asserting his opinion upon all subjects of importance, whether others cared for it or not. Moreover, as he considered his opinions correct, he was naturally desirous of having others adopt them also. Not being ambitious, and asking nothing from the hands of his country or its representatives, he was quite indifferent to the latter, and desired only to serve the former; therefore, he had nothing to fear from either. The "Chronicle" was a spirited little journal, but Freneau's thoughts were ahead of the times, and the fact of its being carried on by one person, and he at some distance from the political centres, prevented it from being a success. Freneau's business affairs were something like Horace Greeley's model farm, whereof it is said everything cost him double what he could get for it; therefore, wearied of providing the public with reading matter at his personal expense, Freneau allowed the paper to die a natural death. Before we bury it, however, we will quote one article contained in its issue of April 16, 1796. The person of whom it speaks, Captain Hodge, was a prisoner in the old sugar-house during the Revolutionary War. The article was copied from an English paper, and runs thus: —

"It is with great satisfaction that we have it in our power to announce to the public the safety of the crew and troops on board the 'Aurora'[1] transport, one of Admiral Christian's fleet, which has for some time been given up as totally lost. Her masts and rudder were carried away by a violent gust of wind about three weeks ago, and from that time she remained a helpless log on the water, kept afloat only by the manual exertions of the people at the pumps. Three vessels bore down to the wreck in this intermediate space, but did not — whether from choice or inability, we do not presume to say — offer her any assistance. On Tuesday last, being about ten leagues west of the Lizards, Captain Hodge of the ship 'Sedgely,' of Philadelphia, was so fortunate as to fall in with her, and without the least hesitation determined, at the hazard of his own life and that of his crew, to rescue these miserable people, one hundred and sixty in number, from that fate which so long had threatened them, and which from that time, they must have met in a few hours. It should be recorded to his honor that his humanity, aided by nautical skill, triumphed over the dangers that awaited his exertions in the boat; for he brought the whole of them safe to his own ship,

[1] This name probably revived in Freneau tender memories of his own beautiful ship, the "Aurora," which, indeed, it may have been.

except one man, who was literally drowned in the boat. The troops are Germans, and have behaved with a sensibility that evinces much gratitude to their deliverers. They have tendered Captain Hodge one thousand guineas, which he has refused, saying that he finds sufficient remuneration in his own breast for the trouble he has had. One of them, on being asked if Captain Hodge treated them well when he had them on board, exclaimed: 'Sir, this brave American does honor to his country; he gave us all he had; he is a king of men, and we are bound to kiss his feet as long as we live.' After the 'Aurora' had parted company with Admiral Christian, she had to encounter most dreadful weather. She soon proved so leaky that the pumps became useless, and it was with the utmost difficulty that she was kept above the water by all hands being employed in bailing. Such was the fatigue experienced by the soldiers and crew, that some are said to have died in consequence. They were all, when taken on board the American ship, reduced to a very feeble state. At the time this friendly ship came up, the 'Aurora' was scarcely afloat, and every further effort to prolong a painful existence had been given up by the people on board."

One may imagine the real pleasure with which Freneau commemorated this noble act in his journal; for no one was ever more willing to give praise when justly due than was he; nor has any one ever more generously brought to light, or before the eyes of others, any heroic or virtuous action. He did not wish this noble deed of his countryman to fall into oblivion, and for this reason we insert it here.

After the obsequies of the Chronicle,[1] Freneau paid a visit to his brother Peter in Charleston, in which city he had many friends and was greatly appreciated. Amongst his acquaintances there were, we learn from

[1] There is a copy of this paper in the N. Y. Hist. Soc.

an old note-book, several with whom he was intimate. They were General Rutledge and the Pinckneys. Charles Pinckney was governor of South Carolina at that time; and Thomas had just returned from Spain, in which country as U. S. minister he had negotiated the treaty of Ildefonso, by which the United States secured the free navigation of the Mississippi. Charles Cotesworth Pinckney had returned lately from an unsuccessful effort, along with Elbridge Gerry and John Marshall, to settle matters between the United States and France, to which country he had been appointed minister. The Directory were demanding an alliance with the United States, or, in lieu of its assistance, a quarter of a million in money, to be paid into their treasury, threatening war in the event of a refusal. It was in reply to this demand that Pinckney uttered these words that have passed into history: "War be it, then! Millions for defence, but not a cent for tribute."

Upon Freneau's return from Charleston in the latter part of December, he formed the project of a co-partnership with Thomas Greenleaf in his two papers, "The Argus," a daily publication, and the "New York Journal," a bi-weekly; but for some reason the project fell through, and he assumed instead the editorship of a miscellaneous paper called "The Time-Piece and Literary Companion." While projecting the co-partnership with Mr. Greenleaf, he wrote to Mr. Madison in regard to it; his letter is preserved amongst the Madison State papers, and reads as follows: —

New York, December 1st, 1796.

Dear Sir, — Having three or four months since formed a resolution to bid adieu for a few years to some old trees in Jersey, under the shade of which I edited, amongst ditching and grubbing, a small weekly paper entitled the Jersey Chronicle, I did not know how to employ that interval better than in striking out here, with some printer, if such could be found, already engaged in supporting the good old Republican cause. After experiencing one or two disappointments in accomplishing this object, I am now, through the kind aid of some friends here, nearly completing the project of a co-partnership with Thomas Greenleaf in his two papers, the *Argus*, a daily publication, and the *New York Journal*, twice a week; both on a pretty respectable footing, and noted for a steady attachment to Republican principles, though open to all decent speculations from any party if they choose to transmit them. In short I would wish to revive something in the spirit of the National Gazette, if time and circumstances allow, and with proper assistance hope to succeed thus, —

A Raven once an acorn took
  From Bashan's strongest, stoutest tree;
He hid it near a murmuring brook,
  And liv'd another oak to see.

As I consider the bargain the same as concluded, my next object is to make all the friends here that I decently can among men of eminence and ability. This I have in some small degree attempted and gained, but for want of certain insinuating qualities, natural enough I suppose to some men, I feel myself sadly at a loss to get acquainted with some characters here to whom I could wish to be known upon motives of public as well as private utility.

Among these is the Chancellor of this state, Robert R. Livingston, with whom, if I recollect right, you are on terms of intimacy. If I am not mistaken in this point, and you can with propriety accede to my request, you would confer a favor upon me by mentioning me to him in your next Letter, in such manner as you may think best, so that this new connexion may attract some share of his attention, and thereby the countenance of the Livingston family in general which would operate greatly through the State at least, in advancing our Subscription and printing Interest in general.

With sincere wishes for your long life, health, and happiness

I am sir, your obliged humble Servt.

PH. FRENEAU.

The "Time-Piece" made its first appearance March 13, 1797, and was issued tri-weekly. It was in form a quarto, and besides editing it, Freneau was associated in its printing and publication. During Freneau's editorship of this paper he had a number of lady contributors, and his office was usually thronged with visitors, many of whom were applicants for favors of one kind or another, as Freneau's kind heart and generosity were universally known. One of these applicants, an eccentric person calling herself Deborah Grennet, informed him that she had served during the Revolutionary War, dressed in male attire; and to corroborate her story, she showed him several wounds that she had received. Freneau drew up a petition for her, and advised her to present it to Congress then sitting in Philadelphia. She did so, and although Freneau had not signed his name, his writing was immediately recognized by several of the members who were his correspondents, and by their head, who was Jefferson, then vice-president. The petition received immediate attention, and Deborah went on her way rejoicing, having received her pension.

In speaking of this journal, an English publisher[1] of one of Freneau's books says: —

> "It appears at this time in America inseparable from the notion of a newspaper to have an opponent, and Freneau's great opponent in the 'Time-Piece' was William Cobbet who started up a few days in advance of Freneau's paper, the Journal called 'The Porcupine Gazette.' If Cobbet discharged any of his porcupine quills at Freneau, it is most probable they were promptly returned; for he was 'always as ready to return a blow with a pen as with a sword, the former being as sharp as the latter.'"

The "Time-Piece" is said to have given evidence of Freneau's ability, and his tact in administering to the

[1] John Russell Smith, Soho Sq., London.

tastes of the public was shown in the skill of the selections and the general elegance of the material. Duyckinck says of it: "As usual, his [Freneau's] part was well done, the Journal being well arranged, judiciously filled with a variety of matter, spirited and entertaining; in fact, what its title promised, — an agreeable companion to an intelligent reader. This at least was its character while in charge of Freneau."

The press at that time was in a primitive state, like all other institutions. Newspapers were few, and managed by ambitious political chiefs; the sheets were small and crowded with advertisements, — the reading matter, what there was of it, contributed by scholars and politicians; but nearly every writer was bound by a party, and many years were to elapse before the germs of what is now one of the chief glories of America acquired anything approximating a full freedom of thought and action.[1] But in that time of political agitation attendant upon Adams' term of office, people did not take much interest in literature, and Philip was ahead of the times in which he lived. The Alien and Sedition Acts were exciting the public, and the latter seriously affected Freneau's freedom of thought and expression, as it threatened fine and imprisonment for the freedom of speech and the press. To live under such a restraint, and moreover to edit a paper, was something like harnessing the American eagle; at least it seemed so to Philip; so, placing the paper in the hands of Matthew L. Davis, a promising young man, Freneau plumed his pinions for flight. This was his last perch in undertakings of this kind.

It would seem that Freneau visited his brother in Charleston, S. C., and that his brother Peter bought and freighted a brig named "Washington" in which Philip, as commander, made many voyages, several of which were to St. Thomas, W. I., and two to

[1] Mrs. Lamb's History of New York.

Madeira; and from a private memorandum in his own hand-writing, we find that he sailed from Teneriffe for Charleston in May of the year 1804. This visit to Teneriffe he has commemorated in one of his poems. Afterwards he sailed between Savannah and the West Indies, and finally to Calcutta, — after which this bold bird of the sea folded his wings on his native shore.

On our desk lie three old volumes once in the possession of the sailor poet; two of them are works on navigation, the one a good-sized book, the second volume of Robertson's "Theory and Practice of Navigation and Marine Fortifications," bearing the print of 1772. On its titlepage is written in large characters the name, "Philip Freneau son livre de navigation," and underneath, the words: "Il faut bien l'esperer, car sans cette consolation il n'y aurait qu'à mourir." Two lines of poetry have evidently been intentionally defaced; the first may with difficulty be deciphered, —

> "If God or Fate to man would give," —

the second is undecipherable. On the back of a chart is written, in his peculiarly beautiful and delicate chirography, in ink paled and yellowed by time, some "Remarks and Observations" which run thus: —

> "The cold is greater in the southern Hemisphere than in the Northern, because, though in the same Latitude of each hemisphere the Position of the Sphere be the same, the Distance of the Earth from the Sun in the Corresponding Seasons is not equal. Winter happens in our hemisphere when the Earth is at its least Distance from the Sun and this circumstance diminishes the cold. In the Southern Hemisphere it is the contrary, winter happens when the Earth is at its greatest distance from the Sun which circumstance augments the force of the cold: add to this, that in the Southern Hemisphere the winter is longer by Eight Days than in the northern."

Philip Freneau

The first volume of this work is missing. Another is " Atkinson's Epitome of the Art of Navigation," an old print of 1749; on the fly-leaf of this book is written, in the same hand-writing, the same name and a "Table of the number of miles contained in a Degree of Longitude In each Parallel of Latitude from the Equator to the Pole." We notice in the extract the custom in those days of beginning every emphatic word with a capital. On the back of two charts in this book is written a poem, if indeed it may be classed as such, which has never seen the light till now, when the poor hand that penned it has returned to the dust. The writing is fast becoming illegible, therefore my readers will bear with me for reproducing it here: —

THE STORM.[1]

Cease, rude Boreas, blustering railer,
List ye Landsmen all to me,
Messmates hear a Brother Sailor
Sing the dangers of the Sea.
From bounding Billows first in motion,
When the distant whirlwinds rise,
From the tempest troubled ocean,
Where the seas contend with skies.

Hark! the Boatswain hoarsely bawling,
By topsail sheets, and halyards stand,
Down topgallants, quick be hauling
Down your staysails, hand, boys, hand!
Now it freshens, set the braces,
Now the topsail sheets let go,
Luff, boys, luff, don't make wry faces
Up your topsails nimbly clew.

[1] Since sending the manuscript of this work to press it appears that the first four lines of this poem are given in Bartlett's "Familiar Quotations" as emanating from the pen of George A. Stevens, an English author who died in 1784. He published a volume of "Songs Comic and Satirical" in 1772, one of which was entitled "A Storm;" it may have been this one, and that Freneau merely copied it. The latter never presented it as his own.

Now all you on down beds sporting,
Fondly locked in Beauty's arms,
Fresh enjoyments wanton courting,
Safe from all but love's alarms,
Round us roars the tempest louder,
Think what fears our minds enthral.
Harder yet it blows, yet harder,
Now again the Bosen calls.

The topsail yards point to the wind, boys,
See all clear to reef each course,
Let the fore sheet go, don't mind, boys,
Tho' the weather should be worse.
Fore and aft the sprit sail yard get,
Reef the mizzen, see all clear,
Hands up — each preventer brace set,
Man the fore yard, — cheer, lads, cheer!

Now the dreadful thunders roaring,
Peal on peal contending clash,
On our heads fierce rain falls pouring,
In our eyes blue lightnings flash.
One wide water all around us,
All above us one black sky,
Different deaths at once surround us,
Hark! what means that dreadful cry?

The foremast 's gone, cries every tongue out,
O'er the Lee twelve feet 'bove deck;
A leak beneath the chest trees sprung out,
Call all hands to clear the wreck.
Quick, the Lanyard cut to pieces,
Come, my hearts, be stout and bold.
Plumb the well, the Leak increases;
Four feet water in the hold.

While o'er the ship wild waves are beating,
We for wives or children mourn,
Alas! from hence there 's no retreating,
Alas! from hence there 's no return.

Still the Leak is gaining on us,
Both chain pumps are choaked below,
Heaven have mercy here upon us,
For only that can save us now.

O'er the Lee beam is the Land, boys,
Let the Guns o'erboard be thrown.
To the pump come every hand, boys,
See, our mizzen mast is gone!
The Leak we've found, it cannot pour fast,
We've lightened her a foot or more,
Up and rig a jury foremast;
She rights, she rights, boys, we're off shore.

Now, once more on joys we're thinking
Since kind fortune saved our Lives;
Come the cann, boys, let's be drinking
To our sweethearts and our wives.
Fill it up, about ship wheel it,
Close to the lips a brimmer join,
Where's the tempest now, who feels it?
None — our danger's drown'd in wine.

Besides different ports mentioned, Freneau visited St. Croix, Guadeloupe, St. Eustatia, Curaçoa, Demerara, Cumana, and Porto Cabello. Upon his return from Calcutta in the year 1809, Freneau, at the age of fifty-seven years, settled down to the management, or mismanagement, of his estate, and the care of his little family, consisting of wife, four girls, and his slaves. Although he understood nothing whatever of farming, he took pleasure in seeing the work progress; and he delighted in feeding the different animals, being a great lover of nature in all its forms. His love for dumb animals and tenderness of heart were such that he always managed to have important business to take him from home during slaughtering season. Mrs. Freneau gave orders to the blacks to have the poultry for the table killed in some place where he would not happen to see them in his walks, or hear their cries during the work of decapitation. Freneau considered his excessive sensibility a weakness, and tried to conceal it, but he could never steel himself to witness any kind of suffering. One day his little granddaughter [1] was busily occupied in endeavoring to capture a fly that was buzzing on the window-pane, but her grandfather speedily put an end to her sport, telling her that there was room enough in the world for everything that God had made. He was a kind and liberal master to his slaves; the miserable condition of the blacks in the different ports he had visited had made an ineffaceable impression upon his mind, which was heightened by the memory of his own cruel captivity on the prison ship; and it caused him unhappiness until he had given freedom to all his slaves, which event occurred some time before the Emancipation Act of New Jersey. After their manumission he continued to support the aged and infirm amongst them. He could say with Dido, "Non [ignarus] mali, miseris succurrere disco." [2]

Freneau frequently visited Philadelphia and New York, where his acquaintance with prominent persons and literary men of the times was extensive.

In 1809 Freneau published a new collection of his poems which constituted a fourth issue; these he entitled "Poems Written and Published during the American Revolutionary War, and now Republished from the Original Manuscripts; interspersed with Translations from the Ancients and other pieces not heretofore in print." The titlepage of this volume bears for its motto,—

"— Justly to record the deeds of fame,
A muse from heaven should touch the soul with flame;
Some powerful spirit, in superior lays,
Should tell the conflicts of the stormy days."

[1] Mrs. Charles Townsend Harris, now living.
[2] I learned from misfortune itself to succor the unfortunate.

An author has said these translations prove that Freneau had not altogether lost the early instruction in the classics which he had received at Nassau Hall. Some of these are from Ovid's "Tristia" and Lucretius. Amongst the Madison Papers is a letter from Freneau dated the same year: —

PHILADELPHIA, April 8th, 1809.

SIR, — I do myself the pleasure to enclose to you a copy of Proposals for the publication of a couple of Volumes of Poems shortly to be put to the Press in this city. Perhaps some of your particular friends in Virginia may be induced from a view of the Proposals in your hands to subscribe their names. If so, please to have them forwarded to this place by Post, addressed to the Publisher at No. 10 North Alley, Philadelphia. — Accept my congratulations on your late Election to the Presidency of the United States, and my hopes that your weight of State Affairs may receive every alleviation in the gratitude and esteem of the Public whom you serve in your truly honorable and exalted Station.

I remain Sir,
with the highest respect and regard,
your humble servant
PHILIP FRENEAU.

Freneau to Madison.[1]

PHILADELPHIA, May 12th, 1809.

SIR, — After a month's ramble through the States of New Jersey and New York, I returned to this place on Saturday last, and found your friendly Letter on Mr. Bailey's table, with the contents. There was no occasion of enclosing any Money, as your name was all I wanted to have placed at the head of the Subscription list. — I hope you will credit me when I say that the republication of these Poems, such as they are, was not a business of my own seeking or forwarding. I found last Winter an Edition would soon be going on at all events, and in contradiction to my wishes, as I had left these old scribblings, to float quietly down the stream of oblivion to

[1] Madison Papers, vol. XXXV. p. 17.

their destined element the ocean of forgetfulness. However, I have concluded to remain here this Summer, and have them published in a respectable manner, and free as possible from the blemishes imputable to the two former Editions, over which I had no controul, having given my manuscripts away, and left them to the mercy of chance. — I am endeavouring to make the whole work as worthy of the public eye as circumstances will allow. 1500 copies are to be printed, only; but I have a certainty, from the present popular frenzy, that three times that number might soon be disposed of. — I will attend to what you direct on the subject, and will forward the ten you mention by the middle of July or sooner. — I will consider of what you say relative to the insertion of a piece or two in prose, but suspect that anything I have written in that way is so inferior to the Poetry, that the contrast will be injurious to the credit of the Publication. — I feel much in the humour of remaining here about two years, to amuse myself as well as the Public, with such matter as that of the fat man you refer to, and if the Public are in the same humour they shall be gratified. But I am intruding on your time and will add no more at present. — I had almost said, —

> Cum tot sustineas et tanta negotia solus
> Res Italas armis tuleris moribus omnes
> Legibus emendes, in publica commoda fecerem
> Si longo sermone mores tua tempora, Cæsar.

My best wishes, Sir, will ever await you, and in particular that your Presidential Career may be equally honourable, though less stormy than that of your predecessor.

My best compliments and respects to Mrs. Madison, and remain with esteem and respect,

Your sincere friend
PHILIP FRENEAU.

Madison's reply to these two letters, if they were preserved by Freneau, were probably consumed in the burning of his house; but Freneau's third letter, proving that there had been such, bears the date of the following August.

Philip Freneau

PHILADELPHIA, Aug. 7th, 1809.

SIR, — The two volumes of Poems that in April last I engaged to have published, are finished, and will be ready for delivery in two or three days. The ten Setts [1] you subscribed for I am rather at a loss how to have safely transmitted to you at your residence in Virginia, where I find by the newspapers, you mean to Continue until the end of September. Will you on receipt of this, send me a line or two informing me whether you would prefer having the Books put into the hands of some Confidential person here, to be sent, or, that they be sent to the Post Office at Washington; or that they be forwarded directly to yourself in Orange County. The precise direction is not in my power.

I am Sir, with respect and esteem,
Your obedient humble Servt.,
PHILIP FRENEAU.

No 80 SOUTH FRONT STREET
or 10 NORTH ALLEY
PHILAD^A.

Letter from Jefferson to Freneau in relation to same work.[2]

MONTICELLO, May 22, 09.

DEAR SIR, — I subscribe with pleasure to the publication of your volumes of poems. I anticipate the same pleasure from them which the perusal of those heretofore published has given me. I have not been able to circulate the paper because I have not been from home above once or twice since my return, and because in a country situation like mine, little can be done in that way. The inhabitants of the country are mostly industrious farmers employed in active life and reading little. They rarely buy a book of whose merit they can judge by having it in their hand, and are less disposed to engage for those yet unknown to them. I am becoming like them myself in the preference of the healthy and cheerful employment without doors, to the being immured within four brick walls. But under the shade of a tree one of your volumes will be a pleasant pocket-companion. Wishing you all possible success and happiness, I salute you with constant esteem and respect.

TH. JEFFERSON.

MR. FRENEAU.

[1] Twenty volumes.   [2] Jefferson Papers. Series 2, vol. 34, p. 135.

Freneau to Jefferson.[1]

PHILADELPHIA, May 27th, 1809.

SIR, — Yesterday your Letter, dated May 22d, came to hand. — Perhaps you a little misunderstood me, when I wrote to you from this place in April last, inclosing the Proposal Paper, respecting the Poems. — I only wished your name to be placed at the head of the list, and did not wish you to be at the pains of collecting Subscriptions, further than as any of your neighbours might choose to put down their names. — Indeed the whole Subscription plan was Set a going without my knowledge or approbation, last Winter. But as I found the matter had gone too far to be recalled, I thought it best to Submit, in the present Edition, to the course and order of things as they are and must be. — Sir, if there be anything like happiness in this our State of existence, it will be such to me, when these two little Volumes reach you in August ensuing, if the sentiments in them under the poetical Veil, amuse you but for a single hour. — This is the first Edition that I have in reality attended to, the other two having been published, in a strange way, while I was wandering over gloomy Seas, until *embargoed* by the necessity of the times, and now again, I fear, I am reverting to the folly of scribbling Verses.

That your shade of Monticello may afford you complete happiness is the wish and hope of all the worthy part of mankind, and my own in particular. In such the philosophers of antiquity preferred to pass life, or if that was not allowed, their declining days.

Will you be so good as to read the enclosed Verses? They were published early in March last in the Trenton True American Newspaper, and in the Public Advertiser, of New York.

I am, Sir, with all esteem
Your obedient humble Servant
PHILIP FRENEAU.

In New York City, Freneau was ever a most welcome guest, at Governor Clinton's and at the residence of Dr. Francis, who then resided in Bond Street.

[1] Jefferson Papers. Series 2, vol. 34, p. 134.

The latter generally had some of the literati to meet him there.

Dr. Francis, in his " Reminiscences," describes Freneau as being somewhat below the medium height and slightly stooped, thin and muscular, with a firm step even in age; his forehead he describes as being very high, with soft and beautiful flowing hair of an iron-gray color; his eyes dark-gray, deeply set, and eyelids slightly drooping; his habitual expression pensive, but lighting up with animation when speaking. He retained the small-clothes, long hose, buckled shoes, and cocked hat of the colonial period until his death.

The same writer also mentions the aversion Freneau evinced to sitting for his portrait, or even having it taken at all. The reason for this peculiarity Dr. Francis could never fathom; and Freneau never gave it. Although not so strikingly handsome as his brother, who was considered the handsomest man in South Carolina, Freneau was, especially in his younger days, considered a handsome man; yet he never wished to have himself reproduced on canvas.[1] Rembrandt Peale once waited upon him with a request from a body of Philadelphia gentlemen to allow his portrait to be taken, but he was " inexorable." At a dinner given by Dr. Hosack of Philadelphia, the artist Jarvis was concealed in the room that he might catch his likeness, but in some way Freneau detected the design and frustrated it. It was caught once in a parlor, and, although he acknowledged it to be a good picture, he compelled its destruction. The picture in this book was executed after his death, from suggestions of the family, and was considered by them to be an excellent likeness.

Freneau, like his brother, was a man of extensive reading; his mind was logical and philosophical

[1] His brother Pierre had this same peculiarity.

rather than credulous; but he was full of imagination and fancy, and withal clear-headed. In manners, we are told, he was courteous and refined; and towards ladies, with whom he was a favorite, he was gallant. His general bearing won the admiration of all parties; his knowledge of the men and events of the times was extensive; and it is said that few knew as much about the early history of our country, the organization of the government, and the origin of political parties; and he could enter into any topic of conversation that interested his companions.

"With Gates he compared the achievements of Monmouth with those of Saratoga; with Colonel Hamilton Fish he reviewed the capture of Yorktown; with Dr. Mitchell he rehearsed from his own sad experience the physical sufferings and various diseases of the prison ships; and he descanted on Italian poets and the piscatory eclogues of Sannazarius, and doubtless furnished Dr. Benjamin Dewitt with data for his dissertation on the eleven thousand and five hundred American martyrs; with Pintard he enjoyed Horace and talked of Paul Jones; with Major Fairlie he discussed the tactics and charity of Baron Steuben; with Sylvanus Miller he compared political clubs in 1795 with those of 1810. He could share with Paine his ideal of a democracy, and with DeWitt Clinton and D. Calhoun debated the project of internal improvements and artificial navigation based upon the former's procedure of the Languedoc Canal; with Francis Hopkinson he talked politics and the poets; with Bishop Provost he interchanged intimate conversation based on kindred sentiments; and with Gulian C. Verplanck, Cadwallader Colden, and Dr. Francis, he discussed old men and old times with rare ability." He could relate Jefferson's account of the hasty signatures affixed to the Declaration of Independence, which he, Jefferson, attributed to the fact of the location being contiguous to a stable, and the signers wearing short clothes; the flies, he asserted, troubled their long hose to such a degree as to keep them continually switching them off with their handkerchiefs. Mr. Jefferson acknowledged that he affixed his signature as quickly as possible and beat a hasty retreat. Old New York was an ever interesting theme with Freneau, and his dear friend and room-mate, James Madison, was a particularly pleasant one; he described him as being of a very retiring disposition and fond of skating, it being his only recreation. According to him, Madison could never be induced to appear upon the stage to debate with the other students, although in after years his training in the House of Representatives and in the various Congresses and councils of state caused him to acquire a habit of self-possession which facilitated the use of the rich resources of his brilliant and discriminating mind; and his extensive information caused him to become the centre of every assembly of which he was a member. His early seclusion had the effect of giving him such a close application to the thread of his subject that he never wandered from it, but ever followed it in the purest and most classical language; and his gentleness and kindly expressions and manner caused even his adversaries to feel kindly disposed towards him. His spotless virtue never allowed calumny a momentary resting-place. He was the only one of Freneau's contemporaries that outlived him.[1]

Extremely hospitable, Freneau always warmly welcomed his friends at Mount Pleasant, where he devoted his declining years to reading and answering his numerous correspondents, and in occasionally penning an article for the press. He always retained his original frankness in expressing himself, but it was

[1] Although Madison graduated the same year with Philip, he remained another year at college.

softened down considerably as he advanced in years. In fact it was his pen, as some author has said, more than his heart that was so acrimonious in his early years; no personal malice ever rested in his mind, and he was ever ready to pardon those who had injured him. Even his adversaries, some of whom he had treated pretty roughly with his pen in early days, in later times claimed him as a friend. In his friendships he was ardent and sincere, and they were usually life-long.

Freneau lived to see his classmate Burr tried for treason, and finally stain his hand in the blood of his own old adversary, Alexander Hamilton. He saw his room-mate on the presidential chair, and others filling the first places in the States; and he rejoiced in their honors, desiring none for himself and refusing those that were offered him. He saw the white sails give place to iron-bound steam, and the old printing-presses he had once manipulated moved by the same power. He saw his contemporaries pass away before him, and he laid in turn his own dear ones to rest. He sang the events of the second great war, and decked with the laurel of his song the brave and gallant deeds of his countrymen. He saw the flames consume the home of his childhood till it lay in ashes at his feet, and his aged hand closed the record his boyish one had commenced in the Bible of his fathers:

> "Old house at Mount Pleasant took fire Sunday afternoon at four o'clock, Oct. 18th 1818. It was burned to the ground with a large quantity of valuable property therein. Said old house was built in 1752 by my father."

Freneau, like most persons of intellect, education, and energy, had from his earliest years of public life associated mostly with persons much in advance of him in years; consequently, as we have seen, many passed away before him; which fact he sadly alludes to in a letter to Madison dated three years before he saw the home of his father laid in ashes. The letter refers to two volumes of poems published by Freneau, commemorating the stirring events of the war of 1812. In these poems, with his usual freedom from all sentiments of jealousy, he celebrates the naval actions of Hull, Porter, and Macdonough. These books were printed by David Longworth in 1815, entitled "A Collection of Poems on American Affairs and a Variety of other Subjects, written between the years 1797 and the present time."

Freneau to Madison.

MOUNT PLEASANT, NEAR MIDDLETOWN POINT.
MONMOUTH COUNTY, NEW JERSEY, JANUARY 12th, 1815.

SIR, — Since my last return from the Canary Islands in 1807 to Charleston and from thence to New York, with my Brigantine Washington, quitting the bustle and distraction of active life, my walks have been confined, with now and then a short excursion, to the neighbourhood of the Never Sink hills, and under some old hereditary trees, and on some fields, which I well recollect for sixty years. During the last Seven Years my pen could not be entirely idle, and for amusement only now and then I had recourse to my old habit of scribbling verses. A Bookseller in New York, Mr. Longworth, by some means discovered this, and has prevailed on me to put my papers into his hands for publication. With some reluctance I consented to gratify his wish, altho' I think after the age of fifty, or thereabouts, the vanity of authorship ought to cease, at least it has been the case with myself. Mr. Longworth informs me the work will be published early in February in two duodecimo volumes. I have directed him, when done, to forward a copy to yourself, of which I beg your acceptance. I do not know that the Verses are of any superior or very unusual merit, but he tells me the Town will have them; and of course, have them they will, and must, it seems. The Work cannot be very tedious, for in two small Volumes there will be upwards of one hundred and thirty

Poems on different subjects, moral, political, or merely amusing, and not a few upon the events of the times since May 1812. However, you know a short production may sometimes be tedious, and a long one very lively and captivating. None of my effusions in these Volumes much exceed two hundred lines, and several do not reach more than the fourth part of that number of lines.

When I left Philadelphia, about the middle of September 1809, the ten copies of the Revolutionary Poems, which you subscribed for, were put into a box well secured, and forwarded according to your direction, under the care of General Steele, then Collector of the Port of Philadelphia; I have not since heard whether they reached you or not.

That Edition was published by *Subscription* merely for the benefit of, and to assist Mrs. Bailey, an unfortunate but deserving widowed female, niece to General Steele, and this consideration alone induced me to pay some attention to that third Edition. — But, in mentioning these matters I fear I am intruding both on your time and patience, constantly, or always perpetually engaged, as you undoubtedly are, in the duties of your station at a stormy period, a tempestuous Presidency indeed! May you weather all the conflicts of these mighty times, and return safe at the proper period to your Virginia Groves, fields, and streams: sure I am, different very different indeed from your long intercourse with political Life and the affairs of a "grumbling Hive." My best wishes attend Yourself, and Mrs. Madison, to whom, tho' I never had the pleasure of her acquaintance, I beg you to present my best compliments and regards.

I remain, Sir, (I hardly need to say)
with great esteem and respect,
Your obedient, humble Servant,
PHILIP FRENEAU.

HONBLE. JAMES MADISON,
Washington.

Freneau to Madison.

NEW YORK, March 3d, 1815.

SIR, — When I mentioned in my few lines to you, dated from my residence in New Jersey on the 22d of January last, the two Volumes of Poems publishing in this city by Mr.

Longworth, I did really think to have had a small box of them at Washington by the middle of February at farthest, with a particular direction of a couple of copies to Yourself bound in an elegant manner. Finding, however, that the business went on slowly here, and a little vexed to be under the necessity of leaving my Solitude and the wild scenes of nature in New Jersey for the ever execrated streets and company of this Capital, I embarked near Sandy Hook in a snow storm, about the last of January, and shortly after arrived here, fortunately unnoticed and almost unknown. . . . At my time of life, 63 ! ! ! abounding however in all the powers of health and vigour, though I consider my poetry and poems as mere trifles, I was seriously out of humour on my arrival here to see my work delayed, as well from the severity of the cold, which has been unremitting for more than a month past, and perhaps to some other causes it would not be prudent *here* to explain.

By my incessant exertions in spurring on the indolence of typography, the work, such as it is, is now finished, in two small Volumes of about 180 pages each. — The moment they are out of the bookbinder's hands, Mr. Longworth will forward you a Copy, and by the first Vessel to Alexandria, Georgetown, or Washington a Box of them to his correspondents in these places. A Copy or two of the Revolutionary poems will be forwarded to your direction. I am sorry the Copies you had were doomed to the flames, but the author had nearly suffered the same fate in the year 1780. Yesterday I received from New Jersey a Copy of your friendly Letter of the 1st. February. A Copy, I say, for my wife, or some one of my four Girls, daughters, would not forward me the original, but keep it until my return for fear of accidents. To-morrow morning I embark again for Monmouth, and among other cares, when I arrive at my magical grove, I shall hasten to exert all the poetical energy I possess, on the grand Subject of the Repulse of the British Army from New Orleans. There is a subject indeed! far above my power, I fear. If there be anything in inspiration, it will be needful on such a theme. Eight hundred lines in Heroic Measure I mean to devote to this animating subject. In due time you shall hear more from me on this business if I am not anticipated by some one more muse beloved than myself. Hoping that all health and happiness may attend you, and that your Libraries in future may escape the ravages of the flames of Goths and Barbarians,

I remain dear Sir
Your obedt. humble servant,
PHILIP FRENEAU.

One more letter to Madison concludes the correspondence on the subject of the poems.

NEW YORK, May 10th, 1815.

SIR, — Mrs. Anna Smyth, the lady of Charles Smyth Esquire, a respectable Citizen of this place, being to set out in a few days on a tour to Virginia, and expecting to be in your neighborhood either at Washington, or at Montpelier, does me the favour to take under her particular care, to put or transmit into your hands, the two little Volumes I mentioned to you in my letter last winter, and to which I received your friendly and obliging Answer. — Be pleased to accept them as a mark of my attention, respect, and esteem, in regard to your private as well as public character. I have written to Mr. Carey, in Philadelphia, a bookseller there, to forward on to you, if he has them, the two Volumes of the Revolutionary Poems published in Philadelphia in the Summer of 1809, and which you wished to regain, since the loss of your copies in the conflagration at Washington last year. I flatter myself, the arrangement I have made with him will replace them in your hand — I will only add, that any attention paid by you to Mrs. Smyth, I will consider as conferred on myself.

I am, Sir, with the highest consideration,
Your obedient humble servant,
PHILIP FRENEAU.

THE HONORABLE JAMES MADISON,
President of the United States.

After the disastrous fire at Mount Pleasant which consumed the fine library mentioned in Mrs. Freneau's letter to her brother, Samuel Forman, and in which much as yet unpublished poetry of Freneau's had been consumed, Freneau with his wife and two unmarried daughters removed, that is, themselves and the clothing they wore, to a house which was building; in which they remained up to the death of Mrs. Freneau's brother, when they took possession of his house, which had formerly belonged to Mrs. Freneau's father and had been the home of her childhood. Freneau lived in this house till his death.

Freneau was naturally sociable, and, being a great walker, he frequently met his friends in the evening at the rooms of the circulating library of the town. On the evening of the eighteenth of December, 1832, he remained there somewhat later than usual, having been interested in a political discussion. The Hon. William L. Dayton, afterwards U. S. Minister to France, offered to accompany him home; but Freneau persistently refused, and started alone. After a time a sudden snow-storm came up and hid from his view the lamp his wife always left burning in a window to light him home. It is supposed that he was blinded by the snow and benumbed by the intense cold, and, falling, broke his hip. He sank down by the side of the road, and, with the snow for his winding-sheet and the wild winter wind singing his requiem,[1] the freedom-loving spirit of Philip Freneau passed into the presence of his Maker.

Mr. Delancey says, "Such was the tragic end of one of the most original and gifted poets that America, up to his day, and I may say to ours, has ever produced."

In speaking of his death the "Monmouth Inquirer" says:—

"Captain Freneau was a staunch Whig in the time of the Revolution, a good soldier, and a warm patriot. The productions of his pen animated his countrymen in the dark days of

[1] They do not err
Who say that, when a poet dies,
Mute Nature mourns her worshipper
And celebrates his obsequies. — Scott.

seventy six, and the effusions of his muse cheered the desponding soldier as he fought the battles of freedom; he was the popular poet of the Revolution."

His death is recorded in the old Bible by his daughter Agnes, and closes the Freneau record.

"My dear father, Philip Freneau, was buried, by his own particular request, in the Locust Grove, very near his beloved mother, on Friday afternoon the twenty-first of December, 1832."

Freneau was buried under the tree of which we have already spoken as being his favorite seat, and under whose shade he composed many of his poems. His tombstone is a very simple one, of marble surmounted by a draped urn, and bears the inscription:

"Poet's Grave.
PHILIP FRENEAU
died December 18th. 1832
ae. 80 years, 11 months, and 16 days.

"He was a native of New York, but for many years a resident of Philadelphia and New Jersey. His upright and honest character is in the memory of many, and will remain when this inscription is no longer legible.

"Heaven lifts its everlasting portal high,
And bids the pure in heart behold their God."

By his side on another tombstone we read,—

"Sacred to the memory of Eleanor, wife of Philip Freneau, and daughter of Samuel and Helena Forman, who died September 1st, 1850, aged 86 years 9 months and 20 days."

The third book we have mentioned as lying on the desk proves that Freneau was not unmindful of his end, and shows his faith in God, and his deep affection for his loved ones. It, strangely enough, is marked by the firm hand of his early youth, and the trembling one of his old age. On its inner cover it bears the date of his entrance to the Penolopen Latin School, that of his initiation into Princeton College, and also that of his graduation. Through it are versified translations of different Latin verses; and in trembling pencil-strokes of later days, the following lines are traced: —

"I am growing fit, I hope, for a better world, of which the light of the sun is but a shadow; for I doubt not but God's works here, are what come nearest to his works there; and that a true relish of the beauties of nature is the most easy preparation and gentlest transition to an enjoyment of those of heaven: I'm endeavoring to put my mind into as quiet a situation as I can, to be ready to receive that stroke which, I believe, is coming upon me, and have fully resigned myself to yield to it. The separation of my soul and body is what I could think of with less pain; for I am sure he that made it will take care of it, and in whatever state he pleases it shall be, that state must be right. But I cannot think without tears of being separated from my friends, when their condition is so doubtful, that they may want even such assistance as mine. Sure, it is more merciful to take from us after death all memory of what we loved or pursued here: for else what a torment would it be to a spirit, still to love those creatures it is quite divided from! Unless we suppose, that in a more exalted life, all that we esteemed in this imperfect state will affect us no more, than what we lov'd in our infancy concerns us now."[1]

On the inner side of the last cover is written, —

"Leaving the old, both worlds at once they view
Who stand upon the threshold of the new."

And again, —

"Stronger by weakness, wiser men become
As they draw near to their eternal home."[2]

[1] Letters of Alexander Pope. [2] Waller.

GRAVE OF FRENEAU

Chapter Eleventh

FOR reasons already given, we deem it best to give the criticisms of others upon the poetry of Freneau, and begin with the remarks of a London publisher[1] who, notwithstanding Freneau's hostile feeling towards all that savored in the least of Great Britain, has had the magnanimity to overlook all such sentiment, and bring before the public, of his own free will, a reproduction of the volume of Freneau's poems, as published by Francis Bailey of Philadelphia in the year 1786. In his introduction to the British public he says: "It has been remarked with justice that, in the states which have arisen out of the British settlements in America, literature as a profession is a thing of recent growth. Till within the present century, it was only taken up as a matter of taste, and at leisure, from time to time, by those whose lives were absorbed in other duties and other pursuits, and most frequently took its character from temporary feelings and impulses. It hence happens that a good proportion of the best of the older American literature was temporary in its character, and has become more or less obsolete even in America, and it is only very considerable excellence that has preserved some of it from comparative oblivion. To this latter class belongs the poet whose works are given in the present volume, and who arrived at fame amidst the turbulence of the revolutionary period."

After giving a synopsis of the poet's varied career, he mentions his first notable poem composed in his

[1] John Russell Smith, Soho Sq., London, 1861.

sophomore year while at Nassau Hall, Princeton College, which, he says, is distinguished both by the vigor and the correctness of its versification. "His poetic satires against the royalists established his reputation in America, and all these show great talent; and some of his severer satires, such as that on his literary opponent whom he addresses under the name of Mac Swiggin, are characterized by great power."

As this poem gives an insight into Philip's character, his intense love for nature in her varied forms, his lack of desire for fame, yet innate knowledge of his own powers, did he desire to gain it, his scorn for all that was low or base in mankind, and his conscious superiority over a rival whom he has it in the power of his two-edged sword to annihilate; and furthermore as it illustrates that which we have already said: his being as much dreaded by a foe, as he was loved as a friend, we will quote some portions of it: —

"Long have I sat on this disast'rous shore,
And, sighing, sought to gain a passage o'er
To Europe's towns, where, as our travellers say,
Poets may flourish, or, perhaps they may;
But such abuse has from your coarse pen fell
I think I may defer my voyage as well,
Why should I far in search of honour roam,
And dunces leave to triumph here at home?
Great Jove in wrath a spark of genius gave,
And bade me drink the mad Pierian wave
Hence came these rhymes, with truth ascrib'd to me.
That swell thy little soul to jealousy:
If thus, tormented at these flighty lays,
You strive to blast what ne'er was meant for praise,
How will you bear the more exalted rhyme
By labour polish'd and matur'd by time?
Devoted madman! what inspir'd thy rage,
Who bade thy foolish muse with me engage?
Against a windmill would'st thou try thy might,
Against a giant would a pigmy fight?

What could thy slanderous pen with malice arm?
To injure him, who never did thee harm?
Have I from thee been urgent to attain
The mean ideas of thy barren brain?
Have I been seen in borrowed clothes to shine,
And, when detected, swear by Jove they 're mine?
O miscreant, hostile to thine own repose,
From thy own envy thy destruction flows!
Bless'd be our western world — its scenes conspire
To raise a poet's fancy and his fire,
Lo, blue-topt mountains to the skies ascend!
Lo, shady forests to the breezes bend!
See mighty streams meandering to the main!
See lambs and lambkins sport on every plain!
The spotted herds in flowery meadows see!
But what, ungenerous wretch, are these to thee!
You find no charms in all that nature yields,
Then leave to me the grottoes and the fields:
I interfere not with your vast design —
Pursue your studies, and I 'll follow mine,
Pursue well pleas'd your theologic schemes,
Attend professors, and correct your themes,
Still some dull nonsense, low-bred wit invent,
Or prove from scripture what it never meant,
Or far through law, that land of scoundrels, stray,
And truth disguise through all your mazy way.
Wealth you may gain, your clients you may squeeze,
And, by long cheating, learn to live at ease;
If but in *Wood* or *Littleton* well read,
The devil shall help you to your daily bread.
O waft me far, ye muses of the west —
Give me your green bowers and soft seats of rest —
Thrice happy in those dear retreats to find
A safe retirement from all human kind —
Though dire misfortunes every step attend,
The muse, still social, still remains a friend —
In solitude her converse gives delight,
With gay poetic dreams she cheers the night,
She aids me, shields me, bears me on her wings,
In spite of growling whelps, to high, exalted things,

Philip Freneau

Beyond the miscreants that my peace molest,
Miscreants, with dullness and with rage opprest.
Hail, great Mac Swiggen ! foe to honest fame,
Patron of dunces, and thyself the same,
You dream of conquest — tell me, how, or whence ?
Act like a man and combat me with sense —
This evil have I known, and known but once,
Thus to be gall'd and slander'd by a dunce,
Saw rage and weakness join their dastard plan
To crush the shadow, not attack the man.
Assist me, gods, to drive this dog of rhyme
Back to the torments of his native clime,
Where dullness mingles with her native earth,
And rhymes, not worth the pang that gave them birth !
Where did he learn to write or talk with men —
A senseless blockhead, with a scribbling pen —
In vile acrostics thou may'st please the fair,
Not less than with thy looks and powder'd hair,
But strive no more with rhyme to daunt thy foes,
Or, by the flame that in my bosom glows,
The muse on thee shall her worst fury spend,
And *hemp* or *water* thy vile being end.
Aspers'd like me, who would not grieve and rage !
Who would not burn, *Mac Swiggen* to engage ?
Him and his friends, a mean, designing race,
I, singly I, must combat face to face —
Alone I stand to meet the foul-mouth'd train,
Assisted by no poets of the plain,
Whose timorous Muses cannot swell their theme
Beyond a meadow or a purling stream —
Were not my breast impervious to despair —
And did not Clio reign unrivall'd there,
I must expire beneath the ungenerous host,
And dullness triumph o'er a poet lost.

. . . . .

Come on, Mac Swiggen, come — your muse is willing,
Your prose is merry, but your verse is killing —
Come on — attack me with your choicest rhymes,
Sound void of sense betrays the unmeaning chimes —

Come, league your forces; all your wit combine,
Your wit not equal to the bold design —
The heaviest arms the Muse can give, I wield,
To stretch Mac Swiggen floundering on the field,
'Swiggen, who, aided by some spurious Muse,
But bellows nonsense, and but writes abuse,
'Swiggen, immortal and unfading grown,
But by no deeds or merits of his own —
So, when some hateful monster sees the day,
In spirits we preserve it from decay,
But for what end, it is not hard to guess —
Not for its value, but its ugliness."

. . . . . .

1775.

"Freneau's longest and most carefully written poems were: 'The House of Night,' 'The Jamaica Funeral,' and 'The Beauties of Santa Cruz;' his most admired is 'The British Prison Ship.'

"The influence of Freneau's wandering and unsettled life is visible in his literary labors, a large portion of which were inspired by the stirring events that were passing around him. For this reason, perhaps, he is not so well known as many other writers to the general reader, even in his own country; while the fierce hostility to England and King George which the great revolutionary struggle had raised in his mind, and which he expresses in very unmeasured language, prevented his being popular among Englishmen, who, indeed, have been generally neglectful of the literature of America. Yet Freneau, as the 'patriot poet,' long enjoyed a very extensive popularity among his own countrymen, and no doubt he deserves to stand among their best poets. There is an ease in his verse, combined with a great command of language, and, at the same time, a simplicity of expression and delicacy of handling, which makes us regret that it was so often employed on subjects the interest of which was of a temporary character. Many of his poems of a more miscellaneous character present beauties of no ordinary kind, while the playful or satirical humour of others is perfect."

On the evening of March thirteenth of the year 1883, Professor James D. Murray of Princeton College delivered a lecture upon the poet and his poetry before the Long Island Historical Society in the society's building. In regard to his poetry, which is the only portion of the lecture that we shall quote in this chapter, he said: "Freneau was a genius in his way, and had brilliant instincts. Some of his poetry sprung from the intense flame of oppression, and as a poet he blew it to a white heat. He was possessed of an impetuous flow of song for freedom, and his wit was pungent and stinging. That he used this with effect can readily be seen by any person who reads his supposed interview with King George and Fox. Then take his exquisite dirge of the heroes of Eutaw Springs, his odes like 'Benedict Arnold's Departure;' some parts of them are unrivalled. His works show that he imitated in some degree both Gray and Shelley. Campbell and Scott did not hesitate to borrow from him. . . . His literary essays were also in this peculiar vein; for instance, his 'Advice to Authors,' his 'Oration upon Rum,' and a series of character sketches. His 'City Burying Places' antedates some of our modern suggestions."

"There was no difficulty in versification with him," wrote Dr. Francis. "I told him what I had heard Jeffrey, the eminent Scotch reviewer, say of his writings, that the time would arrive when his poetry, like that of Hudibras, would command a commentator like Grey."

"The poetry of the revolutionary era was not of an exhilarating character certainly, for with the outbreaking of hostilities there came an outburst otherwise than tuneful of patriotic ballads, songs, and doggerel satires, to all of which at this distance the sounds of the combatants' fife and drum seems a fitting accompaniment. One poet there was, however, who may justly be awarded that title on account of the occasional lyrics which are in pleasing contrast with the verses of his contemporaries; some of which are characterized by a grace and tenderness as well as by a skilful versification that gives them a peculiar charm. Freneau wrote for a purpose, and that purpose accomplished he was satisfied; had he striven to be or become a poet in the best sense of the word, he might have become one, but he used his gift as a means to an end, occasionally solacing his moments of freedom from care by using his pen for his pleasure, but this was seldom."[1]

"He depicts land and naval fights with much animation and gay coloring; and being himself a son of old Neptune, he is never at a loss for appropriate circumstances and expressive diction when the scene lies at sea. — His martial and political ballads are free from bombast and affectation, and often have an arch simplicity in their manner that renders them very poignant and striking. If the ballads and songs of Dibdin have cheered the spirits and incited the valor of the British Tars, the strains of Freneau, in like manner, are calculated to impart patriotic impulses to the hearts of his countrymen, and their effect in this way should be taken as a test of their merit. Many of his compositions relating to persons and things now forgotten are no longer interesting, but he evinced more genius and more enthusiasm than any other poet whose powers were called into action during the great struggle for liberty, and was the most distinguished poet of our revolutionary period.

"It is not to be forgotten, however, that Freneau

[1] Centennial Journals, 188.

had other claims to attention as a poet, than his literary association with the events of the Revolution. He was essentially of a poetic mood, and had many traits of rare excellence in the divine art. His mind was warmed into admiration at the beauties of landscape; his conceptions were imaginative; visionary scenes swarmed before his imagination; and the same susceptibility of mind which led him to invest with interest the fading fortunes of the Indian, and Nature's prodigality in the luxurious scenery of the tropics, made him keenly appreciative of the humble ways and manners of his race. The practical Captain Freneau combined humor with fancy, and his Muse, laying aside what Milton termed 'her singing robes,' could wear with ease the garments of every-day life. The common, once familiar incidents and manners of his time will be found pleasantly reflected in many a quaint picture in his poems."[1]

"The poems of Philip Freneau," if we may be allowed here to repeat our estimate of his powers from a sketch written some years ago, "represent his times, the war of wit and verse no less than of sword and stratagem of the Revolution; and he superadds to this material a humorous simplicity peculiarly his own, in which he paints the life of village rustics, with their local manners fresh about them; of days when tavern delights were to be freely spoken of, before temperance societies and Maine laws were thought of; when men went to prison at the summons of inexorable creditors, and when Connecticut deacons rushed out of meeting to arrest and waylay the passing Sunday traveller. When these humours of the day were exhausted, and the impulses of patriotism were gratified in song, when he had paid his respects to Rivington and Hugh Gaine, he solaced himself with remoter themes: in the version of an ode of Horace, a visionary

[1] Giulian C. Verplanck, in Analectic Magazine.

meditation on the antiquities of America, or a sentimental effusion on the loves of Sappho. These show the fine tact and delicate handling of Freneau, who deserves much more consideration in this respect from critics than he has received. A writer from whom the fastidious Campbell, in his best day, thought it worth while to borrow an entire line, is worth looking into. It is from Freneau's "Indian Burying-Ground," the last image of that fine visionary stanza: —

> "'By midnight moons, o'er moistening dews,
> In vestments for the chase array'd,
> The hunter still the deer pursues,
> The hunter and the deer — a shade.'

"Campbell has given this line a rich setting in 'O'Conner's Child': —

> "'Now on the grass-green turf he sits,
> His tassell'd horn beside him laid;
> Now o'er the hills in chase he flits,
> *The hunter and the deer a shade.*'

"There is also a line of Sir Walter Scott which has its prototype in Freneau. In the introduction to the third canto of 'Marmion,' in the apostrophe to the Duke of Brunswick, we read: —

> "'Lamented chief! — not thine the power
> To save in that presumptuous hour,
> When Prussia hurried to the field,
> *And snatch'd the spear but left the shield.*'

"In Freneau's poem on the heroes of Eutaw, we have this stanza: —

> "'They saw their injur'd country's woe;
> The flaming town, the wasted field,
> Then rush'd to meet the insulting foe;
> They took the spear — but left the shield.'

"An anecdote which the late Henry Brevoort was accustomed to relate of his visit to Scott, affords assurance that the poet was really indebted to Freneau, and that he would not, on a proper occasion, have hesitated to acknowledge the obligation. Mr. Brevoort was asked by Scott respecting the authorship of certain verses on the battle of Eutaw, which he had seen in a magazine, and had by heart, and which he knew were American. He was told that they were by Freneau, when he (Scott) remarked, 'The poem is as fine a thing as there is of the kind in the language.' Scott also praised one of the Indian poems.

"Freneau surprises us often by his neatness of execution and skill in versification. He handles a triple-rhymed stanza in the octosyllabic measure particularly well. His appreciation of nature is tender and sympathetic, — one of the pure springs which fed the more boisterous current of his humour when he came out among men, to deal with quackery, pretence, and injustice. But what is, perhaps, most worthy of notice in Freneau is his originality, the instinct with which his genius marked out a path for itself in those days when most writers were languidly leaning upon the old foreign school of Pope and Dryden. He was not afraid of home things and incidents. Dealing with facts and realities, and the life around him, wherever he was, his writings have still an interest where the vague expressions of other poets are forgotten. It is not to be denied, however, that Freneau was sometimes careless. He thought and wrote with improvidence. His jests are sometimes misdirected; and his verses are unequal in execution. Yet it is not too much to predict that, through the genuine nature of some of his productions, and the historic incidents of others, all that he wrote will yet be called for, and find favour in numerous editions."[1]

"Freneau's originality was very marked. He fol-

[1] Cyclopædia of American Literature. The remainder of this chapter is taken from Mr. Edward Delancey's address to the Huguenot Society.

lowed not in the steps of Dryden, nor any other of the poets of the Augustan age; nor, like his contemporaries Trumbull and Barlow, in those of Young and Pope. Not only did he not follow classic example, but he struck out a style of his own. Free, clear, and expressive, he cast aside the trammels of the stately verse in which his predecessors and contemporaries delighted, and wrote just as he seems to have felt, and in whatever way he deemed most appropriate to his subject. Although careless in his rhymes at times, he was, nevertheless, always effective.

"So long was his life that he wrote some of his finest poems after the advent of that brilliant galaxy of poets who burst forth in the early part of this nineteenth century. But not a trace of Moore, Southey, Campbell, Rogers, Scott, Wordsworth, or Byron, is to be found in the last two small volumes of his poems which he gave to the world in 1815.

"Freneau's prose writings were of two kinds: brief essays on many subjects, after the manner of the *Spectator* and the *Tatler;* and travels and reports of an imaginary character, related and made to their kings by an inhabitant of Otaheite and a Creek Indian, after their return from civilized lands, after the example of Voltaire. To these may be added his political disquisitions and translations from French historical writers. The best of the former were written over the pen-name of 'Robert Slender.' All are pleasing, witty, humorous, easy and agreeable, and show great and close power of observation. His political writings, action, and opinions are a most interesting theme, but they would require a full essay to be adequately presented. The ardor of his nature and the firmness of his opinions, with the vigor and terseness of his style, made him an adversary to be feared.

"During the period of his sea life is to be ascribed

some of his finest and most perfect descriptions of nature, especially of nature in the tropics. Two poems, one styled 'The Beauties of Santa Cruz,' and the other descriptive of the shores of Carolina and Charleston, are instinct with true poetic fire. His versified translations from the Latin show how well his college days were spent, and how late in life he kept up his classic studies. No finer rendition of the fifteenth ode of the first book of Horace, Nereus's prophecy of the destruction of Troy, than Freneau's exists; while his translation of Gray's famous 'Ode written at the Grande Chartreuse,' is as striking and beautiful as the original itself.

"Freneau's poetry may be considered in three classes, — war lyrics and satires; poems on general subjects and descriptions of nature; and translations from the classic poets and those of Italy and France; with a few which do not strictly fall under either of these heads. They vary greatly in style and finish, some wanting much of the latter quality. Freneau was naturally impulsive, inclined to indolence, and often careless; and his verse sometimes reflects his moods. He seems to have written just as the incident or event happened which formed his theme, or as the idea he expressed occurred to him. Like many men of active intellect and quick perceptions, he lacked application. Content to write for the hour, and satisfied if the effect or object aimed at was secured, he little regarded the future of the children of his brain. Hence he has left us no great narrative poem and no epic.

"His verse is wonderful for its ease, simplicity, humor, great command of language, and delicacy of handling. Except Dryden and Byron no poet of America or England has shown himself a greater master of English or of rhyme. The luxuriance of his stanzas is something amazing. Only to the temporary nature of the subjects of most of his verse, especially of his satires, can be ascribed the desuetude into which his poems have fallen. In vigor, sentiment, playfulness, and humor, many of them cannot be surpassed, and their beauties of form and expression are as great now as when they were first given to the world.

"But Freneau possessed other and deeper poetic gifts. We have all wondered at and admired the poems of that strange son of genius of our day, the late Edgar Allan Poe. Yet the strange power of that extraordinary man existed also in the earlier poet. His 'House of Night—a Vision' prefigured the wondrous conceptions of the author of 'The Raven.' Though not at all alike, there is in the supernatural weirdness of each a similarity. Freneau's dreamer, wandering at midnight in a dark wood, comes upon a noble dome. Entering and ascending, he hears 'a hollow voice of loud lament' from out a vaulted chamber, which proves to be that of Death personified in human form, stretched on his dying bed. He is attended by the castle's lord, who has just suffered a heavy affliction; and who, in obedience to the divine precept, 'If thine enemy hunger feed him, if he thirst give him drink,' tries to assuage his sufferings, but at the same time tells him that his end is inevitable. Death gives him certain directions, orders his own burial, and dies in the greatest agony. Then follows a most vivid description of the burial. The vision ends; the dreamer awakes, and the poem closes with some reflections on Death.

"Another, and very different gift which Freneau possessed in an extraordinary degree was his power of invective. In this, some of his satires rival the 'Absalom and Achitophel,' and 'English Bards and Scotch Reviewers' in vigor, as well as in the torrent-like flow of the verse. Listen to these lines upon an opponent who had attacked him in abusive rhyme, and whom, under an odd name, he has immortalized: —

"'Hail, great Mac Swiggen,'" etc.

As Mac Swiggen has already been served up to our readers we will spare them the remainder of the quotation.

"This is certainly equal to Dryden," — that is, Mac Swiggen's eulogy, not our digression, — "yet Freneau wrote it when only twenty-three."

In speaking of another of Freneau's early poems, one written at the age of eighteen while at Nassau Hall, and which we have mentioned in his college life, this author, after quoting several portions of it, says: —

"Is not this true poetry? Is it not extraordinary as the work of a youth of eighteen years? But one other American poet ever wrote anything to compare with it so early in life. Bryant wrote at nineteen his 'Thanatopsis,' and never later did he surpass that poem, although it contains but eighty-one lines.

"Totally dissimilar as these two poets were, in almost every characteristic, physical and mental, Freneau being as warm as Bryant was cold, there was yet a singular parallelism in their literary careers. Both were educated men, both college graduates, Freneau of Princeton, Bryant of Williams; both wrote as mere youths, and wrote then as men of twice their ages might be proud to write. Both studied law and then threw it aside. Both became hot politicians and fierce political writers. Both had an irresistible desire to publish newspapers, and both became editors of their own papers, and editors of power. Both wrote vigorous, nervous, yet polished prose. Both continued to write poetry during their whole lives. Both were eminent as translators of the ancient classics. Both made purely literary ventures, and both wrote satires, and bitter ones. Both became involved in personal conflicts. Both wrote strongly against slavery. Both were eminently worshippers, as well as poets of nature. Both, as their lives grew apace, left the press to others, and passed their latter days in quiet retirement. And both enjoyed almost the longest span of life allotted to man, Freneau dying in his eighty-first, and Bryant in his eighty-sixth year.

"But here the parallel ends, for, unlike Bryant, Freneau wrote better in later life than in youth, and his range of subjects and kinds of verse were wider and more varied. Bryant possessed great application, however, while Freneau had little. In fact the latter was too versatile for his own good.

"Such was the poetry of the Huguenot patriot of the Revolution. Born eight years before the death of George the Second, and living far into the presidency of the seventh ruler of the United States, General Andrew Jackson, Philip Freneau is the only poet whose ringing verse roused alike the hearts and nerved the arms of two generations of Americans against England. He immortalized alike the successes of the Revolution and those of the war of 1812. He sang, with equal spirit, force, and fire, the glory of Trenton and the triumph of Chippewa, the conqueror of Yorktown and the victor of Niagara. He sang, too, the heroic battles of Paul Jones on the German Ocean, and those of Perry and McDonough on the waves of Erie and the waters of Champlain, and also, but in sadder strains, the fate of André and the death of Ross."

We have several times mentioned the poem on the battle of "Eutaw Springs" and as it is, in our opinion, the most beautiful of all Freneau's poems we will close this chapter on his writings by giving it to our readers.

Philip Freneau

EUTAW SPRINGS.

At Eutaw Springs the valiant died:
Their limbs with dust are covered o'er;
Weep on, ye springs, your tearful tide;
How many heroes are no more!

If in this wreck of ruin, they
Can yet be thought to claim a tear,
O smite thy gentle breast, and say
The friends of freedom slumber here!

Thou who shalt trace this bloody plain,
If goodness rules thy generous breast,
Sigh for the wasted rural reign;
Sigh for the shepherds sunk to rest!

Stranger, their humble graves adorn;
You too may fall and ask a tear:
'T is not the beauty of the morn
That proves the evening shall be clear.

They saw their injured country's woe,
The flaming town, the wasted field
Then rushed to meet the insulting foe;
They took the spear but left the shield.

Led by thy conquering standards, Greene,
The Britons they compelled to fly;
None distant viewed the fatal plain,
None grieved in such a cause to die —

But like the Parthians, famed of old,
Who, flying, still their arrows threw,
These routed Britons, full as bold,
Retreated, and retreating slew.

Now rest in peace, our patriot band;
Though far from nature's limits thrown,
We trust they find a happier land,
A brighter Phoebus of their own.

1786.

Chapter Twelfth

IT would seem that the name of Freneau was likely to die out. Philip was the only descendant of the American branch that had a family; and his four children were all daughters. The two younger ones, Catherine Ledyard and Margaret, never married; his eldest daughter, Helen Denise, married Mr. John Hammill, a merchant of New York, and had four daughters; none of whom have left any descendants.

Agnes Watson Freneau, the poet's second and favorite child, is said to have been beautiful in her youth, and she retained much of her beauty even to an advanced age. She was a person of rare intelligence and refinement of taste, and possessed an active and vigorous temperament and a genial and sociable disposition. She inherited from both parents a great love for poetry and other literature, and like them she was a great reader, and a charming conversationalist. Her tastes were much the same as those of her father, which fact seemed to bind them even more closely together, and cause them to be almost constant companions from the time Agnes was old enough to be companionable to him. She frequently accompanied her father to New York to attend dinner and card parties, then greatly in vogue; and her vivacity and personal attractiveness caused her to be much admired.

But, notwithstanding Agnes' love of society, she was capable of deep thought, and her memory was so retentive that even to old age she has entertained her friends by reciting, at some length, passages from her favorite poets that she had committed to memory in her young days. She also composed some creditable poems, but our informant says that she probably either destroyed them, or gave them away, as they were not found among her papers.

In the year 1816 Agnes married Mr. Edward Leadbeater, a prominent merchant of New York, and graduate of Trinity College, Dublin, formerly a surgeon in the British army. He was a son of Dr. Henry Leadbeater, a prominent physician, who owned a fine estate near Coote Hill, County Cavan, Ireland. Dr. Leadbeater was physician to, as well as an intimate friend of, Lord Beresford, who was foremost in church and state. He and his son, Agnes' husband, were fond of fox-hunting, and kept fine hounds for the purpose. An old gentleman, who died within the last decade of years, aged ninety, remembered them well, and enjoyed talking of them; he said they entertained the nobility a great deal.[1]

Mr. Edward Leadbeater's aunt by marriage was an authoress of some note, and was an intimate friend of Miss Maria Edgeworth. Miss Edgeworth wrote the preface for Mrs. Leadbeater's work, entitled "Poems and College Dialogues." Mrs. Leadbeater also left a manuscript history of the events in the family and neighborhood, entitled "Annals of Ballytown," which, with her correspondence with the mother of Archbishop Trench of Dublin, and also with the poet Crabbe, were published in two volumes by Fisher, under the title of "Leadbeater Papers." Many of the anecdotes contained in her "Annals" were gained in her frequent visits among the poor, in company with the wife of the Episcopal minister, the Rev. Mr. Pyncheon. Mrs. Leadbeater was a Miss Shackleton, daughter and sister of the two presidents of Ballytore School, in which Edmund Burke first studied; the second president, son of the former one, was his schoolmate and friend.

[1] Dr. Leadbeater had an offer of knighthood, but he declined the proffered courtesy.

AGNES WATSON FRENEAU LEADBEATER
Favorite Daughter of the Poet

Mr. Edward Leadbeater's sister, Alicia, arrived in America with her husband and son, Henry, the same year in which her brother married Miss Freneau. Alicia had married Mr. Patrick O'Reilly, a merchant, who, in the great financial crisis attending the downfall of Napoleon First, had become seriously involved, and, meeting with little sympathy from their relatives, the young couple emigrated to America. Shortly after their arrival Mr. O'Reilly visited the island of Cuba, where he had relatives, but died of yellow fever almost immediately upon his arrival there. One of the principal streets of Havana is named after the family of the Marquis O'Reilly, formerly Governor-General of Louisiana when under the Spanish rule, and afterwards of Cuba.

There was a little romance in the history of Alicia and her husband; both having drawn upon themselves the great displeasure of their relatives, each being the first to marry into the religion peculiarly obnoxious to their respective families. Alicia's husband was a Catholic, while she belonged to the Church of England, and her family let her feel the weight of their displeasure, while his were even more greatly displeased. That he should unite himself to a heretic, and one of that hated religion that had been the cause of their losing their extensive possessions, titles, and religious rights, was a crime not to be forgiven.

The family of Alicia's husband had suffered greatly from the penal laws, but they were stanch in their faith; their sons, for generations, had been sent abroad to study, and many of them preferred to settle in foreign lands rather than return to a country in which their religion was held in opprobrium, and in which they had been denied their commonest rights, — the possessions and titles of their ancestors, which were the earldom of Cavan and marquisate of Breffney.

Two of the relatives of Alicia's husband had held

the archbishopric of Armagh. The one, Hugh O'Reilly, whose signature is even now seen on the manifestoes of 1741 as Hugo Armacansis, headed the Confederates of Kilkenny when the chiefs of Ulster rose in arms to contend for their rights and religious liberty, and to secure the lands of their ancestors of which they had been despoiled by the confiscation called the "Plantation of Ulster," by which James the First seized on the hereditary possessions of the Irish chiefs and transferred them to his followers.

The other, Daniel O'Reilly, was private chaplain to Maria Theresa, of Austria, and so won her good will that she used her influence with the Holy Father to have him, upon his desire to return to his native land, appointed Archbishop of Armagh. The Empress, however, retained his brother Andrew in her service, appointing him first to the command of her advanced posts in northern Italy and of the fortress of Lecco on Lake Como. She passed him through all the military grades in the Austrian army save that of Field Marshal. Andrew signalized himself in the service of his adopted country, and at the battle of Austerlitz by his bravery and skill saved the last of the army from total destruction. As Governor of Vienna, Count O'Reilly had the difficult task of capitulating honorably with Napoleon.[1]

The late Mr. Henry O'Reilly had in his possession a letter written on vellum from Count Andrew O'Reilly to his brother Daniel, after the latter's return to Ireland as Archbishop of Armagh.[2] Other relics

[1] Napoleon remarked as he entered Vienna, "It is strange that on each occasion — in November, 1805, as on this day — on arriving in the Austrian capital, I find myself in treaty and in intercourse with the respectable General O'Reilly. It was the dragoon regiment of O'Reilly's command, le Troisième Chevaux Légères, that by their brilliant charge at Austerlitz saved the remnant of the Austrian army, December 2, 1805."

[2] Lord Edward Fitzgerald was related to this family. It is said that the White House, Washington, was modelled from his residence. The house of Talbot de Malahide is connected with it by marriage.

Mr. O'Reilly had in his possession, amongst which were a set of etchings to which is attached a history. A grand-uncle, for the great misdemeanor of acting upon his rights as a Catholic priest to say mass, saw, as he was passing through the streets carrying these etchings, placards being posted around for his apprehension, to which a reward was attached. Thinking his best safety lay in flight, he started for the shore, and made arrangements for his passage to a place of safety. During the passage, the sailors were conversing about the reward, and fearing they suspected him, the priest acknowledged his identity, and threw himself upon their protection. He was not mistaken in his countrymen; they landed him out of danger, with the etchings under his arm, and he made his way to Antwerp, where he became president of the university of that city.

Other members of the family went to other countries, in all of which they rose to distinction. There is a pretty legend in the family which runneth thus: —

"At the time of the invasion of Ireland by the Danes, Brian O'Reileigh, as the name was at that time spelled, of Balaraharnahan, was sent out in command of a scouting party by the commander-in-chief of the Irish forces, and at the hour of noon on a very warm day in August stopped to rest on the margin of one of the enchanted lakes of Kilkenny. Enraptured with the romantic scenery and placid waters spread out before him, he lingered long after his allotted time, and the first thing he knew he was surrounded by a large Danish force. Remembering that an old fairy, a particular friend of his family, resided in that vicinity, he called on her for assistance. She appeared to him, and showed him the only way by which he could escape — a narrow pass through the mountains.

"'But,' said she, 'if that be guarded, there is nothing left for you save by the strong arm.[1] Fight your way through, and the fairies will befriend the destiny of the O'Reileighs to the latest generation.'

"He found the pass defended by countless myriads of Danish spears, but he went through by force of the *strong arm*, losing scarcely a man."

It will be seen from the legend that the name has seen some changes from the first, and Henry O'Rielly changed it yet further, as in early days, the Irish names not being so well known as at present, he was constantly called as if the *ei* were double *e*. It was to avoid this pronunciation that he spelled his name contrary to the usual way, reversing the letters *e* and *i*. Probably it was for a similar reason that Philip Freneau left the letter *s* out of his name, as Americans would in all probability sound it as it was spelled, "Fre*s*neau."

On account of the death of his father, Mr. Edward Leadbeater went to Ireland to settle up the estate, but finding that it would cause a greater delay than he had anticipated, he returned to America to put his affairs in order for a prolonged absence; but before he had succeeded in doing so, he fell ill, and died in the spring of the very year in which Philip Freneau died. His death is recorded on the same page with his marriage, and was the last entry made by Philip. His marriage and death read thus:—

"Agnes Watson Freneau, second daughter of Philip Freneau and Eleanor Forman, was married to Mr. Edward Leadbeater, merchant of the city of New York, Nov. 25th, 1816, by the Rev. John Croes, in the twenty-third year of her age."

[1] The name O'Reilly in the Irish language signified "strong arm," and the crest of the arms of the family consists of an arm and hand holding a sword. The arms are preserved in the family and some of the old plate was engraved with it.

After this entry comes that of the marriage of her sister, who although older than Agnes, was not married until later.

"Helen Denise Freneau, eldest daughter of Philip and Eleanor Forman Freneau, was married to Mr. John Hammill, of New York, on Monday eve, Dec. 15th, 1816; both of the above ceremonies at Mount Pleasant, Monmouth Co., N. Y."

"Departed this life on Friday A.M., the 28th day of March, Mr. Edward Leadbeater, at Mount Pleasant in the forty-eighth or forty-ninth year of his age, and interred in the Locust Grove, at his own request, on the Sabbath day following."

Mrs. Leadbeater had six children, the youngest of whom was only about six months old at the time of her husband's death. Her eldest daughter, Jane, was the only one whose birth was recorded by Freneau in the old Bible: "Agnes Leadbeater, my second daughter, had her eldest daughter, Jane Grey Leadbeater, born in New York." The date is not registered. Jane married Dr. Sweeny, and had two children, a son and a daughter. Her eldest son, Philip, to whom was given his grandfather's surname as well as his Christian name, married Helen Denison, and had one daughter. Mrs. Leadbeater's second daughter, Euphemia Kearny, married Mr. Samuel Blatchford, son of Dr. Thomas Windeatt Blatchford, a well-known physician of Troy, N. Y., and grandson of the Reverend Samuel Blatchford of Devonshire, England, who came to America in 1795. The late Judge of the U. S. Supreme Court was his cousin. Mrs. Appleton Bonaparte is likewise a member of this family. Mr. and Mrs. Samuel Blatchford have several children, one of whom is Captain Richard Milford Blatchford of the 11th infantry, U.S.A.

Edward Henry Leadbeater married a daughter of the Reverend Nehemiah Dodge. His daughter married Lieutenant-commander Jacob Noël, U. S. A. Mrs. Leadbeater's third daughter, Catherine Ledyard, married Mr. Edward Biddle, grandson of Clement Biddle of Philadelphia, who was cousin to the celebrated financier, and nephew to Captain Nicholas Biddle,— they have had seven children, all living but one. The youngest child of Mrs. Leadbeater, whom we have mentioned as being only six months old at the time of her father's death, married Dr. Charles Townsend Harris, nephew of Townsend Harris, consul-general to Japan, and the first American envoy to that country.[1]

Dr. Harris, after graduating from the N. Y. University, took a medical course in Paris, and afterwards studied chemistry in Giessen under Baron von Liebig. While in Paris Dr. Harris formed a pleasant acquaintanceship with the Duc. de Montpensier, which they continued by correspondence after Dr. Harris' return to America. Dr. Harris is lineal descendant of Simon Fraser, twelfth Earl of Lovat.[2] The records of this family now in their possession extend back to 1631. Dr. Harris left two sons and two daughters. Mrs. Blatchford, Mrs. Biddle, and Mrs. Harris are yet living.

At the death of Washington, Mrs. Leadbeater was in her sixth year, but her recollection of him was vivid till within the last few years of her life. She remembered distinctly his visiting her father's house in Philadelphia several times, and she always resented any allusion to her father's want of esteem for the first President, whom she admired very much. She always insisted upon her father's sentiments of admiration for General Washington's character, notwithstanding his former violent opposition to his policy. Mrs. Leadbeater lived under every administration from the first till Cleveland's first term inclusive. Notwithstanding

[1] Mr. Griffiths has published the life of Townsend Harris under the title of "Our First Diplomat to Japan."

[2] There is a complete and exhaustive record of the Harris family in preparation for publication.

her great age, she retained the use of her faculties to a remarkable degree until a few years before her death. She could talk by the hour of her dearly loved father, and frequently entertained visitors by repeating conversations she had heard him take part in. She retained much of the vivacity and even freshness of her youthful days till a late period in life. It is related of her, shortly after the death of the wife of her son Philip, that during their summer at Long Branch: The governor, who was a guest of the same hotel, announced that he would open the "hop" that evening with the handsomest lady there. As the hour approached, and none of the beauties had been bespoken, there was considerable wonderment as to who the unknown one could be. Philip was in mourning for his wife, and as his daughter was quite young, they did not make their appearance; but Mrs. Leadbeater, yielding to the urgent solicitations of His Excellency, entered the room leaning on his arm. Very lovely she looked, too, in her silver-gray silk and snowy crape turban, which rivalled her silvery curls; and at the appearance of her sweet face all sentiments of former jealousy were allayed. She was quite unconscious of the joke, but when His Excellency insisted upon her opening the evening, she yielded his arm to a more youthful aspirant for the honor.

A few years before her death the exceptionally brilliant faculties of Mrs. Leadbeater became clouded, owing partly to a serious disaster which caused two apoplectic strokes. During her last illness she received unremitting care from the members of her household, which consisted of a daughter, two granddaughters, and two great-grandchildren. This family presented the rather unusual sight of four generations living together.[1]

[1] At the present time there are living fifty-three lineal descendants of the poet Freneau.

On the sixth day of August in the year 1888, the dear old lady peacefully resigned her soul into the hands of her Maker. She was buried in the family vault of Dr. Charles Townsend Harris at Ocean Hill, Greenwood.

Among her papers we have found an account of the exhumation of the body of her father's old and valued friend, James Madison, the fourth President of the United States.[1] The account contains a moral good for us to learn, — the nothingness of all that is created, and that God alone is great.

"In digging for the foundation for the monument erected over the grave of President Madison the coffin was exposed to view. The appearance of the remains is thus described: 'The board placed above the coffin had decayed, but no earth had fallen in upon it, and everything appeared to be as when the coffin was deposited there, except that the coffin was slightly out of place, allowing a partial view of the interior. As there was no fastening to prevent it, the part of the lid covering the superior portion of the body was raised, and several gentlemen present looked in upon the remains of the great Virginian. The coffin itself, of black walnut, was in perfect preservation and the interior was nearly filled with a species of moss, which adhered tenaciously to the wood. Beneath this, and partially hidden by it were a few of the largest and hardest bones. The lower jaw had fallen away, the bones of the breast and ribs were gone and the only parts of the skeleton which remained were the skull and portions of the cheek bones, the vertebræ of the neck, the spine and the largest bone of the arms. All else of the upper part of the body had returned to the dust whence it was taken, and in a few years more every trace of the body will disappear, until the trump of the resurrection shall unite the scattered particles.'"

Mors ultima linea rerum est. — HORACE.

[1] James Madison died in the year 1836, and was exhumed twenty-one years after burial.

THE RISING GLORY OF AMERICA

[Poem composed and recited by the poet at his graduation, Class of 1771.]

Venient annis
Sæcula feris, quibus oceanus
Vincula rerum laxet, et ingens
Pateat tellus, Typhisque novos
Detegat orbes; nec fit terris
Ultima Thule.

SENECA, MED. Act. III. v. 375.

ARGUMENT.— The subject proposed — The discovery of America by Columbus — A philosophical enquiry into the origin of the savages of America — The first planters from Europe — Causes of their migration to America — The difficulties they encountered from the jealousy of the natives — Agriculture descanted on — Commerce and navigation — Science — Future prospects of British usurpation, tyranny, and devastation on this side of the Atlantic — The more comfortable one of Independence, Liberty, and Peace — Conclusion.

Acasto

Now shall the adventurous Muse attempt a theme
More new, more noble, and more flush of fame
Than all that went before —
Now through the veil of ancient days renew
The period fam'd when first Columbus touch'd
These shores so long unknown — through various toils,
Famine, and death, the hero forc'd his way,
Thro' oceans pregnant with perpetual storms,
And climates hostile to advent'rous man.
But why, to prompt your tears, should we resume
The tale of Cortez, furious chief ordain'd
With Indian blood to dye the sands and choak,
Fam'd Mexico, thy streams with dead? or why
Once more revive the tale so oft rehears'd
Of Atabilipa, by thirst of gold,
(All conquering motive in the human breast)
Depriv'd of life, which not Peru's rich ore
Nor Mexico's vast mines could then redeem?
Better these northern realms demand our song,
Design'd by nature for the rural reign,

For agriculture's toil. — No blood we shed
For metals buried in a rocky waste. —
Curs'd be that ore, which brutal makes our race,
And prompts mankind to shed a brother's blood!

Eugenio

But whence arose
That vagrant race who love the shady vale,
And choose the forest for their dark abode?
For long has this perplext the sages' skill
To investigate. — Tradition lends no aid
To unveil this secret to the mortal eye
When first these various nations, north and south,
Possest these shores, or from what countries came? —
Whether they sprang from some primeval head
In their own lands, like Adam in the east, —
Yet this the sacred oracles deny,
And reason, too, reclaims against the thought:
For when the general deluge drown'd the world
Where could their tribes have found security,
Where find their fate, but in the ghastly deep?
Unless, as others dream, some chosen few
High on the Andes 'scap'd the general death,
High on the Andes, wrapped in endless snow,
Where winter in his wildest fury reigns,
And subtile aether scarce our life maintains.
But here philosophers oppose the scheme:
This earth, say they, nor hills nor mountains knew
Ere yet the universal flood prevail'd;
But when the mighty waters rose aloft,
Rous'd by the winds, they shook their solid base,
And, in convulsions, tore the delug'd world,
'Till by the winds assuag'd again they fell,
And all their ragged bed expos'd to view.
Perhaps, far wandering toward the northern pole,
The streights of Zembla, and the frozen zone,
And where the eastern Greenland almost joins
America's north point, the hardy tribes
Of banish'd Jews, Siberians, Tartars wild
Came over icy mountains, or on floats
First reach'd these coasts, hid from the world beside. —

And yet another argument more strange,
Reserv'd for men of deeper thought, and late,
Presents itself to view: — In Peleg's[1] days,
(So says the Hebrew seer's unerring pen)
This mighty mass of earth, this solid globe
Was cleft in twain, — " divided " east and west,
While straight between, the deep Atlantic roll'd.
And traces indisputable remain
Of this primeval land, now sunk and lost. —
The islands rising in our eastern main
Are but small fragments of this continent,
Whose two extremities were New Foundland
And St. Helena. — One far in the north,
Where shivering seamen view with strange surprise
The guiding pole-star glittering o'er their heads;
The other near the southern tropic rears
Its head above the waves — Bermuda's isles,
Cape Verd, Canary, Britain and the Azores,
With fam'd Hibernia, are but broken parts
Of some prodigious waste, which once sustain'd
Nations and tribes, of vanish'd memory,
Forests and towns, and beasts of every class,
Where navies now explore their briny way.

Leander

Your sophistry, Eugenio, makes me smile:
The roving mind of man delights to dwell
On hidden things, merely because they 're hid:
He thinks his knowledge far beyond all limit,
And boldly fathoms Nature's darkest haunts —
But for uncertainties, your broken isles,
Your northern Tartars, and your wandering Jews,
(The flimsy cobwebs of a sophist's brains)
Hear what the voice of history proclaims —
The Carthagenians, ere the Roman yoke
Broke their proud spirits, and enslav'd them too,
For navigation were renown'd as much
As haughty Tyre with all her hundred fleets,
Full many a league their vent'rous seamen sail'd

[1] Gen. x. 25.

Thro' streight Gibralter, down the western shore
Of Africa, to the Canary isles:
By them call'd Fortunate; so Flaccus[1] sings,
Because eternal spring there clothes the fields
And fruits delicious bloom throughout the year.—
From voyaging here, this inference I draw,
Perhaps some barque with all her numerous crew
Falling to leeward of her destin'd port,
Caught by the eastern *Trade*, was hurried on
Before the unceasing blast to Indian isles,
Brazil, La Plata, or the coasts more south—
There stranded, and unable to return,
Forever from their native skies estrang'd
Doubtless they made these virgin climes their own,
And in the course of long revolving years
A numerous progeny from these arose,
And spread throughout the coasts—those whom we call
Brazilians, Mexicans, Peruvians rich,
The tribes of Chili, Patagon and those
Who till the shores of Amazon's long stream,
When first the power of Europe here attain'd
Vast empires, kingdoms, cities, palaces,
And polish'd nations stock'd the fertile land.
Who has not heard of Cuzco, Lima and
The town of Mexico—huge cities form'd
From Europe's architecture; ere the arms
Of haughty Spain disturb'd the peaceful soil.—
But *here* amid this northern dark domain
No towns were seen to rise.—No arts were here;
The tribes unskill'd to raise the lofty mast,
Or force the daring prow thro' adverse waves,
Gaz'd on the pregnant soil, and crav'd alone
Life from the unaided genius of the ground,—
This indicates they were a different race;
From whom descended, 't is not ours to say—
That power, no doubt, who furnish'd trees and plants,
And animals to this vast continent,
Spoke into being man among the rest,—
But what a change is here! what arts arise!

[1] Hor. Epod. 16.

What towns and capitals! how commerce waves
Her gaudy flags, where silence reign'd before!

Acasto

Speak, my Eugenio, for I 've heard you tell,
The dismal story, and the cause that brought
The first adventurers to these western shores;
The glorious cause that urg'd our fathers first
To visit climes unknown, and wilder woods
Than e'er Tartarian or Norwegian saw,
And with fair culture to adorn a soil
That never felt the industrious swain before.

Eugenio

All this long story to rehearse, would tire,
Besides, the sun toward the west retreats,
Nor can the noblest theme retard his speed,
Nor loftiest verse — not that which sang the fall
Of Troy divine, and fierce Achilles' ire.
Yet hear a part: — by persecution wrong'd,
And sacerdotal rage, our fathers came
From Europe's hostile shores, to these abodes,
Here to enjoy a liberty in faith,
Secure from tyranny and base controul.
For this they left their country and their friends,
And dar'd the Atlantic wave in search of peace;
And found new shores, and sylvan settlements,
And men, alike unknowing and unknown.
Hence, by the care of each adventurous chief
New governments (their wealth unenvied yet)
Were form'd on liberty and virtue's plan.
These searching out uncultivated tracts
Conceiv'd new plans of towns, and capitals,
And spacious provinces. — Why should I name
Thee, Penn, the Solon of our western lands
Sagacious legislator, whom the world
Admires, long dead: an infant *colony*,
Nurs'd by thy care, now rises o'er the rest
Like that tall pyramid in Egypt's waste
O'er all the neighbouring piles, they also great.

Philip Freneau

Why should I name those heroes so well known,
Who peopled all the rest from Canada
To Georgia's farthest coast, West Florida,
Or Apalachian mountains ? — Yet what streams
Of blood were shed ! what Indian hosts were slain,
Before the days of peace were quite restor'd !

Leander

Yes, while they overturn'd the rugged soil
And swept the forests from the shaded plain
'Midst dangers, foes, and death, fierce Indian tribes
With vengeful malice arm'd, and black design,
Oft murdered, or dispers'd, these colonies —
Encourag'd, too, by Gallia's hostile sons,
A warlike race, who late their arms display'd
At Quebec, Montreal, and farthest coasts
Of Labrador, or Cape Breton, where now
The British standard awes the subject host.
Here, those brave chiefs, who, lavish of their blood,
Fought in Britannia's cause, in battle fell ! —
What heart but mourns the untimely fate of Wolfe
Who, dying, conquer'd ! — or what breast but beats
To share a fate like his, and die like him !

Acasto

But why alone commemorate the dead,
And pass those glorious heroes by, who yet
Breathe the same air, and see the light with us ? —
The dead, Leander, are but empty names,
And they who fall to-day the same to us,
As they who fell ten centuries ago ! —
Lost are they all, that shin'd on earth before ;
Rome's boldest champions in the dust are laid,
Ajax and great Achilles are no more,
And Philip's warlike son, an empty shade ! —
A Washington among our sons of fame
We boast conspicuous as the morning star
Among the inferior lights —
To distant wilds Virginia sent him forth —
With her brave sons he gallantly oppos'd

The bold invaders of his country's rights,
Where wild Ohio pours the mazy flood,
And mighty meadows skirt his subject streams. —
But now, delighting in his elm tree's shade,
Where deep Potowmac laves the enchanting shore,
He prunes the tender vine, or bids the soil
Luxuriant harvests to the sun display. —
Behold a different scene — not thus employ'd
Were Cortez, and Pizarro, pride of Spain,
Whom blood and murder only satisfy'd,
And all to glut their avarice and ambition! —

Eugenio

Such is the curse, Acasto, where the soul
Humane is wanting — but we boast no feats
Of cruelty like Europe's murdering breed —
Our milder epithet is merciful,
And each American, true hearted, learns
To conquer, and to spare; for coward souls
Alone seek vengeance on a vanquish'd foe.
Gold, fatal gold, was the alluring bait,
To Spain's rapacious tribes — hence rose the wars
From Chili to the Caribbean Sea,
And Montezuma's Mexican domains:
More blest are we, with whose unenvied soil
Nature decreed no mingling gold to shine,
No flaming diamond, precious emerald,
No blushing sapphire, ruby, chrysolite,
Or jasper red — more noble riches flow
From agriculture, and the industrious swain,
Who tills the fertile vale, or mountain's brow,
Content to lead a safe, a humble life,
Among his native hills, romantic shades
Such as the muse of Greece of old did feign,
Allur'd the Olympian gods from chrystal skies,
Envying such lovely scenes to mortal man.

Leander

Long has the rural life been justly fam'd,
And bards of old their pleasing pictures drew

Of flowery meads, and groves, and gliding streams;
Hence, old Arcadia — wood-nymphs, satyrs, fauns,
And hence Elysium, fancied heaven below! —
Fair agriculture, not unworthy kings,
Once exercis'd the royal hand, or those
Whose virtue rais'd them to the rank of gods!
See, old Laertes [1] in his shepherd weeds
Far from his pompous throne and court august,
Digging the grateful soil, where round him rise
Sons of the earth, the tall aspiring oaks,
Or orchards, boasting of more fertile boughs,
Laden with apples red, sweet scented peach,
Pear, cherry, apricot, or spongy plumb;
While through the glebe the industrious oxen draw
The earth-inverting plough, — Those Romans too,
Fabricius and Camillus, lov'd a life
Of neat simplicity and rustic bliss,
And from the noisy Forum hastening far,
From busy camps, and sycophants, and crowns,
'Midst woods and fields spent the remains of life,
Where full enjoyment still awaits the wise.
How grateful, to behold the harvests rise,
And mighty crops adorn the extended plains!
Fair plenty smiles throughout, while lowing herds
Stalk o'er the shrubby hill or grassy mead,
Or at some shallow river slake their thirst. —
The inclosure, now, succeeds the shepherd's care,
Yet milk-white flocks adorn the well stock'd farm,
And court the attention of the industrious swain —
Their fleece rewards him well; and when the winds
Blow with a keener blast, and from the north
Pour mingled tempests through a sunless sky
(Ice, sleet, and rattling hail) secure he sits
Warm in his cottage, fearless of the storm,
Enjoying now the toils of milder moons,
Yet hoping for the spring. — Such are the joys,
And such the toils of those whom heaven hath bless'd
With souls enamour'd of a country life.

[1] Hom. Odyss. lib. 24.

The Poet of the Revolution

Acasto

Such are the visions of the rustic reign —
But this alone, the fountain of support,
Would scarce employ the varying mind of man;
Each seeks employ, and each a different way :
Strip Commerce of her sail, and men once more
Would be converted into savages —
No nation e'er grew social and refin'd
'Till Commerce first had wing'd the adventurous prow,
Or sent the slow-pac'd caravan, afar,
To waft their produce to some other clime,
And bring the wish'd exchange — thus came, of old,
Golconda's golden ore, and thus the wealth
Of Ophir, to the wisest of mankind.

Eugenio

Great is the praise of Commerce, and the men
Deserve our praise, who spread the undaunted sail,
And traverse every sea — their dangers great,
Death still to combat in the unfeeling gale,
And every billow but a gaping grave ; —
There, skies and waters, wearying on the eye,
For weeks and months no other prospect yield
But barren wastes, unfathom'd depths, where not
The blissful haunt of human form is seen
To cheer the unsocial horrors of the way —
Yet all these bold designs to science owe
Their rise and glory — Hail, fair Science ! thou,
Transplanted from the eastern skies, dost bloom
In these blest regions — Greece and Rome no more
Detain the Muses on Cithaeron's brow,
Or old Olympus, crown'd with waving woods,
Or Haemus' top, where once was heard the harp,
Sweet Orpheus' harp, that gain'd his cause below,
And pierc'd the heart of Orcus and his bride ;
That hush'd to silence by its voice divine
Thy melancholy waters, and the gales,
O Hebrus ! that o'er thy sad surface blow. —
No more the maids round Alpheus' waters stray,
Where he with Arethusa's stream doth mix,

Or where swift Tiber disembogues his waves
Into the Italian sea, so long unsung;
Hither they wing their way, the last, the best
Of countries, where the arts shall rise and grow,
And arms shall have their day — even now we boast
A Franklin, prince of all philosophy,
A genius piercing as the electric fire,
Bright as the lightning's flash, explain'd so well
By him the rival of Britannia's sage. — [1]
This is the land of every joyous sound
Of liberty and life, sweet liberty!
Without whose aid the noblest genius fails,
And science irretrievably must die.

Leander

But come, Eugenio, since we know the past —
What hinders to pervade with searching eye
The mystic scenes of dark futurity!
Say, shall we ask what empires yet must rise,
What kingdoms, powers and states, where now are seen
Mere dreary wastes and awful solitude,
Where Melancholy sits, with eye forlorn,
And time anticipates, when we shall spread
Dominion from the north, and south, and west,
Far from the Atlantic to Pacific shores,
And shackle half the convex of the main! —
A glorious theme! — but how shall mortals dare
To pierce the dark events of future years,
And scenes unravel, only known to fate?

Acasto

This might we do, if warm'd by that bright coal
Snatch'd from the altar of cherubic fire,
Which touch'd Isaiah's lips — or if the spirit
Of Jeremy and Amos, prophets old,
Might swell the heaving breast — I see, I see
Freedom's establish'd reign; cities, and men,
Numerous as sands upon the ocean shore,
And empires rising where the sun descends! —

[1] Newton.

The Ohio soon shall glide by many a town
Of note, and where the Mississippi stream,
By forest shaded, now runs weeping on,
Nations shall grow, and states, not less in fame
Than Greece and Rome of old! — we too shall boast
Our Scipios, Solons, Catos, sages, chiefs,
That in the womb of time yet dormant lie,
Waiting the joyous hour of life and light.
O snatch me hence, ye muses, to those days
When through the veil of dark antiquity
Our sons shall hear of us as things remote,
That blossom'd in the morn of days — Alas!
How could I weep that we were born so soon,
Just in the dawning of these mighty times,
Whose scenes are panting for eternity!
Dissensions that shall swell the trump of fame,
And ruin brooding o'er all monarchy!

Eugenio

Nor shall these angry tumults here subside
Nor murders[1] cease, through all these provinces,
Till foreign crowns have vanish'd from our view
And dazzle here no more — no more presume
To awe the spirit of fair Liberty —
Vengeance shall cut the thread — and Britain, sure,
Will curse her fatal obstinacy for it!
Bent on the ruin of this injur'd country,
She will not listen to our humble prayers,
Though offer'd with submission:
Like vagabonds, and objects of destruction,
Like those whom all mankind are sworn to hate,
She casts us off from her protection,
And will invite the nations round about,
Russians and Germans, slaves and savages,
To come and have a share in our perdition —
O cruel race, O unrelenting Britain,
Who bloody beasts will hire to cut our throats,
Who war will wage with prattling innocence,

[1] The massacre at Boston, March 5, 1770, is here more particularly glanced at.

And basely murder unoffending women ! —
Will stab their prisoners when they cry for quarter,
Will burn our towns, and from his lodging turn
The poor inhabitant to sleep in tempests ! —
These will be wrongs, indeed, and all sufficient
To kindle up our souls to deeds of horror,
And give to every arm the nerves of Samson
These are the men that fill the world with ruin,
And every region mourns their greedy sway —
Nor only for ambition.
But what are this world's goods, that *they* for them
Should exercise perpetual butchery ?
What are these mighty riches we possess,
That they should send so far to plunder them ? —
Already have we felt their potent arm —
And ever since that inauspicious day,
When first Sir Francis Bernard
His cannons planted at the council door,
And made the assembly room a home for strumpets,
And soldiers rank and file — e'er since that day
This wretched land, that drinks its children's gore,
Has been a scene of tumult and confusion ! —
Are there not evils in the world enough ?
Are we so happy that they envy us ?
Have we not toil'd to satisfy their harpies,
King's deputies, that are insatiable ;
Whose practice is to incense the royal mind
And make us despicable in his view ?
Have we not all the evils to contend with
That, in this life, mankind are subject to,
Pain, sickness, poverty and natural death —
But into every wound that nature gave
They will a dagger plunge, and make them mortal !

Leander

Enough, enough — such dismal scenes you paint,
I almost shudder at the recollection —
What, are they dogs that they would mangle us ? —
Are these the men that come with base design
To rob the hive, and kill the industrious bee ! —

The Poet of the Revolution

To brighter skies I turn my ravish'd view,
And fairer prospects from the future draw —
Here independent power shall hold her sway,
And public virtue warm the patriot breast :
No traces shall remain of tyranny,
And laws, a pattern to the world beside,
Be here enacted first.

Acasto

And when a train of rolling years are past,
(So sung the exil'd seer in Patmos isle)
A new Jerusalem, sent down from heaven,
Shall grace our happy earth — perhaps this land,
Whose ample breast shall then receive, tho' late,
Myriads of saints, with their immortal king,
To live and reign on earth a thousand years,
Thence called Millennium. Paradise anew
Shall flourish, by no second Adam lost.
No dangerous tree with deadly fruit shall grow,
No tempting serpent to allure the soul
From native innocence. — A *Canaan* here,
Another *Canaan* shall excel the old,
And from a fairer Pisgah's top be seen.
No thistle here, nor thorn nor briar shall spring,
Earth's curse before : the lion and the lamb,
In mutual friendship link'd, shall browse the shrub,
And timorous deer with softened tygers stray
O'er mead, or lofty hill, or grassy plain :
Another Jordan's stream shall glide along,
And Siloah's brook in circling eddies flow :
Groves shall adorn their verdant banks, on which
The happy people, free from toils and death,
Shall find secure repose. No fierce disease,
No fevers, slow consumption, ghastly plague,
(Fate's ancient ministers) again proclaim
Perpetual war with man : fair fruits shall bloom,
Fair to the eye, and grateful to the taste ;
Nature's loud storms be hush'd, and seas no more
Rage hostile to mankind — and, worse than all,
The fiercer passions of the human breast

Shall kindle up to deeds of death no more,
But all subside in universal peace —
                                        Such days the world,
And such, America, thou first shalt have,
When ages, yet to come, have run their round,
And future years of bliss alone remain.

1771.

Appendix

Appendix

[*See page 6*]

"ON a exagéré infiniment le nombre des huguenots qui sortirent du royaume à cette occasion, et cela devoit être ainsi. Comme les interessés sont les seuls qui parlent et qui crient, ils affirment tout ce qui leur plait. Un ministre qui voyoit son troupeau dispersé publioit qu'il avoit passé chez l'etranger. Un chef de manufacture qui avoit perdu deux ouvriers faisoit son calcul comme si tous les fabricans du royaume avoient fait la même perte que lui. Dix ouvriers sortis d'une ville où ils avoient leurs connoissances et leurs amis faisoient croire, par le bruit de leur fuite, que la ville alloit manquer de bras pour tous les ateliers. Ce qu'il y a de surprenant, c'est que plusieurs maîtres des requêtes, dans les instructions qu'ils m'adressèrent sur leurs généralités, adoptèrent ces bruits populaires, et annoncèrent par là combien ils etoient peu instruits de ce qui devoit les occuper; aussi leur rapport se trouva-t-il contredit par d'autres, et démontré faux par la vérification faite en plusieurs endroits. Quand le nombre des huguenots qui sortirent de France à cette époque monteroit, suivant le calcul le plus exagéré, a soixante-sept mille sept cent trente-deux personnes, il ne devoit pas se trouver parmi ce nombre, qui comprenoit tous les âges et tous les sexes, assez d'hommes utiles pour laisser un grand vide dans les campagnes et dans les ateliers, et influer sur le royaume entier. Il est certain d'ailleurs que ce vide ne dut jamais être plus sensible qu'au moment où il se fit. On ne s'en aperçut pas alors, et l'on s'en plaint aujourd'hui! Il faut donc en chercher une autre cause: elle existe en effet, et, si on veut le savoir, c'est la guerre. Quant à la retraite des huguenots, elle coûta moins d'hommes utiles à l'Etat, que ne lui en enlevoit une seule année de guerre civile." [1]

[1] Vie du Duc de Bourgogne, tome ii. p. 108.

[*See page 6*]

"S'il falloit écouter certains déclamateurs, on croirait que les richesses et la prospérité avoient fui la France avec les protestans réfugiés; et cependant, je le demande, le commerce et l'industrie ont-ils cessé de prendre des accroissemens? Dans le cours du dix-huitième siècle, n'a-t-on pas vu se multiplier de toutes parts les étoffes précieuses, les meubles superbes, les tableaux des grands maîtres, les maisons richement décorés?

"A l'époque de la révocation, notre commerce, à peine sorti des mains de Colbert, son créateur, étoit encore dans l'enfance. Que pouvrons-nous apprendre à nos rivaux, de ce qui nous avions tout appris? L'Angleterre, la Hollande, l'Italie, nous avoit devancés dans la carrière; les manufactures de Louviers et de Sédan ont eu leurs modèles chez nos voisins. Le nom seul d'un très grand nombre de nos fabrications rapelle Londres, Florence, Naples, Turin, et décèle ainsi une origine étrangère." [1]

[*See page 7*]

"Les arrêts et les édits se succédoient rapidement, on pensoit alors que les édits précédens de tolerance et de pacification n'etoient pas des traités d'alliance, mais des ordonnances faites par les rois pour l'utilité publique, et sujets a revocation lorsque le bien de l'Etat le demande. Tel étoit le sentiment du docteur Arnauld, et, ce qui est plus remarquable, de Grotius lui-même. Le gouvernement français paroissait suivre le même système politique que les gouvernements protestans avoient mis depuis longtemps à exécution contre leurs sujets catholiques; et même, en comparent leur code pénal avec celui de la France, il seroit facile de prouver qu'il se montra plus indulgent et plus tolerant." [2]

[*See page 47*]

"The Blue Bells" was at the present Washington Heights, on the east side of the old Kingsbridge road, and opposite the Bennett place, formerly owned by Mr. Henry O'Reilly. We are told by Mr. Blasie Ryer of that vicinity that it was a long, low-roofed frame house, and was demolished many years ago.

[1] Conférences par M. I. Frayssinous, liv. iii. p. 127.
[2] Histoire de Bossuet, tome iii. p. 87.

This tavern was kept during the Revolution by one Wilson, an Englishman and a Tory. It was a favorite rendezvous of British officers, who there once concocted a night job for the capture of Washington; discovered, however, in time to save him, by a Scotch servant girl of the house, by the name of Douglas. She let out the secret to a good patriot woman, Mrs. Bauer, living across the street, — our informant's grandmother, — who contrived to send word to the General by her little Christine, to keep out of the way that night." — *Magazine of American History, vol. vi.* 1.

[*See page 52*]

Etienne DeLancey[1] was descended from Guy DeLancey Viscount de Loval and de Nourion. At the time of the Revocation of the Edict of Nantes he and his widowed mother, being stanch Protestants, were obliged to seek flight or concealment for safety. Etienne, then at the age of twenty-three, chose the former. Before parting, his mother gave him the family jewels, they being the most available property for him, and he succeeded in escaping with them to Holland, and from there went to England, where he embarked for America, after obtaining letters of denization. By the sale of his jewels he obtained a considerable sum that enabled him to enter a profitable commercial business. His rank and high personal character acquired for him a high position amongst the French refugees in New York, and he was one of the first anciens of the French Church. He married a daughter of Stephen Van Cortlandt and founded a family of social and political distinction. His son James became Chief Justice and Lieut. Governor of the province. This family is now represented by Edward Floyd Delancey, Esq., of New York, who is the head of this branch, all the other branches having become extinct in the male line. — *Baird's Huguenot Emigration.*

[*See page 63*]

Jacques Desbrosses was a Huguenot refugee from Monchamp, France, and arrived in the city of New York in 1701. He married Hélène Gaudineau in 1703. She was the

[1] Like many other names this has changed from its original form.

daughter of a Huguenot physician of Sigournais, France, who was very active during Leisler's time; and the latter threw him into prison for refusing to surrender his commission. He was an ancien of the French Church and obtained the freedom of the city in 1702. He was afterwards a vestryman of Trinity Church.

Jacques and Hélène had six children all of whom were baptized in the French Church. Their eldest son, likewise Jacques, was an ancien of that congregation, and the youngest, Elie, was a vestryman and warden of Trinity Church, New York City. In his will he left to the corporation of the latter church a fund for the use and benefit of such French clergy as should perform divine service in the French language, but according to the liturgy of the Church of England. One of the streets in New York is named after this family. — *Baird's Huguenot Emigration.*

[*See page 63*]

John Fanning Watson, the antiquary and annalist, was born at Batsto, Burlington County, New Jersey, in 1780, and died in Germantown, Pennsylvania, December 23, 1860. He had a bookstore in Philadelphia for many years, and employed his leisure in gathering items of interest in regard to the early history of Philadelphia; which he published under the title of "Annals of Philadelphia," 8vo, 1830; and a second edition in two volumes in 1844. The success of this work led him to collect and publish some incidents of early and revolutionary history pertaining to New York and Pennsylvania under the title of "Historic Tales of the Olden Times in Pennsylvania, 1833." In 1846 he published "Annals of New York City and State," and in 1856 a "History of the United States." — *American Cyclopædia.*

[*See page 89*]

The family of Morin was from Niort, one of the former Huguenot strongholds in France. Upon escaping from the latter country in the year 1685, the Morins, along with the Quintards, with whom they were related, sought refuge in Bristol, England, where Sir Jonathan Trelawney procured for the use of the refugees the beautiful Church of St. Marks, or the Gaunt Chapel.

The Morins and the Quintards belonged to the Narragansett Colony, but finally came to New York, where Pierre Morin married, in the year 1700, Esther, daughter of Elie Charron. By her he had nine children, three boys and six girls, two of the latter being twins.

The Right Rev. Ch. T. Quintard, D.D., LL.D., of the Protestant Episcopal Church, Bishop of the diocese of Tennessee, is a descendant in the fifth generation of this family. The Quintards finally moved to Stamford, Conn., where their descendants yet live.

[*See page 95*]

On May 26, 1775, the British warship "Asia," of sixty-four guns, arrived with orders to take on board the Royal Irish Regiment, which was quartered at the Upper Barracks in the Park. The departure of this detachment almost led to bloodshed. The committee had issued an order permitting the troops to leave unhindered, with such arms and accoutrements as they carried on their persons.

The people gathered in the streets to see the departure of the thoroughly unpopular redcoats, and were astonished to see, directly behind the first lines, a number of carts containing stacks of arms. Among those who noticed this unexpected feature of the procession was Marinus Willett, a prominent "Son of Liberty" and Captain in the First Regiment, "New York Line." He immediately gave the alarm and began collecting a force to prevent the troops from carrying off their spare arms.

"The way I took," to quote his own words ("New York in the Revolution," Mercantile Library Collection), "brought me to the front of the troops, as they were marching, before any of the other persons who set out on the same business. On my arrival in their front, which was at the corner of Beaver Street, in Broad Street, I stopped the horse that was drawing the front cartload of arms. This, of course, occasioned a halt of the troops, and brought the Major of the regiment, who was the commanding officer, in front to inquire into the cause of the halt. I had the horse by the head, and on the appearance of the Major informed him that the halt was made to prevent the spare arms from being carried off, as the act of the committee did not authorize the troops taking any other arms than such as they carried on their backs.

"While I was making this explanation to the Major, David Matthews, Esq., came up and accosted me in the following words: 'I am surprised, Mr. Willet, that you will hazard the peace and endanger the lives of our citizens when you know that the committee has directed that the troops shall be permitted to depart unmolested.' As Mr. Matthews was a Tory and zealous supporter of the measures of the British Government, his presence or opinion could have no influence with me, and I very unhesitatingly assured him . . . that, considering the bloody business which had taken place among our brethren in Massachusetts, whom we were bound by ties of honor as well as interest to support, I deemed it my duty to prevent these arms from being used against them, and conceived that it would be much more reputable for us to employ them in the defence of our injured country.

"While this question was agitating with the Major and the Mayor, [Matthews,] Mr. Gouverneur Morris made his appearance, and, to my great astonishment, joined the Mayor in opinion. Mr. Morris's situation was very different from that of the Mayor's. He was a Whig of very respectable connections and young, of brilliant talents. To be opposed by Mr. Morris staggered me — And I doubt whether all my zeal and enthusiasm would have supported me had it not been for the arrival at that critical moment of John Morin Scott, who was an influential member of the committee, and whose reputation for talents was as great as any in the city. He came up just as I was repeating to Mr. Morris the reasons of my conduct, and exclaimed in a loud voice: 'You are right, Willett; the committee has not given them permission to carry off any spare arms.' By this time the throng of people around us had greatly increased and were pressing in on every side. Mr. Scott's opinion was scarcely proclaimed when I turned the front cart to the right and directed the cartman to drive up Beaver Street; the other carts, which were loaded with arms, were made to follow."

At the suggestion of Scott, Willett jumped in one of the carts and announced to the soldiers that if they were ready to aid in the bloody business the patriots were ready to meet them "in the sanguine field," but if any of them felt a repugnance to the work of shedding their countrymen's blood they would be protected. One redcoat came forward and was received with great cheers.

The carts, accompanied by the continual huzzas of the people, were thereupon turned back, and, making their way through Beaver Street and upon the Broad Way, deposited their chests in a ball alley at the corner of John Street. These arms were afterward used by the first troops raised in New York by the Committee.

The forbearance of the British Major on this occasion has always been a cause of great surprise. It was perhaps due to his sympathy with the American cause, as shortly after he resigned his commission.

No doubt the advice of the sage and patriotic Morris in this instance was eminently proper, but as sometimes happens the rash and audacious deed of Willett bore good fruit and rendered his name and his service immortal.

During the Revolutionary War, Willett became one of the most efficient officers in the American army. Subsequently he occupied the position of Sheriff, and in 1807 was Mayor of the City. Sheriff and Willett Streets were both named in his honor. He died at the ripe old age of ninety, and was buried in a coffin made of pieces of wood collected by himself from various Revolutionary battlefields. — ALBERT ULMANN, *in the New York Times — Saturday Review.*

[*See page 105*]

As many seem to identify privateering with piracy, a word on the subject may not be inopportune.

According to the law of nations, when one power has declared war against another, all the subjects of the one are enemies to the subjects of the other, and consequently the subjects of one power may not properly complain of hostile acts done by those of the adverse power, even though such acts should not have been specially commanded by the power. Usually, however, unsanctioned inimical acts have been practically condemned by nearly all civilized nations, for, although not looked upon as piracy, yet they would be irregular. The universal rule is that, except in case of self-defence, only those regularly enrolled by their respective powers should take part in warfare. To the sovereign power it belongs to make war, and in doing so it may employ what means it sees fit. It may limit itself to its own resources, or it may make use of those of others, either by land or sea; it may employ only its public vessels, or it may avail itself of vessels belonging to private persons; and in doing the latter, the fact of giving them a commission forms of such forces in respect to the navy what would compare with a volunteer force in respect to the regular army, for in both of these cases the commissions they bear make of them servants of the State. To guard against the abuses incident to piracy, such sea forces are subject to certain regulations.

Unprepared as were the colonies for warfare on land, to a greater degree were they so by sea. Warfare against the French, Spanish, and Indians had necessarily imparted to the colonists a certain degree of experience and discipline, but never having entered into contest with these foes on the sea, they had consequently no advantage whatever. Far easier was it for them to raise an army, and to drill it on firm land which had been their basis in every operation since their advent, than to build and equip vessels, and perform evolutions on such an unstable and unaccustomed element as water. Subjects also could be found more ready to rise up and equip themselves to defend their hearth-fires than to leave them to the mercy of their enemy and go forth to meet such of them as were already considered masters of the sea.

The origin of the United States navy dated only from 1775, in which year Congress authorized two cruisers to be built, the one carrying ten, the other fourteen guns; soon after, fifteen other vessels were authorized to be built, carrying from twenty to thirty-six guns, — the colonies of New England, New York, Pennsylvania, and Maryland bearing the expense of their construction. On December 22, 1775, Esek Hopkins and Paul Jones were appointed, respectively, commander-in-chief and lieutenant; there was also appointed a corps of naval officers. By October, 1776, the infant navy numbered twenty-six vessels, mounting 536 guns, and with this ineffectual armament, the colonies were to meet the superior force of Great Britain, until such time as the French fleet came to assist them in their efforts. They were utterly unable to succeed in combined operation against the British, as in the very few encounters they had, the colonists came off conquered; consequently the sea-coast was at the mercy of the oppressors.

Seeing the necessity of enlarging their force, Congress gladly granted letters of marque to any well-known patriots who should be venturesome enough to undertake the work of assisting their country on the sea. Without these letters of marque such vessels would have been treated, when captured, as ordinary pirates. The instructions issued by Congress to all privateers during the Revolution were as follows: —

"I. You may by force of arms attack, subdue, and take all ships and other vessels belonging to the inhabitants of Great Britain, on the high sea, or between high water and low water marks, except ships and vessels bringing persons who intend to settle and reside in the United States; or bringing arms, ammunition or warlike stores to the said colonies, for the use of such inhabitants thereof as are friends to the American Cause, which you shall suffer to pass unmolested, the commander thereof permitting a peaceable search and giving satisfactory information of the contents of the ladings and the destination of the voyages.

"II. You may by force of arms subdue and take all ships and other vessels whatsoever carrying soldiers, arms, gunpowder, ammunition, provisions, or any other contraband goods to any of the British armies or ships of war employed against the colonies.

"III. You shall bring such ships and vessels as you shall take, with their guns, tackle, apparel, furniture and lading, to some convenient port or a port of the united Colonies, that proceedings may thereupon be had in due form before the courts which are or shall be then appointed to hear and determine causes civil and maritime.

"IV. You or one of your chief officers shall bring or send the master and pilot and one or more principal person or persons of the company of every ship or vessel by you taken, as soon after the capture as may be, to the Judge or Judges, of such court as aforesaid to be examined upon oath and make answer to the interrogatories which may be propounded touching the interest or property of the ship or vessel and her lading, and at the same time you shall deliver or cause to be delivered to the Judge or Judges all Passes, Sea Briefs, Charter-Parties, Bills of Lading, Lockers, Letters and Documents, and Writings found on Board, proving the said Papers by the Affidavit of yourself, or of some other Person present at the Capture, to be produced as they were received, without Fraud, Addition, Subtraction, or Embezzlement.

"V. You shall keep and preserve every Ship or Vessel and Cargo by you taken until they shall by Sentence of a Court properly authorized be adjudged lawful Prize, not selling, wasting, or diminishing the same or breaking the Bulk thereof, not Suffering any such Thing to be done.

"VI. If you or any of your Officers or Crew shall in cold blood, kill or maim, or, by Torture or otherwise, Cruelly, inhumanly, and contrary to common usage and the Practice of civilized nations in war treat any Person or Persons surprised in the Ship or Vessel you shall take, the offender shall be severely punished.

"VII. You shall by all convenient Opportunities, send to Congress written accounts of the Capture you shall make, with the number and names of the Captives, Copies of your Journal from time to time, and Intelligence of what may occur or be discovered concerning the Design of the Enemy and the Destinations, motion and Operation of their Fleets and armies.

"VIII. One third, at least of your whole company shall be Land men.

"IX. You shall not ransom any Prisoners or Captives, but shall dispose of them in such manner as the Congress, or if that be not sitting in the Colony whither they shall be brought, as the General Assembly, Convention or Council or Committee of Safety of such Colony shall direct.

"X. You shall observe all such further instructions as Congress shall hereafter give, in the promise you shall have notice thereof.

"XI. If you shall do anything contrary to these instructions or to others hereafter to be given, or willingly suffer such things to be done, you shall not only forfeit your commission and be liable to an Action for Breach of the Condition of your Bond, but be responsible to the Party aggrieved for Damages sustained by such malversation."

[*See page 138*]

The following letter[1] goes to prove that Peter Freneau did not go to South Carolina till after the year 1780; it was written just two weeks before the capture of the "Aurora."

PHILADELPHIA, May 13th, 1780.

SIR, — With this you will receive a Cask containing 14 Galls of Wine which is due you for two Guineas that you gave me on the other side you have your Account — I am informed that you have recd £50 for the Horse that I lost in Mr. Budinots service, this sum is so far from making me any satisfaction that I am determined not to take it, the Horse cost me upwards of £20 in Specie, I think it is Just that I should have more than £50 Continental which at the present Exchange is only $\frac{16}{8}$ a very Small Compensation for lying out of my property upwards of two years. I would therefore beg that if you do not get more for me that you will inform Mr. Budinot that I had rather Loose the horse than take a mere Shaddow in pay for him. — I have nothing more to add only that I am

Very Respectfully
Your most obedient
Humble Servant
PETER FRENEAU.

JOHN COVENHOVEN ESQR.
Freehold
Monmouth County.

[*See page 187*]

Chief Justice Pinckney was the son of Thomas Pinckney and Mary Cotesworth. In 1752 he was made Chief Justice of the province. His wife, Eliza Lucas, daughter of Colonel Lucas of the British army, was the first to introduce the cultivation of indigo into the United States. He had two sons Charles Cotesworth and Thomas Pinckney; both brothers

1 The original letter is in the possession of Mr. Weymer Jay Mills.

practised law in Charleston, and at the breaking out of the Revolution took up arms in defence of their country. Charles accepted in 1796 the post of Minister to France; he was afterwards appointed major-general in the army. In 1800 he was a candidate for the presidency. Thomas became aid to General Lincoln the commander of the Southern army. In 1789 he was elected Governor of South Carolina, and in 1792 was appointed Minister to Great Britain, and afterwards was appointed to fill the same position in Spain. He was appointed major-general in 1812.

[*See page 228*]

In the preface to one of Edmund Burke's works we find this allusion to Mrs. Leadbeater: —

"Edmund Burke was at Ballytore school under its founder, and its founder's son and heir was then among his schoolfellows and comrades. Its founder's daughter, Mary, became afterward Mrs. Leadbeater, and when Burke was a great man in London, Richard Shackleton having come also to be head of the Ballytore school, it was his rest and happiness to Burke, to take a holiday at Ballytore with its president who had been his schoolfellow and to correspond with Mrs. Leadbeater."

[*See page 229*]

"At the age of seventeen years Henry O'Rielly became the assistant editor of the 'New York Patriot,' the organ of the 'People's Party,' which elected De Witt Clinton governor of the State of New York in 1824. When in 1826 Luther Tucker & Co. established the 'Rochester Daily Advertiser,' the first daily newspaper published between the Hudson River and Pacific Ocean, young O'Rielly, then not twenty-one years of age, was chosen to be its editor. 'About this time he married Marcia, eldest daughter of General Micah Brooks, of Brooks' Grove, Livingston County, a pioneer settler from Brooks' Vale, Connecticut. General Brooks' father, a graduate of Yale, as a minister preached resistance to injustice with picket guards around his church, and held such different positions of trust in the New Haven colony as were compatible with his profession. He was related to Maj.-Gen. David Wooster. General Brooks filled many prominent positions and exercised a great influence in the early days of the State and the Republic. In our State Legislature, and Constitutional Convention, in the National Congress, as Judge for over twenty years, and served several campaigns on the British frontiers during the war of 1812. While in Congress he was chairman of the "Committee on Internal Improvements," which committee was composed of Henry Clay, Daniel Webster, John C. Calhoun, Wm. Henry Harrison, Richard M. Johnston, and others.'

"Mr. O'Rielly resumed his editorial labors in 1832, and became an active leader in all public enterprises. In 1833, as chairman of the Executive Committee of Rochester on Canal Affairs, he wrote the first memorial presented to the Legislature and the Canal Board, in favor of rebuilding the failing structures of the Erie Canal. He then proposed a judicious plan for the enlargement of the Canal, which, if it had been adopted, might have saved the State millions of dollars. He was a zealous advocate of such enlargement, and he was chairman of the first State Executive Committee appointed by the first Canal Enlargement Convention in 1837. In that capacity he served many years with great efficiency. In 1838 he was appointed postmaster of Rochester. At the same time his never-wearied pen prepared pamphlets and newspaper essays, filled with cogent arguments in favor of reform in the methods of popular education. In these efforts he was ably seconded by the venerable James Wadsworth, Senior,[1] of Genneseo; and their joint labors led to the legislation that fashioned the present common-school system of the State of New York. Mr. O'Rielly earnestly advocated the introduction of works on agriculture into the school-district libraries of the State, and his wise suggestions in his reports as Secretary of the State Agricultural Society have been practically carried out in the establishment of State Agricultural Colleges in every commonwealth in the Union. He was the originator of the State Constitutional Association which was the means of bringing about the reforms in the Constitution of the State of New York in 1846. He was also the originator at about the same time, of a project for the establishment of a private telegraph system for a range of about eight thousand miles in length connecting

[1] Father of General James Wadsworth.

all sections of the United States east of the Mississippi River. For this purpose he secured the right to the use of all the telegraph patents which had then been granted. This system was known as the 'Atlantic, Lake, and Mississippi Telegraph Range,' the earliest lightning range in America or the world, and it was carried into effect by his individual effort, without governmental direction or subsidies.

"In 1853 Mr. O'Rielly was engaged by the State of Iowa to improve the navigation of the Des Moines River, but circumstances caused a suspension of the work. A few years later the railroad interest in the State of New York took an attitude decidedly hostile to the great Erie Canal, a powerful commercial rival. That interest conspired to destroy its credit and to make the people believe that it was the source of burdensome taxation. The completion of its enlargement was opposed, and a scheme was devised for controlling legislation so as to deprive the people of this great property by its sale to the highest bidder. In the fall of 1859 Mr. O'Rielly sent forth a stirring address to the people of the State on the subject. They were aroused. The 'Clinton League' was formed, with Mr. O'Rielly as chairman, and, by their untiring efforts, this scheme, which if carried out, would have disgraced the Commonwealth, was frustrated. When the late Civil War broke out he was one of the most active promoters of measures for the preservation of the Union, and was secretary of the 'Society for Promoting the Enlistment of Colored Troops.' He originated in 1867 an organized movement for reforming and cheapening the operations of the Railroad system of the United States. Mr. O'Rielly has deposited with the New York Historical Society, of which he had been a member since 1840, almost two hundred volumes, partly in manuscript and partly in print, containing well-arranged documents and other papers relating to the history of important public events in which he has participated. These form authentic materials of inestimable value, especially to the future historian, of the early operations of the Canal and Telegraph systems of the United States."[1] About 1838 he prepared and published a volume of five hundred pages entitled "Sketches of Rochester, with Incidental Notices of Western New York." It was the first

[1] Harper's Cyclopædia of American History.

work of its kind ever published in the interior of the continent. Mr. O'Rielly was also the author of "Personal Recollections of Major Van Campen, the Guide and Chief Quartermaster of General Sullivan;" "The Personal Recollections of William Wood;" "Personal Recollections of Thomas Morris," the son and representative of Robert Morris; "Personal Recollections of John Greig, M. C.;" "Sketch of the Formation of the First Regiment of the National Guards," now the Seventh Regiment, of which he was Orderly Sergeant.

"Memoir" concerning American Journalism.

"Memorial" concerning Public School System.

"Memorial" in regard of right of Telegraph Constructors.

"Memorials" to President Polk, to Congress, National Conventions, and State Legislatures to urge the stationing troops for security of travellers and settlers between the Mississippi and Pacific Ocean.

"Memorial to Supreme Court against Telegraph Monopoly."

"History Getting Right," rendering justice to Prof. Joseph Henry, of Smithsonian Institute, and Mr. Alfred Vail.

"Resolutions and Correspondence," New York State Agricultural Society 1844–5.

"American Political Anti-masonry."

"Origin of Mormonism and its Golden Bible."

"True Causes of the Great Rebellion."

"Historical Sketch of the Origin of Enlisting Colored Troops."

Mr. O'Rielly was also the compiler and author of various publications issued by the "Democratic League" and the compiler and annotator of more than fifty volumes of papers and documents concerning "Public Improvement Enterprises" in which he had taken part. He also composed many poems, usually patriotic, some of which were set to music. He also frequently contributed articles to the public press, and at the close of the war he published a "memento of Captain Brooks O'Reilly," his eldest son, who after the besieging of Yorktown fell during the attack upon Williamsburgh, Va.

[*See page 233*]

Thomas Windeatt Blatchford, M.D., was born in Topham, Devonshire, England, on the twentieth of July, 1794. His father, the Rev. Samuel Blatchford, removed to this country when Thomas was an infant, and first settled in Bedford, N. Y., and afterwards in Greenfield Hill, Conn., to which place he was called as the successor of Dr. Dwight, who had accepted the presidency of Yale College. He was subsequently called to the pastoral charge of the united congregations of Lansingburgh and Waterford, N. Y., in 1804, where he spent the most of his useful life.

Dr. Blatchford's early studies were prosecuted under the direction of his father, in Lansingburgh Academy, of which his father was the principal. In 1810 he commenced the study of medicine under Dr. John Taylor of Lansingburgh, and in 1813 he matriculated at the "College of Physicians and Surgeons." In 1815 he went to England and attended two courses of lectures at the united schools of Guy's and St. Thomas' hospitals, given by Sir Astley Cooper and Professor Cline. In 1816 he returned to New York and after attending another course of lectures he graduated in 1817. His graduating thesis was upon "Feigned Diseases," being the result of his observations and experience while attending the State Prison. The paper was printed and gives evidence of that judicious observation and accuracy of diagnosis which distinguished his subsequent career as a medical man. After receiving his degree of M.D. he opened an office in New York City. He afterwards removed to Jamaica, Long Island, where, gaining the confidence of the residents, he had an extensive and arduous practice. In 1819 he married Harriet, the daughter of Thomas Wickes, a descendant of one of the original patentees of the town of Huntington in 1666, and one of the leading men on Long Island, who took a prominent part in our revolutionary struggle, being connected with the American army during the entire war, in the quartermaster's department, with the rank of major. While in Jamaica the doctor identified himself with the interests of the town, being a trustee in Union Hall Academy, and an active laborer in works of religion and general benevolence.

In 1828, after the death of his father, Dr. Blatchford removed to Troy for the purpose of being near his widowed mother. The successful treatment and cure of a clergyman there whom several other physicians had treated unsuccessfully, caused him to become very popular, and for a period of about forty years he was looked upon as a highly successful practitioner and a cultivated and scientific medical man.

His intercourse with his associates was uniformly marked by the amenities and courtesies of one who appreciated and loved the honor of his profession. While jealous of his own reputation, he paid a scrupulous regard to the reputation and rights of others. He took great pleasure in rendering aid and encouragement to his professional juniors, and even assisted them materially. His interest in the advancement and welfare of his profession was manifested in his efforts for the promotion of medical association. The State and county medical societies, and the American Medical Association, were regarded as worthy of his active efforts for their promotion. He was rarely absent from their meetings, and their records bear evidence not only of his interest in their welfare, but of his sound judgment in the adoption of measures calculated to promote the cause of medical science.

Dr. Blatchford is favorably known by his published papers and essays, which are as follows: "Inaugural Dissertation on Feigned Diseases," in 1817; "Letters," &c., 1823; "Letters to Married Ladies," 1825; "Homœopathy Illustrated," 1824. One of the earliest discussions of the delusion which was published and which has always been regarded as possessed of peculiar merit, "Equivocal Generation," 1844. "Inaugural Address before the Medical Society of the State of New York;" "Memoir of Charles Lyman, Esq.," 1849; "Two Cases of Hydrophobia," 1854; "Report on Hydrophobia," 1856, read before the American Medical Association, and published in their Transactions; "Report on Rest and the Abolition of Pain, as Curative Remedies," 1856; "Eulogy on Dr. Samuel McClellan," 1859; "Alumni Oration before the College of Physicians and Surgeons," New York, 1861; besides many articles for newspapers, and papers contributed to the medical and surgical journals.

Dr. Blatchford kept a meteorological journal from the year 1824; noting the range of the thermometer and barometer, direction of the wind and aspect of the weather, account of rain, snow, &c. His accuracy and care in these observations were well known, and the testimony of his record on these subjects, was regarded as conclusive. He was a philanthropist in the highest sense of the term. The temperance cause received his earnest and most systematic efforts for its promotion. Every enterprise for the advancement of the well-being of his fellow-men, at home or abroad, found in him an earnest friend, and active and consistent colaborer.

Dr. Blatchford was connected with the Marshall Infirmary of Troy from its foundation. The Lunatic Asylum connected with the Infirmary was projected by him. Upon his death the governors, in their tribute to his memory, express their "irreparable loss" in the death of their associate, and declare that his place in their councils "can never be wholly filled," and that his labors in the care of the institution "have been such that few can ever equal." He left his valuable medical library of over six hundred volumes to the institution. The bequest was accepted by the governors, who resolved to place the books in a separate apartment to be known as the "Blatchford Medical Library of the Marshall Infirmary."

The doctor was connected for a period of seven years with the Board of Education of the city of Troy, and was its presiding officer during most of that time. To the cause of education he gave his untiring energies. Regarding the health of the body as essential as the improvement of the mind he drew the plan of most of the schoolhouses of the city, so as to secure pure air and thorough ventilation. One of the public schools was named, in 1862, the Blatchford School. He was also a trustee of the Rensselaer Polytechnic Institute, and of the Troy Female Seminary.

Dr. Blatchford's reputation as a man of science was recognized in the degree of A.M., by Union College in 1815; in his election as Fellow of the Albany Medical College in 1834; President of the Rensselaer County Medical Society 1842–3; Permanent member of the Medical Society of the State of New York, 1845, and its President in 1847; Member of the American Association for the Advancement of Science, 1849; Corresponding Fellow of New York Academy of Medicine, 1847; Vice-president of the American Medical Association, 1856; Corresponding Member of the Academy of Science, St. Louis, 1857; Fellow of the College of Physicians and Surgeons, New York, 1861; Honorary Member of the Medical Society of New Jersey, 1861, and of the Medical Society of Connecticut, 1862.

As a Christian a uniform and consistent piety formed a part of the man. In his daily round of duties, professional, civil, social, as well as in those more peculiarly religious, his aim seemed always to be to "do all things to the glory of God." He seldom absented himself from the services of the sanctuary. So unusual was his absence that when at rare intervals it did happen, the minister would send to his residence, under the apprehension that he was ill. It is said that a certain physician in Troy had been admonished for his uniform absence from services on Sundays, and he excused himself on the ground of professional duty, and he was asked why Dr. Blatchford could attend church so regularly, whereupon he acknowledged that he could not understand it, as his practice was not so large as Dr. Blatchford's. He was advised to learn the doctor's secret, and upon calling upon the latter for the purpose, the doctor said to him: "You always attend your consultations, don't you, doctor?" "Oh, yes," he replied. "And you aim to be always punctual to your appointments, don't you?" He answered in the affirmative, and with emphasis. "Well," said Dr. Blatchford, "I have a consultation with my Divine Master at ten o'clock every Sunday morning, and I make all my arrangements to meet my appointment."

His piety was not severe, but always beautiful; ever cheerful, often jocose and eminently social, his society was welcome to every circle. He fell asleep in Jesus Jan. 7th, 1866. — *Memoir by Stephen Wickes, A.M., M.D.*

[*See page 234*]

In the notes to "The Lord of the Isles" we find an account of the cruel execution of Sir Simon Frazer, called in the poem the "flower of chivalry."

NOTE. — "Sir Simon Frazer, or Frizel, ancestor of the family of Lovat, is dwelt upon at great length, and with savage exultation, by the English historians. This knight, who was renowned for personal gallantry, and high deeds of chivalry, was made prisoner, after a gallant defence, in the battle of Methuen. Some stanzas of a ballad of the times give minute particulars of his fate. It was written immediately at the period, for it mentions the Earl of Athole as not yet in custody. It has been translated out of the rude orthography of the times to make it intelligible."

"This was before Saint Bartholomew's mass,
That Frizel was y-taken, were it more other less,
To Sir Thomas of Multon, gentil baron and free,
And to Sir Johan Jose be-take tho was he
To hand
He was y-fettered wele
Both with iron and with steel
To bringen of Scotland.

"Soon thereafter the tiding to the King come,
He sent him to London, with mony armed groom,
He came in at Newgate, I tell you it on a-plight,
A garland of leaves on his head y-dight
Of green,
For he should be y-know
Both of high and of low,
For traitour I ween.

"Y-fettered were his legs under his horse's wombe,
Both with iron and with steel mancled were his hond;
A garland of pervynk [1] set upon his heved,[2]
Much was the power that him was bereved
In land
So God me amend,
Little he ween'd
So to be brought in hand.

"This was upon our lady's even, forsooth I understand,
The Justices sate for the knights of Scotland,
Sir Thomas of Multon, an kinde knyght and wise,
And Sir Ralph of Sandwich that mickle is told in price,
And Sir Johan Abel,
Moe I might tell by tale
Both of great and of small
Ye know sooth well.

"Then said the Justice, that gentil is and free,
Sir Simond Frizel the king's traiter hast thou be;

[1] Periwinkle. [2] Head.

In water and in land that mony mighten see,
What sayst thou thereto, how will thou quite thee,
Do say.
So foul he him wist,
Nede war on trust
For to say nay.

"With fetters and with gives [1] y-hot he was to draw
From the Tower of London that many men might know,
In a kirtle of burel, a selcouth wise,
And a garland on his head of the new guise.
Through Cheape
Many men of England
For to see Symond
Thitherward can leap.

"Though he cam to the gallows first he was on hung,
All quick beheaded that him thought long;
Then he was y-opened, his bowels y-brend, [2]
The heved to London Bridge was send
To shende.
So evermore mote I the,
Some while weened he
Thus little to stand. [3]

"He rideth through the city, as I tell may,
With gamen and with solace that was their play,
To London-bridge he took the way,
Mony was the wives child that thereon lacketh a day [4]
And said alas!
That he was y-born,
And so vilely forlorn,
So fair man he was. [5]

"Now standeth the heved above the tu-brigge,
Fast by Wallace sooth for to segge;
After succor of Scotland long may he pry;
And after help of France what halt it to lie
I ween
Better him were in Scotland
With his axe in his hand
To play on the green," &c.

[1] He was condemned to be drawn. [2] Burned.
[3] Meaning that he little thought ever to stand thus.
[4] Saith lack a day.
[5] The gallant knight was pitied by the female spectators.

"The Friday next, before the assumption of Our Lady, King Edward met Robert the Bruce at Saint Johnstowne in Scotland, and with his company, of which company King Edward qvelde seven thousand. When Robert the Bruce saw this mischief and gan to flee, an hov'd him that men might not him find; but Sir Simond Frisell (Frazer) pursued was so sore, that he turned again and abode bataille, for he was a worthy knight and a bolde of body, and the Englishmen pursuede him sore on every side and qvelde the steed that sir Simon Frisell rode upon, and then toke him and led him to the host. And Sir Symond began to speke fair, and saide, Lordys, I shall give you four thousand marks of silver, and myne horse and harness, and all my armoure and income. Tho', answered Thobaude of Pevenes, that was the king's archer, now, God me so helpe, it is for nought that thou speakest, for all the gold of England I would not let thee go without commandment of King Edward. And tho' he was led to the king, and the king would not see him, but commanded to lead him away to his doom in London, on our Lady's even nativity. And he was hung and drawn and his head smitten off, and hanged again with chains of iron upon the gallows and his head was set at London-bridge upon a spear, and against Christmas the body was burnt."

We have quoted these notes in full for three reasons: of which the first is that there are many of Sir Simon Frazer's descendants living in America who may not have read them before; to picture the extreme cruelty with which brave men were treated in those times; and to show the changes the English language has undergone, when even this version has been "translated out of its rude orthography."

[*See page 234*]

The family of Biddle have added many important names to the roll of honor of their adopted country. In what year any of its members first came to America we know not, but they were settlers and proprietaries of western New Jersey before the war of independence. Clement Biddle, in 1764, united with others to form a military corps for the protection of the friendly Indians against the zealots called Paxton boys. He and his brother, Owen Biddle, identified themselves with the non-importation resolutions of 1765. During the Revolution, Clement was instrumental in forming the body of Quaker volunteers of which he was colonel. He took part in the battle of Trenton and was appointed by Washington to receive the swords of the Hessian officers. He also served in the battles of Princeton, the Brandywine, Germantown, and Monmouth. He, as well as his brother Owen, had a share in framing the revolutionary State constitution of 1776.

Edward Biddle was an officer in the French war, 1756-63. He was speaker in the Assembly, and a delegate from Pennsylvania to the Continental Congress 1774-6 and 1778-9.

Nicholas Biddle entered the royal navy in 1770 and was made captain in the U. S. Navy in 1776 and took several prizes from the English. Freneau commemorated his death in the following poem, although with too great poetical license he represented him as falling in the moment of victory. Captain Biddle met the adversary in a very unequal contest and acted with great gallantry.

On the Death of

CAPTAIN NICHOLAS BIDDLE

Commander of the Randolph Frigate, blown up near Barbadoes

What distant thunders rend the skies,
What clouds of smoke in columns rise,
What means this dreadful roar!
Is from his base *Vesuvius* thrown,
Is sky-topt *Atlas* tumbled down,
Or *Etna's* self no more?

Shock after shock torments my ear;
And lo! two hostile ships appear,
Red lightnings round them glow:
The *Yarmouth* boasts of sixty-four,
The *Randolph* thirty-two — no more —
And will she fight this foe!

The Randolph soon on Stygian streams
Shall coast along the land of dreams,
The islands of the dead!
But Fate, that parts them on the deep
Shall save the Briton yet to weep
His days of victory fled.

Philip Freneau

Say, who commands that dismal blaze,
Where yonder starry streamer plays;
  Does *Mars* with *Jove* engage!
'Tis Biddle wings those angry fires,
Biddle whose bosom Jove inspires
  With more than mortal rage.

Tremendous flash! and hark, the ball
Drives through old Yarmouth, flames and all:
  Her bravest sons expire;
Did Mars himself approach so nigh,
Even Mars, without disgrace, might fly
  The Randolph's fiercer fire.

The Briton views his mangled crew,
"And shall we strike to *thirty two*
  (Said Hector, stain'd with gore)
"Shall Britain's flag to *these* descend—
"Rise and the glorious conflict end,
  "Britons, I ask no more!"

He spoke—they charg'd their cannon round,
Again the vaulted heavens resound,
  The Randolph bore it all,
Then fix'd her pointed cannons true—
Away the unwieldy vengeance flew;
  Britain, thy warriors fall.

The Yarmouth saw, with dire dismay,
Her wounded hull, shrouds shot away,
  Her boldest heroes dead—
She saw amidst her floating slain
The conquering *Randolph* stem the main—
  She saw, she turn'd—and fled!

That hour, blest chief, had she been thine,
Dear *Biddle*, had the powers divine
  Been kind as thou wert brave;
But Fate, who doom'd thee to expire,
Prepar'd an arrow, tipt with fire,
  And mark'd a wat'ry grave.

And in that hour, when conquest came
Wing'd at his ship a pointed flame,

That not even he could shun—
The battle ceas'd the Yarmouth fled,
The burning Randolph ruin spread,
And left her task undone.

James Biddle entered the navy in 1800. He served against Tripoli, where he was taken prisoner and detained over a year and a half. He served with great distinction in the war of 1812. For his services he received a gold medal from Congress, besides other honors. Captain Biddle was afterward Commissioner to Turkey, China, etc.

Clement Cornell Biddle entered the naval service of the United States in the beginning of the last century, but retired to the study of law. He served in the war of 1812 with the rank of colonel.

Richard Biddle was a lawyer and writer; he served in Congress from 1837 to 1841.

Nicholas Biddle, the great American financier, was named after his uncle, the naval officer. After graduating from Princeton College he studied law, but being too young to practise he went to France as Secretary to General Armstrong, U. S. Minister. He afterwards went as Secretary to Mr. Monroe, U. S. Minister to England. He travelled extensively in Europe and gained a knowledge of the modern languages. In 1810 he was in the House of Representatives of Pennsylvania, and in 1812–15 was State Senator. In 1819 President Monroe appointed him government director of the United States Bank, and upon the resignation of Mr. Cheves, he was elected its president. The old charter expiring in 1836, the bank ceased to exist. Its success, however, caused the Legislature of Pennsylvania to create a State bank, called the U. S. Bank, and Mr. Biddle reluctantly accepted its presidency. In 1839, by reason of his failing health, Mr. Biddle resigned, leaving the bank in an apparently prosperous condition. Two years after his resignation it became insolvent. Mr. Biddle's character won high eulogiums from even his political opponents. Mr. Biddle, as president of the trustees of Girard College, planned the building, as also that of the U. S. Custom House, which was formerly the U. S. Bank. His speeches, essays, and letters are said to exhibit great elegance with vigor of style. He married Miss Craig of Philadelphia, and after his resignation retired to his country seat of Andalusia and devoted himself to literary pursuits.

George W. Biddle practised law in Philadelphia. Besides holding many minor offices in that city, he was a member of the constitutional convention of Pennsylvania in 1873. He became the leader of the bar of the State and was retained in most cases of importance in the Supreme Court of the State. Besides contributing numerous legal papers, he wrote translations of the Greek orations of Demosthenes, and Æschines on the Crown.

Col. James Biddle, of the Ninth Cavalry, U. S. A., served in many engagements during the Civil War. His son, David Harmony Biddle, is at the present time (1901) serving in Manila.

Index

Index

Index

Index